Predestined to Reign

From: National Author,
Crystal ...

Crystal McDaniel

Predestined to Reign

FOR SUCH A TIME AS THIS

Tate Publishing & *Enterprises*

Predestined To Reign For Such a Time as This
Copyright © 2009 by Crystal McDaniel. All rights reserved.

No part of this publication may be reproduced, stored in a retrieval system or transmitted in any way by any means, electronic, mechanical, photocopy, recording or otherwise without the prior permission of the author except as provided by USA copyright law.

The opinions expressed by the author are not necessarily those of Tate Publishing, LLC.

Published by Tate Publishing & Enterprises, LLC
127 E. Trade Center Terrace | Mustang, Oklahoma 73064 USA
1.888.361.9473 | www.tatepublishing.com

Tate Publishing is committed to excellence in the publishing industry. The company reflects the philosophy established by the founders, based on Psalm 68:11,
"The Lord gave the word and great was the company of those who published it."

Book design copyright © 2009 by Tate Publishing, LLC. All rights reserved.
Cover design by Amber Gulilat
Author Photo by Tony Lunnie
Hair Stylist Corletha Hill
Interior design by Stefanie Rooney

Published in the United States of America

ISBN: 978-1-61566-544-0
1. Biography & Autobiography, Women
2. Religion, Christian Life, Women's Issues
09.12.02

Table of Contents

Acknowledgements 7

Foreword 9

Preface 11

Introduction 15

CHAPTER ONE: FROM BAD TO WORSE 19
   The Root of Anger 19
   The Scent of Change 25

CHAPTER TWO: A NEW START 31
   The Journey 31
   Just When I Thought It 39
      Couldn't Get Worse
   A Glimpse of Hope 52
   The Same Old Thing 61
   A Second Chance 67
   Surrounded by Greatness 73
   The Prophetic Dream 78
   Back in Egypt 82
   The Free Gift 86

CHAPTER THREE: THE TRAP 93
   New Beginnings 93
   The Opened Door 97

Warning: Destruction Ahead!	104
Satan's Bait	110
The Rapid Decline	115
The Antidote	121
The Escape	129
Marked by God	137
A New Found Love	142

CHAPTER FOUR: IT'S A SETUP! 155

A Strange Land	155
Black Crows	161
The New Groups	165
Déjà vu	167
Instructions	176
A Fire Kindled	178
Help, I've been Robbed!	182
Walking by Faith	184

CHAPTER FIVE: THE CROSSROADS 203

Reunited	203
The Birthday to Remember	210
The Face of Death	214
So Long, Fair Love	216
At Death's Door	238
The Transformation	264
Predestined to Reign	269

Letter from the Author	275
Discussion Questions	277

Acknowledgment

First, I would like to start by thanking God for birthing a passion to write this book. I would also like to thank him for giving me a life interesting enough to write about. Next, I would like to say that, without a doubt, I couldn't have completed this task without the strength and encouragement of my dear mother, Stella McDaniel, who loves me and believes that "I can do all things through Christ, which strengthens me" (Philippians 4:13 KJV). Mom, you are my greatest inspiration as well as my hero. I love you. To my brothers and sisters, Freddie Jr., Enda, Kevin, Gloria, Starles, and Tommy McDaniel: I just want to say that all of you are destined for greatness. I love you guys very much. Although my flaws, struggles, and addictive cycles are more vivid up close and personal, you all continue to love me unconditionally. As I go up, each of you shall go up.

Now, I want to take the time to send a shout out to my relatives as well as my best friends, Erica Lynn Hare-Young and Laverne McNutt. Ladies, we've been to hell and back together. Although we're separated by distance, I'll always love you both and be here when you need me. Thanks to Daniel Lamont Drew, who taught me to love through my pain. I pray that wherever you are, you will take your rightful place in God's kingdom and become the mighty man of God that I know you were created to be. Thanks to evangelist Chris Parson, my mentor and friend, who taught me to deal with issues from the past while residing at the Serenity House in Schenectady, NY. You taught me through example what true wholeness is all about and how to become a woman of excellence.

It is needful that I take out time to honor Bishop Thomas A. Jackson of Earle Lighthouse Temple of Deliverance (my first true, spiritual dad). Special thanks to Apostle Lincoln and Lynetta Dent of Dominion and Praise Global Ministries, Pastor Kenneth and Angela Evans of Restoration Ministries, and last but not least, my new spiritual parents, Pastor Cedric and Karen Hayes, the overseers of Gloryland Family Fellowship Ministries. Together, you shall take the nation by storm with your profound teachings! Thank you both for imparting spiritual blessings, wisdom, and sound teaching into my life. You challenged me to relinquish fear and walk on water. I pray that each leader that spoke into my life will receive a hundred-fold in your ministries in the name of Jesus Christ. Thanks for feeding me with the meat of God's Word. Continue to lift me up and to hold me accountable.

Thanks to all of my family and friends who make my life more fulfilling. I love all of you. Without everyone's prayer and support on this long journey, perhaps the fruits of my labor would never have flourished. May God bless and strengthen you all. "[Be] not...weary in well doing: for in due season [you] shall reap, if [you] faint not" (Galatians 6:9 KJV).

Foreword

Welcome to one of the greatest books ever written! This book will amaze you, excite you, encourage you, and motivate you. As you follow Crystal through her incredible journey of discovering hidden treasures within the mishap of being rejected, misused, and abused, you will gain the courage to face your circumstances head on and not run from them, because running wastes time. This book will cause readers to snap out of denial, confront their issues, and then deal with them so that true healing can take place. Although someone can be broken into many pieces, Predestined to Reign shows that pieces can fit back together—and once reconnected, they do create a whole! After having an encounter with God, he then becomes the healing agent that can mend a broken heart, a distorted mind, low self-esteem, and a lack of courage. If you are willing to be remolded, you will still find your purpose in life. A life fulfilled and running over with joy will be your prize.

Without a doubt, you will not be able to put this book down until you have completed it in its entirety! Crystal McDaniel is an astonishing prolific writer. Look for other books by her in the future. From me to you, enjoy!

—First Lady, Karen Hayes

Preface

Sometime during my journey in life, I knew God was calling me to greatness. While wrestling with the weights of generational curses and cycles of addiction, God was setting me up a platform constructed carefully from the rudiments of my pain. It was during this process of warring that a message for the nations was born.

Before I proceed with my "story before the glory," I deem it helpful to give a brief synopsis of the life of Queen Esther. It can be seen in this concise illustration how, like she, God handpicks his elite and mishaps out of brokenness and uses them to profit his kingdom for an appointed time.

Esther, also known as Hadassah, was initially carried away out of Jerusalem and into captivity right by the side of her cousin Mor'decai. He had taken her as his own after the death of both her parents. As they were pushed and shoved into exile, it probably never occurred to any of the people around Esther that this dusty and scared little girl would one day become queen to deliver them all from complete annihilation. Maybe some even looked down on her because she was nothing more than an orphan–an outcast. She was just a pretty face with no hope but to become a maidservant in someone's home whenever they reached their new land.

During her dark days of losing both parents, being forced out of her homeland, and being pushed into slavery, God began to instill something in this little girl that was naked to the eye. Without a doubt, she had a beautiful countenance, but the beauty Esther contained within was far beyond comparison. Magnificent strength and boldness developed within her. But out of respect for Mordecai and due to humility, she constrained it. The fullness of her time had not yet come. Her appointment with destiny was the only way the substance God was birthing in her could be manifested.

When word got out that King Ahasuerus was summoning all the fair young virgins to come into his palace while seeking the next queen, I imagine Mordecai's heart beating rapidly. He had always seen a glimpse of greatness in his little cousin. He possibly paused for a few seconds to contemplate on whether putting Esther on display would be good for her or not. But after noting her large, dark-brown, almond-shaped eyes, and her midnight-black hair hanging below her waist, his reluctance dissipated. Everything about her hinted at royalty.

Possibly many nights as he prayed towards the east, he had fragmented visions of her ascension into royalty. Somehow he knew it was Esther's time to step through destiny's door.

Perhaps Mordecai remembered images of Esther running to him after coming back from the evening sacrifice with loose tendrils dancing against her cheeks and the sun's rays illuminating her small frame. Maybe, he imagined her dark, smooth skin basking in pure radiance as each pump of her Jewish blood reached its surface after a hard day in the fields. Her lips, as red as rubies, guarded the wisdom that God placed in her heart, waiting for the moment when she would become queen.

Immediately upon entering the marvelous palace, with its green marble floors and chalk white columns, Esther could feel eyes roaming across her body, mesmerized by her beauty. It surprised her that she didn't retreat back to the side of Mordecai who stood at the gate's entrance. She continued to walk with her head held high and with her back arched as if she were born a queen. Finally, she stood alongside the other young maidens to be chosen by the king. After being picked as a contestant, Esther was given favor by God and was placed in the palace's best room to complete a year of purification.

When her time of purification was up, she stood before the king again. His heart pulsated with desire unlike any he had ever known before. All he knew was that this young girl was the one. She would be his queen.

When Esther rose to become queen, she was translated into a symbol of hope to the Jews. These words came from her cousin Mordecai's mouth: "and who knoweth whether thou art come to the kingdom for such a time as this" (Esther 4:14 KJV). These words possibly cut Esther like a knife. It slapped reality back into her soul. Those very words made her realize that she didn't arrive at a place of prestige so that she might get glory for herself, but so that God could get the glory through her. After accepting her purposed assignment, Esther nullified Haman's plot to destroy the Jews. It was God's ultimate plan to use her as the vehicle to accomplish this goal.

Esther was an orphan, a Jew, and a female. Culturally, those were three strikes against her, but God saw otherwise. He took her garments of shame and rejection and exposed to her the garments of glory and majesty.

Just like Esther, I am someone who has been raised out of ashes and clothed with "garments of praise" (Isaiah 61:3). Not by our own doings but by a God that was leading us to do great things for him.

And what is the significance of the statement, "for such a time as this?" The answer: Esther and her people were living in a time when the enemy was attacking everyone that followed after the true and living God—the Jewish race in particular. They were living in a time of famine and great persecution. God needed an instrument that he could use in delivering his chosen people from their adversaries by giving them hope concerning his promises.

Nothing Esther could have done made him choose her—no religious acts such as praying three times a day or fasting five times a week. She was predestined before the hands of time. All throughout her life, the mark of God was upon her to carry out his task. He already had an appointed time when she would become queen. Her exaltation was destined to emerge during an era of great persecution, a time when the enemy was in hot pursuit of God's chosen people. Esther would be the vehicle of hope in which deliverance would spring forth.

On Sept. 11, 2001, only seconds after the announcement of the destruction of the Twin Towers, God spoke to my spirit, "I've called you for such a time as this." God made it visible to me that, like Esther and her people, we are living in evil times. The enemy desires to destroy families with the stench of abuse, rape, molestation, low self-esteem, drug addiction, and pornography. But just like Esther reveals, prayer, fasting, and obedience are weapons to nullify the enemy's plans.

God raised me up to declare war on the enemy and to sound the alarm to his end-time warriors that the violent must take back the kingdom of God from the forces of darkness. Now is the time to cry loud and spare not! I decree and declare that this book will carry the weight of a breaker's anointing. Bad relationships shall be severed. Generational curses shall be destroyed. Opened doors of perversion shall be closed. All addictions shall lose their power over you. I declare your freedom today in the name of Jesus Christ!

To protect identities, most names have been changed.

Introduction

Worn, weary, and battered—all of these characteristics were found in the same broken vessel. I was that broken vessel. For years I listened to prophetic lies spoken over my life, lies from people that said I would never amount to anything, that I was ugly, and that I wasn't worth two dead flies. I believed them for years. I became what they said. I was nothing. I was ugly. I wasn't worth two dead flies. My entire thought pattern was filtered through these "deceptive facts." I became my worst nightmare—the female version of my father. Like him, I ended up turning to drinking and smoking, not caring about the people that loved me. Things I looked down upon were the very things I started entertaining. Many addictive substances became my lifestyle, my consolation, and my masquerade from reality—pain.

Throughout my life, past failures kept me condemned and traditional mindsets left me confused. There was nowhere to turn. Finally, after living in turmoil for years, my soul began seeking after God and the gods I was serving began loosening their hold on me. I wanted to be healed. I started declaring my soul free from bondage, and little by little, their strongholds began to loosen.

After sitting down and facing my issues, I was able to see cycles that had become major themes in my life. I saw cycles of addictions, generational curses, and strongholds. Each time, before getting entangled with another cycle, I realized that God always provided spiritual road signs that declared: *Drive Slow, Danger's Ahead,* but because I naively overlooked them and ventured on, I made unnecessary mistakes prolonging my maturity. It wasn't until I came face to face with the "naked" truth concerning my life that God truly began healing me of emotional scars and breaking those cycles of addictions, "for such a time as this."

All across this world, God is preparing a people of great valor who will arise out of their hurt, their addictions, their oppressions, and will possess their rightful place in the kingdom. This great mass of people will declare war on the enemy and will nullify his plans of destroying families through sexual perversion, drugs, and domestic violence. These chosen vessels will speak out and declare to Satan that enough is enough!

If you are reading this book, it is because God wants to heal you of wounds, generational curses, strongholds, legalism; anything that is deeply rooted that has kept you imprisoned from walking in complete wholeness. He wants to break through your masquerades and reach the soul part of you; the created-in-his-likeness version of you; the person he saw on the sixth day when he declared, "It is very good."

Restoring you to the father was Jesus' main objective for coming to earth. It was his humbleness, quiet boldness, and his broken and contrite spirit that drew people to him. Although Jesus is King of kings and Lord of lords, he could have come in a bodily fashion as a handsome man, but he chose not to. He grew up in an ordinary family. He could have made himself some great physician like Luke, but he didn't. He was a carpenter. He appeared common to reach a common people. That's where he did his greatest work—among the forsaken, lost and rejected.

Sifting through years of pain and isolation, God began making me aware of true humility. He needed to show me that Christian "life" isn't about having a strong demeanor. It isn't about smiling when you really want to cry, but it is about recognizing that "all our righteousness [is] as filthy rags" (Isaiah 64:6 KJV). It's about knowing that without him we can do nothing. It's about knowing that it's only by grace that we are saved. Only when recognizing these facts and intertwining them into one's spirit can a victorious life be obtained. With the acceptance of grace, one's failures or mistakes can then be seen for what they really are—a means of keeping us humble. This acceptance of our humanness isn't meant to justify living a sinful life, but it's meant to bring about a more fulfilled one. This acceptance allows us to rest in the fact that "he which hath begun a good work in [us] will perform it until the day of Jesus Christ" (Philippians 1:6).

CHAPTER ONE

From Bad to Worse

> Behold, I was shapen in iniquity; and in sin did my mother conceive me."
>
> Psalms 51:5

The Root of Anger

From the moment I was nestled in my mother's womb, the enemy was after me. My mother, Stella McDaniel, recounted various incidents in which she was near death while carrying me. On three of these occasions, the elders of the church had to come and pray over her to revive her strength. Also, for three days, I lay motionless inside her womb terrifying her with the uncertainty of my well-being. Despite the enemy's attacks, I was born. He couldn't abort what God had planned. But of course, he didn't stop trying.

Shortly after my birth, on December 17, 1978, the doctor walked into my mother's hospital room and announced, "Sorry to give you this news, Mrs. McDaniel, but your daughter has been diagnosed with leukemia." Miraculously, as the result of a praying mother and the grace of God, I was pronounced cured of cancer not many days hence. Although cured from that disease, the enemy plagued me with various others. As a result, my mother became very protective of me. Despite my sickness and my mother's overprotectiveness, I developed the determination of a bull.

I grew up in the small town of Wynne, Arkansas. Partial segregation was still seen throughout the city. A railroad track separated the whites from the blacks, but for the most part, everyone got along. All around me was the smell and talk of poverty. Litter and glass occasionally arrayed the ground of the small park that stood as the gazebo in "our" neighborhood. And just like that park, my family's unity started deteriorating rapidly. All hopes of a normal childhood seemed bleak.

Times were devastating for our family due to my parents' low income, but simultaneously, they were the best years of my childhood.

The downfall of my family wasn't poverty, but it was the fact that my father didn't make living in it any better. Oftentimes, when he got a well paying job, he would only work until payday. Sometimes he lasted a few months. Either way, when he got fed up with the boss or decided to go on a drinking binge, he wouldn't return to work. This routine became very difficult on my mother.

My father, a retired Vietnam War veteran, stood about 6'4 and weighed almost 300 lbs. He was a brilliant man. His intellect and musical abilities didn't go unnoticed by many. He also had the ability to build almost anything, fix-up cars, sing, write poetry, and play most musical instruments by ear. As a result of his many different talents, he was often blessed with very good jobs.

Stemming from his gift as a carpenter, he built the house my family and I resided in. I watched in amazement as it began to transform by his hands. I remember with explicit imagery as he turned our three-bedroom trailer into a full four-bedroom house. It included a living room, a dining room, a den, a bigger kitchen and a full back and front porch.

But despite all of the good skills he possessed, he had his fair share of flaws. With a history of Post-traumatic Stress Syndrome, my family spent many Fourth of Julys trying to convince him that he was not in Vietnam and that he was not being shot at. He often used alcohol to drown out the last breath of those dying around him that were yet trapped in his head. Supposedly a remedy, it eventually began ruling his life.

On many occasions, in a drunken rage, his voice would roar through the entire house as if traveling from the abyss of hell. Truthfully, I used to wonder if he was Satan himself. He oftentimes said bizarre things like, "I am the Messiah" or "I'm Lucifer," and then he'd quote scriptures from the Bible. Many times he would curse my mother in a slurred frenzy. "Nobody would ever want you! If you ever try to leave me, I'll kill you and the kids," he'd scream. For fear that he would carry out his threats, my mother held onto the marriage. This left my family and me living in fear and seclusion.

His alcoholic episodes caused the police to come to our house constantly. The word of the cop's arrival often circulated throughout town so fast that I usually ended up ashamed to face my classmates the following day. We became the rejects of our town. If one spoke of the McDaniel Family, it was usually because of three reasons: we were poor, we could fight, and we had an alcoholic father.

Although my father knew that my mother was sickly, he didn't refrain from blowing cigarette smoke around her. These consistent, inconsiderate acts resulted in her spending many nights in the hospital with asthma attacks. Holiday after holiday, she would end up there only moments away from death. I was so afraid of losing her that I started petitioning God to spare her life. I really didn't know much about prayer personally, but from what I had watched her do, I mimicked.

As our family's name lay amongst the ruins, my mother fought to maintain her sanity. Many days, I watched her time-withered face darken as the yearly hardships began dimming the gleam in her eyes. She tried hard to uphold her composure in front of us, but every now and then, a tear of desperation would trickle down her sugar-brown face. Oftentimes, I would catch her staring into space while she hummed from the deepest part of her being. Like the furniture in the house, she had become weary and worn.

One day, out of curiosity, I asked, "What are you doing?" "Calling on God," was her reply. She never missed a beat while rocking back and forth on the dusty plaid-colored couch.

It wasn't until I got older that I discovered that this form of expression was her way of getting strength from God. God was her main injection of fuel. She didn't have to go to a support group to pull through life's hardships, but she did have to continue to fall on her knees and remain steadfast in the faith in which she was professing. She stopped praying for God to change our father and started praying that God would change her negative thinking about her situation. After a paradigm shift, God granted her peace to endure. He needed to prove to her that she could remain a Christian in any situation. By watching and examining her life, I began to see and understand just what God was capable of doing in my own.

Though I was raised in church, the lives of the saints didn't influence me as much as my mother's did. Watching her pray to someone she couldn't see along with her consistency in good works was astonishing to me. Yet I was confused how someone could go through so much pain and still have peace in the midst of it. It was her lifestyle that taught me about God and the peace that he could provide regardless of life's circumstances. Words alone couldn't convey to me his omnipotence in her life. It was her daily lifestyle of purity in the midst of adversity that taught me lessons on faithfulness, hope, and the power of prayer.

Nevertheless, due to misplaced anger, I began to build up

secret resentment towards my mother even more than what I had for my father. In my heart, I felt that if she were so strong in the Lord, then she should've been strong enough to protect me from his mental and physical abuse and herself for that matter. It wasn't fair that she was so at peace, and I was left feeling like an unwanted vagabond.

Where was her God when I was getting slapped for no reason, or when I was being called ugly and stupid by dad? Better yet, where was he when classmates were ridiculing me for being poor? I concluded that it was her fault that my life was so miserable. I refused to let go of the bitter accusations that I had against her. I couldn't—didn't want to—accept the fact that she was suffering just as much as I was because of him. I needed someone to blame for the pain that stole my youth. At the time, she was the perfect candidate.

In addition to my emotional battle with my mother, many different emotions circulated throughout our house daily. Resentment grew towards my father from all of my brothers and sisters, and along with resentment, I was confused. I didn't know whether to be angry or feel sorry for him. Because of my family's unhealthy suppression of emotions, a whirlwind of chaos arose constantly, resulting in many outbursts of rage. Over time, the atmosphere became so damp and clammy that our place of residence became more like a house instead of a home.

No one was brave enough to admit it, but our family was falling apart fast. It had happened over a span of years, but our unity was dispersing. The closeness that we once shared was ruined. There no longer remained an interest in trying to eat dinner together and engage in conversation—two ingredients that are essential in keeping a family knit together. It was saddening to see my family being overtaken by so much pain. Our family structure had been shaken at its core. Because I didn't know how to deal with my own emotions, there was absolutely nothing I could do about it.

As years went by, I turned the majority of my frustrations of being abused and of feeling neglected inside and began to suppress them. I knew it was harmful and that too much built up pressure would blow sooner or later. Nevertheless, all the anger that was embedded within me caused me to eliminate anyone from getting close to me. It soon started to deteriorate my self-image as well as my social skills. Since I was the baby girl of six siblings, it was very easy to conceal my hurt. Everyone was too busy with their own problems.

Since my home life was exposed to the community, by the age of ten, I stopped trying to fit into groups at school. Distancing became a method to cover up the abuse my father was inflicting on my family. I craved to fit in with classmates, but by then I was already labeled as "weird," so I grew accustomed to being alone. I gave up trying to fit in. I learned to build up barriers to protect myself from becoming susceptible to getting hurt in order to survive at home.

Often, when I would come in from school, I could tell by the atmosphere in the house if my parents had been fighting. An eerie quietness usually settled around me, paving the way for the boisterous doom that was to follow. As if waiting for my death sentence, I would walk down the long corridor to my bedroom, dump my books on the bed, and wait for the screaming and yelling to begin.

If they happened to fight at night, I usually ended up hiding in the back of my room's dark and damp closet. With stifled asthmatic coughs, I lay underneath as many blankets as possible, so my father wouldn't find me, afraid he would carry out his threats of killing us.

A few mornings before school, my mother would find me asleep in the closet only moments away from an asthma attack. As she dug under the piles of covers to discover my sickly body, the wheezing sounds from my lungs would fill the room. There were a few incidents when she had to rush me to the emergency room because of a fever I had developed along with persistent nonproductive coughs that shook my frail body.

There were only a few incidents that I can recall when my father actually physically abused me. He mostly picked fights with my eldest sister, Marsha. "Why did I have girls? They're all stupid. I wish I had all boys," he often retorted at Janet, Marsha, and me. This oftentimes was followed by a smack across Marsha's face. My father seemed to take pleasure in making us pay for our gender. Although we had four brothers in the house, it seemed he were easier on them than us girls. We had to go out into the snow, chop wood, bring it in, and sometimes even start the fire. Many days, because of his mistreatment, I ached to be a boy.

The Scent of Change

It didn't happen over night, but it was the result of years of mental and physical abuse. The anger and bitterness, both of which had manifested in my childhood, had lingered on after I turned into an adult. They grew as malignant substances, confiscating every portion of my being. The anger lurked at a stance behind my desolate eyes, waiting to strike at any moment; ready to sink its venomous teeth into anybody that crossed its path wrongly. The innermost part of my being wreaked death. I was dying. I was so accustomed to being unhappy and miserable that happiness fled from me. I felt cursed. I believed I was the fury of God in flesh and that he had shaped me in his anger to live all my days bound underneath a curse—perhaps originally like Jabez.

Bitterness became my daily condolence. He was my protection, my clothing from rejection and pain. He shielded me. I soon became imprisoned within my own dilapidated self. As hard as the spirit-part of me wanted to break free from bondage, I was constrained by the soul part of me—stinking thinking and emotional roller coasters. I longed to feel joyous emotions, but they rarely surmounted. They were subdued to my every command. With mastery, I learned how to numb my feelings. During those stormy seasons in my life, I started praying to God in those "secret places," and slowly, he began filling voids that had engulfed my life with a hunger and thirst for him.

Unconsciously, God began giving me secret treasures during those midnight experiences in my life. In the midst of my hurt and built up frustration, he started cultivating fruit I thought would never do anything but rot. It was as if I could hear a faint whisper speaking over my situation, "Can these bones live again?" I was hurting, but God wanted me to keep pushing. I was scared and scarred, but God wanted me to keep pushing. I was tired and alone, but God wanted me to keep pushing. Only he knew what he was trying to birth out of me. It's hard to explain, but even then in my why-can't-I-be-normal years, I knew God's hands were cradling me in the womb of destiny.

Many nights, I awakened to dreams that were both frightening and exciting. As I began to get older, I realized that many of the dreams were prophetic and that God was showing me where he was about to take me in life. At the age of eleven, I saw visions of myself in New York. In these visions, I was a reformed person, no longer looking like the poverty-stricken girl who was uneducated and withdrawn. Instead I was a woman that had high standards and appeared self-assured. I was no longer the shy girl who held her head down low and refrained from making eye contact, but I was a powerhouse who declared the power of a loving God.

I can recall a series of revivals that were being held in our church in Cherry Valley, Arkansas, which was about fifteen minutes from Wynne. The anointing was so great in those services. One particular night I watched out of curious tear-brimmed eyes, as some were being "slain in the Spirit" and speaking in tongues. I was sitting on a cold pew in the middle of winter, but for some reason, I was burning up inside. It felt as if my soul was on fire. I could not comprehend what was going on, but I knew I didn't want the feeling of warm peace that I was experiencing to subside.

One night during a weekly revival, Pastor Davis (which was also my uncle) voice boomed out, "You can't go to heaven without God's Spirit!" There were eruptions of Amen's and Hallelujahs. He continued. "Is there anyone here that wants to receive the baptism of the Holy Ghost? Come to the altar, and someone will tarry with you so that you may receive it." His fire and brimstone voice was so convicting.

My legs weakened underneath me, but before the spirit of doubt could keep me seated, I rose and inched my way to the front of the sanctuary. To my surprise, many of my relatives all across the congregation got up and made their way down to the altar as well. It seemed as if we moved in unison. Tears streamed down my face as I pressed my way through the crowd. Each of our cries began to blend together as our souls wailed out to the Lord. Suddenly, as if a great weight had fallen from my shoulders, an immense sense of freedom overtook me. Next thing I knew, I began to dance before the Lord as if he and I were the only two in the room.

Time seemed to have stood still as I pranced in the presence of God. After noticing that the sound of the people around me began to grow faint, I peeked out of one of my eyes. There were only two of us remaining at the altar. Quite awkwardly, I walked back to my seat. As everyone began regaining their composure, Pastor Davis, radiating from the anointing, stepped up to the podium and asked, "Does anyone want to share with us what God has done for them tonight?"

Four of my relatives simultaneously leaped up. "Praise the Lord, saints!" Amanda Baily, the first to speak, erupted with a voice of pure ecstasy. Tears of joy begin streaming down her rich dark skin. "God has filled me with the Holy Ghost!" Immediately, she began shouting and speaking in tongues. Almost everyone in the church began rejoicing on her behalf. It felt as if my heart had sunk to the bottom of my stomach. I was so hurt. The spirit of defeat befriended me. *"Why didn't I get it? Why didn't I speak in tongues like everybody else? Something must be wrong with me."* The thoughts seeped inside my mind. Just as soon as they came, I relinquished the negative thoughts and decided that no matter what it took and how long it took, I would get the full manifestation of the Holy Spirit.

After everyone had finished shouting and giving their testimonies, the pastor stood up once more to take the mike. "Don't be discouraged. If any of you didn't get it tonight, just come back tomorrow night with your mind on God." At that moment, I vowed that I would find out what the Holy Ghost really was and see for myself if it really was as powerful as people portrayed.

Revival after revival, I continued to seek after the endowment of the Holy Spirit. While waiting for it, God kept revealing to me that I had to deal with the buried anger that I held against my mother. It was causing my prayers to be hindered. God wasn't going to allow me to shout over my mess. He refrained from pouring something holy into something that was so foul—my heart. There was no way around it. I had to deal with my issues.

I allowed the enemy to let resentment build up so long that I literally despised my mother. The bitterness was so great that I completely shut myself off from verbally communicating with most people. I was afraid that someone would discover the depth of my anger. The magnitude of my wrath was dangerous; it gnawed at me constantly. I yearned to be free of its heinous grasp but didn't know how.

I had a long road to travel to get to freedom. Anger was simply one hurdle that I had to conquer. Abandonment, guilt, low self-esteem, and fear were other giants that were lurking near the surface waiting to abort my kingdom assignment. Even in the midst of my inner battles, God began giving me sneak previews of the glory that was going to be revealed in me.

Eventually, in the place of outbursts of rage, I gravitated towards other coping methods. Eating, sleeping, and reading became my methods of escape. Eating seemed to comfort me momentarily, but in reality, it left me feeling worst. The binging only made me obese, killing the little self-esteem I had left. I felt ugly and fat. I was ugly. I was fat. There were moments when I refused to look at myself in a mirror. I stopped caring about life, and it showed.

Sleeping was my biggest comfort. Since I didn't have any friends, I tried to escape reality by living in a delusional world that was void of pain. I often got excited about coming home from school just to jump in the bed and daydream that I was pretty and well liked among my peers. I enjoyed fantasizing more than living in the real world.

During this time of sleeping to escape, God began to deal with me even more vividly through my dreams. He dealt with me on a level that I could comprehend. He spoke hope to my spirit. He showed me that he was going to take me through many things but was going to reconstruct me into something new for his glory.

I started having visions that I was standing in front of large audiences speaking. I often spoke about my deliverance from drugs, alcohol, abusive relationships, and a promiscuous lifestyle. The strange thing about these visions was that I had never done any of those things before. I was the type that looked down on people who did those things. So just dismissing those visions as "delusional thoughts," I brushed them off.

To gain some sense of control in my life, I began stuffing myself with knowledge. Being smart gave me a sense of power. If I made any grades lower than a *B*, I'd look in the mirror and tell myself that I was stupid and a failure at everything. Those were the repeated words that my father had constantly told me. I believed them.

During that period in my life, God began to work through my love for knowledge. An interest in reading the Bible developed. Slowly, the words that were found on its pages began to carve themselves inside my heart. Without even really noticing, my life began to change. I found myself lying upon my bed, and instead of fantasies popping up, all I could see before my eyes were Scriptures. Over and over again, they begin replaying themselves in my head, becoming intertwined into the deep core of my being.

I got excited just anticipating reading all of the many stories that the Bible had. It contained romance, mystery, and horror all in one. The best part is that all of the stories are true. I began to dissect section after section. So engrossed in its stories, I started hiding the Bible in my book bag so I could take it with me to school.

During recess, I would stray away from everyone on the playground and lay upon the ground. Sometimes I would look up into the clouds and watch the clouds transform themselves into many shapes. I begin to realize how beautiful everything was that God created and how unique he was in his artistic displays.

Some days, I would pull out my Bible and sit upon the damp grass as I practiced how to meditate on God. I particularly loved the scripture written by King David, "Thy words have I hid in my heart that I might not sin against thee" (Psalms 119:11). It was during these moments of meditation that I begin to realize how important the Word of God really was. Because I was turning into a walking Bible, many of the school kids thought I was strange. When we divided up into groups, I would usually end up being the last one picked.

Bit by bit, my wounds began to heal as I allowed God to become my "invisible friend." I ate with him. I talked to him. I learned how to cry to him. For years I felt that it was wrong to cry because it showed my weakness. But through the adventures of pain and hardship, God resurrected all the hurt that was suppressed in me so that I would deal with them in order to be healed.

CHAPTER TWO

A New Start

> Behold, I will do a new thing; now it shall spring forth; shall you not know it? I will even make a way in the wilderness, and rivers in the desert."
>
> Isaiah 43:19

The Journey

When I was about thirteen or fourteen, my parents mentioned moving to Orlando, Florida. I never expected them to actually carry out their plans since they often complained about a lack of funds. To my surprise, one cool morning in the middle of April, Mom crept silently into my bedroom and spoke slightly above a whisper, "Wake up. Wake up." Even while sleep held me captive, her quiet humility and gentleness momentarily overwhelmed me. Thinking that I was dreaming, I continued to lie there upon my hard bed snuggled up underneath the covers.

"We're finally moving," she said. "Get up. We have a lot of packing to do." The voice sounded far away, but its persistence finally jolted me to reality.

I sat upright, staring bewilderedly into my mother's face. "Did I hear you right?" I yawned. "Did you say we're moving?" I rubbed frantically at my eyes trying to make sure I was really awake.

"Yes," she replied as a smile crept upon her face. "Hurry and get up. We have a lot of packing to do."

"When are we leaving?" I asked throwing the covers back.

"As soon as your father feels rested enough to drive," she replied.

I hurriedly got out of bed and jumped up and down across the bedroom floor in pure bliss. Apparently, I was the last to know because my sisters were already rambling through dresser drawers trying to decide what they would pack or throw away. "I can't believe it!" I screamed. "We're finally moving out of this boring old town!" I joyously flung my suitcase open and started throwing cloths into it. Halfway through packing, I decided to call some of my relatives to share the good news about our soon departure.

When I made it to the telephone, my brother, Melvin, was already engrossed in spreading the news. I stood by anxiously waiting for him to get off. As I listened, a cold and sullen loneliness descended over me. It suddenly dawned on me that I would miss hanging out with my relatives.

As soon as Melvin got off the phone, the dread I was starting to feel dispersed temporarily. Felicia, a very close relative of mine, was the first person I called. Once I gave my farewell speech, I could tell by the tone of her voice that she was going to miss us deeply.

One by one, everyone in my family took turns using the phone. Afterwards, we resumed taking pictures off the walls and packing the remainder of our belongings. The rest of the day stretched forward in silence. The sound of zippers and drawers shutting along with a few muffled grunts here and there were the only noises that filled the rapidly barren house.

Many images of Orlando, Florida crept into my head that night. The colorful mirages made it almost impossible to fall asleep. Every time I tried to picture the pretty sunsets and the palm trees I saw on television, images of hurricanes kept destroying the scene washing away any signs of paradise with it. Next, questionable thoughts followed. *What if everyone is mean and the kids don't like me at school? What if everyone think I'm strange like they do here in Wynne?* The questions flowed continuously. I silently prayed that God would make this journey a fun experience for my family and me. Soon after the petition, calmness came.

The next thing I knew, it was the next day, and I was rousing to the smell of bacon and the sound of loud talking from outside my door. I opened one eye and quickly shut it to block out the glare of the sun's radiant light. With squinted eyes, I dangled my feet over the side of the bed, sat up, and looked at my surroundings. *"Goodbye, house,"* I exhaled. One by one, I named everything I was leaving behind, uncertain if I would ever see it all again. The sadness I felt the previous day began to resurface. I could feel it moving at the bottom of my stomach, snaking its way upward towards my throat. Before it could completely evade me, I leapt up and joined the rest of my family to find out the reason behind all of the commotion. My father had decided we would be leaving the following morning.

While eating breakfast, I was reminded of Jesus' Last Supper. Each of us ate in silence as our minds took us to different avenues of our adventure that lay ahead and to the love ones we were leaving behind. We soon learned that Marsha and Ray would be staying behind since they were in their senior year in high school. Although anticipating the unknown, I was overjoyed that God had made a way of escape from the extreme poverty we were living in. I concluded that since we were going to the city where there were bigger and better opportunities, everything would be better for our family. After eating, each of us loaded the van with the packed items.

It was in the wee hours of the morning when we set out towards our destination. Although we were moving forward in hopes of better things, the chains of oppression shackled me to my past. I reclined back into the velvety seat of our minivan and replayed the last few days in my head over and over again. The further we drove down the road, the deeper I felt like I was living in the twilight zone. After hours of watching houses and streetlights whiz by, sleep came.

I awakened to the suns' rays pounding against my face. It was as if its fervent heat were trying to awaken me to see the splendor of my surroundings. I glanced out the window. A sign read: *Chattanooga, Tennessee.* I gasped in astonishment. Soon all traces of sleep fell from me like dirty garments. Our vehicle drove upward on a steep mountain, traveling towards its apex. I watched in wonder as we ascended into the clouds. I wanted so badly to stretch out my fingers and stroke the white "cotton puffs" while feeling their fluffiness caress the sensitive part of my hands. In amazement, I looked down and saw just how high up in altitude we were.

After riding for about another hour, my father's voice sliced into my thoughts as he boomed out, "This is called, *Lookout Mountain*. People from all over the world come here to see this." I didn't want to blink, too afraid of missing something. The very scene was a poem in itself. All of my five senses were in action. The sky was a shade of blue that impersonated a sparkling river that had no beginning or end. The trees seemed to bow down to us as if reverencing and acknowledging our deity over their own. The air, so cool and crisp, danced its icy fingers through the loose tendrils that had fallen at the nape of my neck. I stared spellbound, digesting every detail that unfolded before me.

As my family and I continued on throughout the journey, we began to share with each other the things that were on our minds. "I'm excited about starting a new school," exclaimed Janet. She was two years older than I. Excitement as well as desire for adventure could be easily seen as her slanted eyes glistened. Her pretty, dark-brown eyes resembled those of a feline, almost oriental-like. Her teeth were like white columns that hung in perfect symmetry constructed with the finest marble. Her skin tone was the color of rich almonds that had been baked with such tenderness—almost an image of perfection.

"I don't have anything to wear," she shrieked as if suddenly aware that her fantasy of pure bliss had been crushed by reality, poverty. She leaned over and whispered in my ear. "I hope Daddy will get a good job and take us shopping."

"How likely is that?" I whispered back sarcastically. "You already know that when he get some money, he'll only get drunk and lose his job."

With that comment, we both erupted in laughter. We glanced up and saw our father looking at us through the mirror as if trying to pierce his eyes through our minds to detect what we were laughing about. Janet and I immediately stifled our laughter. Deep down, we were both terrified of him. My father knew he instilled terror within his family. Even when he was sober, his eyes had the look of a madman. The pain he inflicted upon us, both physically and mentally, flashed through my mind like lightning. While watching him, anger brewed within me as the sun's heat began to mingle with my own.

I watched my father's strong, massive fingers grip the steering wheel as if holding on to dear life. I wondered what was going on in his mind. *Does he feel that things would be different this time around?* I wondered. *Does he have any intentions of changing his alcoholic behaviors?* I could only hope for the best.

Melvin's loud and obnoxious snores broke into my thoughts. "Boy, is he sleeping hard," Janet said.

"He sure sounds like it," I replied sluggishly yet irritated by previous thoughts of my father. I pressed my face against the window, trying to see everything that passed by. I decided to release the painful memories from my mind and enjoy the journey.

After having driven for hours, my father pulled over to a rest area, so we could take a break from riding and stretch our tired muscles. Having stopped, we all spilled out of the van. As I got out, a loud popping noise erupted from my knee. "Ow!" I yelped. "These old bones are so stiff."

"You sound like a bowl of Rice Krispies," Melvin teased.

I rolled my eyes at him and hobbled over to Janet's side. "By this time tomorrow, we'll be at our new home in Florida," I said flexing my legs.

She shook her head in disbelief. "I never thought I'd ever leave Wynne, Arkansas," she replied lazily. "Well, we better go to the bathroom before Daddy starts fussing," I said, breaking into her moment of reflection.

While walking towards the building, I turned around and saw Janet following me. Mother smiled as she exited the bathroom's entrance and headed towards the van. It amazed me how sweet and humble she was. Though her character was quiet and discrete, my mother's smiles spoke volumes. Whenever in distress, her smile spoke of peace. Whenever discouraged, her smile spoke of hope. Whatever the situation, her smile seemed to have its own special prophetic message. My mind raced back to a specific time when her smile silenced the fear in my soul:

> The Persian-Gulf War was in full effect. Young and high-spirited, I could see myself then trying to conquer life even though the scent of war was in the air. I recalled watching and listening silently to the rain as it tapped against my windowpane. While staring blindly out the window, vivid images of war that could not be specifically detailed flashed through my mind. As soon as the imagery had begun, dread overtook my thoughts. It moved like a cancerous tumor, slowly upward, until it had conquered every part of my body. Frightened and awestruck, I turned on the television. Graphic pictures of men who had lost their lives in the fast spreading war once again filled the small screen.
>
> During that season of war, night after endless night, I lied on my time-withered bed, watching the dancing shadows formed by my sisters' hands, attempting to override my fears. I imagined the blood that twirled around bodies that had been slain and envisioned souls that had been forever engraved within its crimson components. To no avail, I often cried myself to sleep seeking peace of mind.
>
> One particular night, while peering through crystallized droplets from my bedroom window, I prayed for God's protection for my family and myself through the treacherous night. A wisp of cool air from beneath the windowpane sent chills racing down my spine. A mild scent of mildew crept into the room. With great fear, I stood.
>
> As I walked down the long dark hallway, I peered into my mother's room. She was kneeling beside the bed. The faint sound of an anchorman was announcing another victim of the war. I could see her tear-stained face as her mouth formed words but nothing was uttered. The television's glare allowed the silhouette of mother's oval face to be traced. While stand-

ing there and looking at her, all of the yearly hardships could be seen intertwined with every curve of her rounded face. At that precise moment, our eyes fell upon one another unifying our souls. She smiled softly. It was a beacon of light that helped me find my way through those remaining dark days of violence. It was then, suspended by a smile on a dark night, when I realized that regardless of whatever alarming situation life had in store for me, my mother's smile would always linger and provide me with the strength and courage I needed to survive it.

I smiled in memory of that cold night in October. After using the bathroom, I walked over to the sink, washed my hands, and looked into the mirror. I ran my fingers through my thick locks as I tried to undo the damage the wind had caused. My sister did the same.

After freshening up, we returned to where the rest of the family was. They were lounging around on a nearby picnic table eating lunch. I picked through a box of potato chips that was sitting on the hood of our van, found my favorite Doritos, grabbed a soda, and then took one of the sandwiches that my mother had made.

Everyone ate in silence. The humidity along with the exhaustion from the ride had depleted our energy. Although I sat under the pavilion, the sun's rays seemed to follow me. I chunked down the remainder of my hardened sandwich and climbed into the van to escape the sun's rays. "I'm ready to go," I said aloud to no one in particular. "At least maybe some air will circulate." I climbed into the van and stretched out on the back seat. Just as I was getting comfortable, the side door abruptly pulled open.

"Get up," Melvin teased. "We're getting ready to go."

I agitatedly got up and slid towards the window as my brothers and sister began to pile into the van.

The whole excitement of the trip had faded. I didn't realize how hot and long the trip would be. Watching objects through the window was fun at first, but after nine hours, things were getting pretty boring. As we pulled back off onto the main freeway, I began to fantasize about how my new school would be. After a while, sleep slowly took over. It was only in dreamland that I was able to escape the furious heat.

I awakened the next morning with the sun's rays beaming through the window. I slightly opened my eyes, so they could adjust to the brightness. To my amazement, I saw white stuff all over the ground. I knew it was too hot for snow.

"What's that white stuff on the ground?" I asked to anyone that would answer.

"That's sand," my father answered in excitement.

I glanced up into the front view mirror. He had a sparkle in his eyes as if he was thinking about his new life that lay ahead for him. I looked back out the window.

The sand was so white that it looked unreal. It was the color of chalk. Once I saw the palm trees, I knew we had finally arrived in Florida. They were like huge pineapples stuck in the ground. The sun sent shimmering sparkles dancing across the surface of the ocean's cerulean body. I could hardly believe that it was only yesterday I was in Wynne, the pun of poverty. All across the blue sky were large seagulls flapping their mighty wings as they hovered over the ocean's body while scouting for food. "Yes," I decided, "*this would definitely be a better life for my family.*"

Just When I Thought It Couldn't Get Worse

When we made it to Orlando, it was pitch black outside. As dad pulled over to a gas station, he said, "This is where we'll sleep for the night." I didn't dare ask why we were sleeping in our van instead of a nice, cozy hotel. I threw a look of confusion in Janet's direction. Both of us tried our best to stifle our laughter. I quickly ducked my head, so dad wouldn't discern that the escaped laughter had come from me.

"What are y'all doing back there?" His voice boomed in rage. Everything got silent. I didn't even dare to breathe. As he saw that no one was going to speak, he roared, "I don't want to hear anything else out of any of you. Go to sleep!"

Afterwards, I was afraid to move too much, afraid the noise might irritate him. That night, it was hard to sleep due to a roaming mind and a bad stomachache. It was almost time for my menstrual cycle to start. I silently prayed it would be irregular and not come. I spent the remainder of the night in a tight ball trying to bear the pain of premenstrual cramps.

The next morning I awakened and glanced around me. Mom was preparing sandwiches for us to eat. I peered out the window. It actually seemed as if steam was coming up out of the pavement. I picked up a nearby piece of paper and began fanning myself. The humidity was unbelievable. I literally felt as if I was being cooked alive.

After dad finished eating, he started up the van. "Let's go see the town. After that, I'm going to try and find work, so I can get us a place to live."

No one uttered a word, not even Mom. We pulled out of the parking lot and drove off into the traffic. I couldn't focus on anything except the words that my father had just spoken. *What did he mean about going to find work to get us a place to live?* I juggled the question over and over in my head. *I can't believe he moved us here before securing a job first.* Every ounce of joy I had left came to a complete halt. I was furious. I sat on the backseat, staring at the back of my father's head. *How can you do this to us?* I screamed at him inwardly. *How could you take your family from our home and have us living on the streets? Just because you want to be a homeless low-life doesn't give you the right to do the same to us!"* I wanted so badly to smack him in the back of the head in a fit of premenstrual frenzy.

After he had driven for a while, he pulled up in front of a Labor Ready overcrowed with Mexicans. "I'm going in to see if they have any jobs available," he announced. As soon as he disappeared into the building, everyone started talking at once.

"Momma!" I shrieked. "You mean to tell me, we don't have anywhere to stay?"

Before she could answer, Melvin interrupted. "I can't believe this mess! I should have stayed in Wynne with Marsha and Ray."

Mom turned around in her seat to face us. "We just have to keep praying. Hopefully we'll find a place soon," she chuckled halfheartedly. I could hardly believe that she was taking it so calmly. "We will have to just see what happens."

All of a sudden, I burst out laughing. Ted, my youngest brother who was two years younger than I, looked at me strangely. "What's so funny?" he asked.

"We are bums! We are bums!" I chanted over and over in a fit of laughter. Soon everyone started laughing. "We are homeless bums!" Janet emphasized the word homeless while bursting in an array of giggles.

After what seemed like hours, my father finally walked back outdoors. He had a huge grin plastered on his face. "I got it!" he exclaimed as soon as he pulled the van's door open. I rolled my eyes upward. "Hold these directions Stella," he said, while handing her a piece of crumpled paper. "I'm going to be working at Pleasure Island located at Disney World. I have to be there first thing tomorrow morning. We're going to go find the place now, so I'll know where it is." He jumped in the front seat and drove off.

Once again, we were on the road. After a few hours of driving, dad pointed a finger out his window, "Look!" he beamed. My eyes followed his fingers and spotted a massive white ball that towered above the trees. "That's Epcot Center!" he exclaimed.

He continued to drive on, and within minutes, we arrived at Pleasure Island. It was gorgeous. There were pretty flowers and trees all over the place. The buildings looked like miniature castles.

"This is it, everyone. This is where I'll be working," Dad

said while parking in front of a tan-colored building. Without another word, he got out the van and strolled towards the building's entrance. Once he was no longer in view, I shouted with pleasure, "Wow, it's pretty here!"

"It sure is," Janet breathed as we looked around at the well-manicured lawn. Tulips, daffodils, roses, and many other exotic flowers were displayed as far as the eyes could see. After a moment of silence, Janet said to no one in particular, "I wonder where we'll be staying while Daddy is at work?"

"I really don't care as long as he is away from me," I sneered.

"I know that's real," she interjected.

After a few minutes of being gone, my father walked briskly back towards the vehicle. "Yes," he said as he climbed in. "This is where I'll be working." Afterwards he cranked the van up and drove off into the sunset.

It was dark outside when we made it back to the gas station where we had slept the previous night. *"Oh, brother, not this place again,"* I thought. After parking, each of us took turns using the restroom. When I went in, I saw specks of blood on my underwear. "Great. What am I going to do now?" I mumbled. I didn't have any money to buy pads or tampons, so I placed fifty-cents in the sanitary machine and purchased a package of feminine napkins. After washing my hands, I stepped back into the humid night.

Once inside the van, I stretched out onto the back floor. By now, my stomach was cramping badly. *"I must be cursed,"* I declared inwardly. *"Everything that concerns me seems to go wrong. Maybe, I was born to suffer?"* I quickly wiped away any trace of tears that had escaped. I fell asleep trying to delude both the physically and mentally anguish from my mind.

After hours of sleep, I awakened to the sound of our vehicle being ignited. Moments later we were moving. It was yet dark outside, but now a hint of blue was breaking through the sky. I refused to wake up entirely and soon drifted back into a deep sleep.

After hearing the van's door slam shut, I momentarily sat up. We were at Pleasure Island. My father no longer sat in the vehicle with us.

"Is Daddy gone to work?" I whispered to Mom.

"Yes," she said as she leaned back in her chair. I drifted back off to sleep.

A few hours later, I awakened to the sound of Janet's voice. "Do we have to stay here all day?" she asked.

"I don't know my way around Florida," my mother replied with a hint of sarcasm. "Your father would be mad if he got off of work to find us gone." Agitated from being woken, I got up from the floor, sat down, and stared out the window, daring someone to irritate me any further, so I could give them a piece of my mind.

Hour after hour, we sat in that hot van. "Open the side door, so the air can ventilate in here," Mom said. After obeying, it yet seemed there was hardly any air circulating. Soon, I became so engrossed in my romance novel that I stopped focusing on the heat. In fact, I was too enraptured with the heat generating between the book's main characters.

About four o'clock that evening, Dad returned. "I sure am hungry," he said. "What does everyone want to eat today?" Thinking it was a trick question, no one said anything. After his second attempt, everyone blurted out his or her requests. After finally agreeing on chicken, Dad drove us to Popeye's, where we ate to our heart's content.

The next evening, after Dad got off work, he drove us to a City Mission for dinner. After walking through the graffiti-decorated doors, he steered us towards a half-occupied table where each of us took a seat. My heart filled with sadness for the little kids that sat around the room with their parents. *"So this is how homeless people live,"* I thought, looking down at the strange-looking food. I couldn't imagine living like that everyday. Well, whether or not I accepted it, I was now no different than any of them; I too was homeless and hungry.

It took me a minute to muster up enough courage to actually bite into the food. When I finally did, I was surprised to find that it didn't taste like garbage. It was actually delicious.

The people we sat with seemed to be very friendly. My father fit in well with them like the missing piece to their puzzle. He and some of the other guys began to engage in conversation.

"Wow, this is where he belongs," I chuckled underneath my breath towards Janet's ear. "He fits right in." We both snickered.

After finishing our meal, we pulled into a deserted parking lot for the night. The area looked very dangerous, but I knew better than to voice my opinion. There were homeless people all around us. Some were sleeping in cardboard boxes, and others were just stretched out on the ground close to their buggies. In the distance, arguing could be heard.

It was hard for me to sleep that night because of all the commotion that was going on outside. I trembled as I watched a shadow approach my window. It was a man. At the same time, Melvin noticed him also. I guess the prowler didn't know our vehicle was occupied because he stood directly at the window and peered inside.

"Look, Daddy!" Melvin and I both shouted.

As my father turned around, he saw the man. He flung the door open and yelled, "Get away from here!" Startled, the man took off running.

"These people are crazy here," I said, not caring if my father heard.

I guess Dad could sense everyone's anxiety because he soon drove off in search of another location for the night. He pulled up at a dark secluded place on the side of the road and parked.

"We can sleep here tonight." He let out a sigh of desperation then continued. "This can't go on. I have to get us a house to live in."

I wanted to scream, "It's about time you got some sense! You should have thought about that before moving us down here," but of course, I didn't. Instead, I peered out the now foggy window to examine our new resting location. It was spooky here as well, but I lay on the floor and prayed that God would protect us throughout the night. I kept my eyes open until they became too heavy. Before I knew it, I had drifted off.

It was yet dark outside when I awakened to the sound of my mother's scream. I jolted upright and saw a man running down the street.

"He was staring in my window!" she wailed, "and was pulling up on the door handle trying to get in. When I awoke, he nearly scared me to death!"

"Get some sleep," Dad said, obviously frustrated by the endangerment he was placing on his family. "I'll stay awake tonight, so everyone can get some rest."

Early the next morning, I awakened to a sticky substance trickling down my legs. I looked down in horror afraid of what I'd find. To my dismay, my skirt was covered in blood. Nauseous, I mumbled underneath my breath, "Lord, you have to help us. I refuse to live like this any longer." Before anyone awakened, I grabbed some clean cloths from my suitcase and changed into them. Next, I took my soiled skirt and used it as sanitary protection. It was disgusting, but I didn't have much of a choice. We were so poor that I couldn't even afford tampons.

The remainder of that day and many to follow, I refrained from speaking to anyone. I sat in silence and stared out the window at the smoldering pavement. For about a month, my family and I were homeless. This journey was definitely not turning out the way I expected.

And just when I thought it couldn't get any worse, it did. One evening after my father got off of work, he seemed overly excited. "Let's go find a place to live." He beamed. I could hardly believe my ears. I was so tired of living in our hot and stuffy van void of privacy.

Within minutes of searching for an apartment, he pulled up next to a small yellow duplex that read: *For Rent*. He got out and jotted the telephone number down. After reentering, he said, "I'm going to a payphone, so I can call and find out how much they're asking for." Next, he drove over to the gas station across the street from the apartment.

After stopping, everyone got out to stretch. *Please, let us get it, Lord. I'm so miserable,* I pleaded with God. All I wanted was to sleep in a soft bed and use a decent bathroom.

After we had all piled back into the van, my mother turned towards my father and asked, "What did they say?"

My father replied joyfully, "They weren't asking for much. In fact, the man said that he would meet us over at the duplex in a few minutes. He said the apartment is already furnished." I remained calm. I was happy about the good news but was afraid of getting my hopes up too high.

By now, darkness was starting to clothe the sky, and the streets were beginning to light up with nightlife. Within minutes of our waiting in front of the apartment, a short chubby blond-haired man pulled up beside us with his window down.

"Come on." He motioned to my father as he got out his muddy Dodge truck.

After being in the house for a while, the man and my dad came out talking amongst themselves. Finally, Daddy left the man's side and walked over to Mom's window.

"Stella," he said, "we can move in tonight if we don't mind cleaning the house up ourselves. It's apparent a homeless person has been living in the house because the apartment is in pretty bad shape. After overhearing that portion of the conversation,

I figured it couldn't be too bad. I mean how could anything be worse than living in a vehicle while on your period?

"Get out and tell me what you think," he said, opening her door. When she got out, the rest of us immediately started piling out the side door behind her.

When I looked into the front door of the house, I could hardly believe my eyes. The Sci-Fi channel couldn't even conjure up a picture like the one that lay before me. Huge cockroaches, gigantic dead spiders, and overstuffed maggots littered the floor. I turned and rushed back outdoors. I hoped that just maybe I could persuade my mother to talk my father out of it.

"Mom, please don't make me stay there!" I begged and pleaded with her. "I'll be willing to sleep in the van longer. I won't complain anymore. Just please don't make me sleep in there!"

I quickly straightened my face up as my father walked out the door and came towards my mother and me. "I know it'll take a lot of cleaning up, but this is all we have right now," he said.

I abruptly walked back into the house.

"He makes me sick," I said to my brothers and sister, who was busy dumping paper and things into garbage bags. "Just because he's used to nastiness...why does he want us to be like him? This is so disgusting that it's absolutely horrific!" I announced brusquely.

No one else said a word but continued to work. I couldn't tell if they were upset and didn't want to talk, or if they were making the best out of a horrible situation.

Filled with nausea, I stepped outside to get some fresh air. I wanted to burst out crying with all of my might, but once again, I knew it wouldn't make a difference. I didn't have any choice in the matter. We were definitely moving in the house whether I liked it or not.

I walked back inside and looked around. Ted, Melvin, and Janet were submissively helping my parents clean up the filthiness. There was a lot to do, so I humbly picked a spot on the living room floor and started there. Suddenly, out of the corner of my eye, I noticed big, furry things in the corner of the room. I could have sworn they had moved. I inched closer to get a better look. Thinking they were huge balls of hair and that my eyes were playing tricks on me, I bent over to discard of them. When I made it close enough to see what they were, I realized they were huge tarantulas—almost the size of Thing on *The Addam's Family*. Their furry feet fluttered as the last breath of life was sucked from them, obviously from poison. I took off running out of the apartment as fast as I could into the moonlight. I shook with such a violent array of tremors that I could have easily gone into a state of shock. Spiders terrified me. The typical arachnophobia victim had nothing on me. I was so afraid of spiders that I probably would have jumped in front of a moving vehicle just to keep one from getting on me.

After my initial shock, I mustered up enough courage to go back into the unrealistic domain and plunged back into the gruesome work. Garbage bags began to fill rapidly. I shuttered in disgust as the flying coach roaches wings flapped against the sealed trash bags trying to break free. Every time I filled a bag, I ran outside to gasp for air. It felt as if germs and bugs were crawling all over me. Although I was exhausted, I didn't see any way I could sleep in the house that night.

As my mother walked outside to discard some garbage, I followed close behind. I pulled her to the side and spoke as quietly as I could so my father wouldn't overhear the conversation. Without raising my voice, I did my best in allowing her to know I was upset. It was hard to do while whispering.

"Mom, please let me sleep in the van tonight? I'll get sick if I stay in there," I pleaded.

"No." she replied calmly. "You'll sleep with everyone else, in this house and in a bed."

"But Mom, there's spiders in there. I'm scared of them. They're gigantic," I continued to whine. At that moment, my father came outside, carrying a trash bag. I rolled my eyes upward and briskly stomped back into the house.

The sky was charcoal black with fragments of shimmering diamond-like stars when I hauled the last garbage bag outside. Daddy decided to wait on unpacking our belongings with the exception of our night cloths and personal items until the next day. I was relieved because there wasn't much strength left in me.

Things couldn't have possibly gotten any worse than living in a vehicle for about a month and walking into a nasty house with maggots, huge spiders, and huge coach roaches on the floor, so I thought.

"You all will be sleeping together," my mother announced after all of us had gathered in the living room.

"What!" I exclaimed. "How in the world do you think all of us are going to sleep in the same bed?" I questioned, wanting her to explain the procedure to me. She proceeded to do just that.

"Janet and you will sleep in the middle; Ted and Melvin will sleep on the outside," she said having it all figured out.

There wasn't anyway I could change her mind, arguing was senseless. All that would do was get me in trouble. At this point, getting a "beat down" for being sassy probably would have provoked me to runaway.

With my lips poked out, I walked towards the bedroom. I grabbed my night clothes out of my suitcase and went into the bathroom. *"Why can't I just die?"* I thought leaning against the cold door. *"Anything would be better than living like this."* I glanced into the mirror and was disgusted with what I saw. My jerry curl was nappy and my eyes had dark circles around them.

"Look at me. Everyone at school is going to think I'm ugly," I ranted out loud. "It's always either I'm too fat, too dark, too tall, or something. I'm tired of being ridiculed because of my looks. One day, I'll be pretty, and I'll have lots of guys liking me," I declared while undressing. Within minutes, I was dressed for bed.

While walking to the bedroom, I could hear my mother and father talking behind their closed door. It seemed they already started to accept that this was home. *"This would never be my home,"* I thought rebelliously. Although Wynne was boring, poverty-stricken, and brought many bad memories, it would always be a place where I could call home.

That night, I lay in the bed by my sister and between my two brothers and stared at the ceiling. There was hardly any room to turn. I was getting claustrophobic, which made it almost unbearable to fall asleep. My eyes strained from trying to see if I could see any black, hairy, things crawling on the floor or ceiling. I was so terrified of the big spiders I had seen earlier that now I was paranoid. Their vivid imagery would forever be imprinted within my mind.

After only being in bed for about thirty minutes, heavy breathing could already be heard from around me. I guess due to the strenuous work of the day, my brothers and sister's young bodies were worn out. I stayed in the position of lying on my back for as long as I possibly could and finally gave in to turning on my side. I was tired but continued to restlessly rotate from my back and onto my side until my brother Melvin woke up.

"Will you stop moving around so much?" he asked his voice dry and raspy.

"I'm trying to get comfortable," I explained. "I can't sleep."

There wasn't any response, nothing but quietness, so I figured he had drifted back off to sleep. I lay there once more on my back staring up into the ceiling. I refused to close my eyes until they were too heavy to keep open.

When morning came, the aroma of food awakened me. I almost forgot where I was until I opened my eyes and saw a big cockroach zoom by my face and land on the wall. Suddenly, reality struck me. There was no mistake that I was in the yellow duplex that had been totally infested the night before. I slid on my tennis shoes to walk to the bathroom. I didn't want to get my feet contaminated. I had turned into a germ freak for sure.

After taking care of my personal hygiene, I joined the rest of the family in the kitchen. They were all sitting down eating cereal and bacon.

"Hurry up, and finish eating," my father said rising from the table. "We have a lot of unpacking to do."

I hurried and ate the bowl of cereal, while staying alert for roaches that would inevitably come zooming by. The smell of their bacteria infested little bodies, along with the images that had invaded my mind about the previous night, nauseated me.

I ran outside and threw up by the side of the house. "Time to get to work," My sister's voice teased as she walked out the front door behind me. By the look on my face, she knew I was really sick. I didn't respond but continued to lean against the cold, damp bricks. She walked pass me, opened the van's side door, and loaded some of the boxes and other items in her arms to carry inside the house. Within minutes, Melvin and Ted joined her. When I heard the front door slam shut again, I assumed it was my father and immediately jerked upright. I rushed over to the van and began helping out.

With the help of everyone, we unloaded the items very quickly. Trying to decide where everything should go was the time-consuming part. Once everything was in its place, the infested duplex looked more like a nice home, but in my heart, it would never be home.

My mother finally made arrangements for Janet and me to keep one of the bedrooms, and Melvin and Ted would sleep in the living room on the couch. I agreed to that plan just fine. I didn't want to get used to waking up next to drooling and morning breath.

A Glimpse of Hope

After living there for a week, I awakened to the sound of voices outside our bedroom window. I peeked outside and saw four guys unloading furniture in the duplex next to ours. I wondered if they were moving in. I nudged my sister in the side to wake her up.

"Janet, Janet. Wake up." I said with excitement. Rubbing her eyes, she rolled over and glared at me. "Look! I think we're getting new neighbors," I whispered as if they could hear me. "Look outside for yourself."

"You woke me up just to tell me that?" she asked rolling back on her side.

"Ooh, that guy is so cute!" I spat out lustfully as my eyes fell on a tall and dark-skinned guy. His whole demeanor declared GQ. At that comment, Janet leaped out of bed and peered through the blinds alongside me. When she saw that there were four guys outside, her mouth fell open. "Let me get up and put some cloths on!" she sang out in anticipation.

"I thought so," I said laughing hysterically.

We both jumped from the bed and started pulling open drawers to find something to wear. I found a two-piece green and black wool skirt set and threw it on.

"Boy, I look good," I said, modeling the outfit in front of the mirror. It fitted so tightly that my too-grown-for-my-age hips were easily revealed. I was only fourteen at the time, but I had the body of a twenty-five or thirty year old. Although I was yet a virgin, my full, wide hips and breasts declared a sexually-active lifestyle. Oftentimes, it was older men that approached me.

Janet rapidly threw on a short, blue-jean skirt with a matching top and ran to the window to see if the guys were still outside. Upon seeing that they were, she ran to the bathroom and started doing her hair and making up her face. While she was in the bathroom, I began to tidy the room up.

When she returned and saw that the room was clean, she ran

to the window, pulled the blinds all the way up, and then opened the window. Immediately, the eyes of the guys turned towards our direction. I ducked in embarrassment as Janet waved and smiled from ear to ear. When I saw them waving back and looking with interest, I stood and started doing the same. When two of the guys walked up to the window, I was terrified. One of them was the tall, dark brother who I had found to be very handsome. I had no clue as what to do next.

"Hi, there," one of them said holding his mouth close to the glass. "We're your new neighbors."

"Janet, what if Daddy sees them over here?" I muffled under my breath while maintaining my smile.

"Run and go see what he's doing," she uttered never losing her poise.

"What's your name?" the other short, light-skinned guy asked Janet as I fled to go spy on my father.

I walked into the living room. Dad, Melvin, and Ted were sitting there eating breakfast on the couch. I sat down as if interested in what they were watching on television. I waited until a commercial came on and jumped up to go back into the bedroom.

"He's eating," I said bursting back into our room. Afterwards, I closed the door and locked it behind me. "Janet, you better hurry up. You don't know when Dad will finish." I protested.

Obviously having overheard my statement, both guys said simultaneously, "Well, it was nice meeting you lovely ladies. We need to finish our work, but we'll definitely be talking to you both again."

As they turned to leave, the tall chocolate brother stopped in his tracks. "By the way, what's your name?" he asked as he looked straight into my eyes.

"Crystal," I breathed.

My legs weakened underneath me. This was the first time a guy had ever made me feel that way or even made it that obvious he noticed me for that matter. After hearing my name, he had the audacity to smile at me and then wink. By now, my heart was pounding so fast that every thud resounded in my ear. This brother was fine. His rich, chocolate skin was blemish free, and his white teeth dazzled as he spoke.

"It was verrrrrry nice to meet you," he growled.

All I could do was stand there with a silly grin on my face. I was blushing ridiculously, but of course, he couldn't tell because I was too dark to notice. This was one time I was very happy for my blue-black complexion.

When he walked away and was no longer in sight, I started jumping all over the room.

"He came back just to ask for my name," I sang gleefully. "And did you see how he looked at me?" I stopped jumping for a split second to grab onto Janet's arm.

"You're silly," she said chuckling at my immaturity. I walked back and forth by the mirror, so I could see how I looked.

"I'm so sexy!" I announced while observing my image from each angle.

"Yeah, right," Janet sneered as she rolled her eyes upward and walked out the room.

"Quit hating!" I screamed after her.

While searching for Mom, I found her in the kitchen.

"Where's Daddy?" I asked.

"He went to the store," she replied while washing dishes that were in the sink. "Tomorrow, I'm going to take all of you to get your physical exams, so you guys can get back into school," she stated.

"Can we go and see what the school looks like?" I asked.

"Yes, tomorrow after y'all take your physical exams." She replied continuing to wash the dishes.

Suddenly sadness surrounded me. "We don't have any good clothes to wear for school. Everyone's going to laugh at us," I complained remembering our poverty.

"You have to use what you got or ask your father." She added.

Before she could change the subject, "Mom, you know Daddy won't buy us any clothes." I interjected. "When has he ever bought us any?" She had to see my point because not once did I remember Dad buying us clothes.

"Well, regardless, ask God to bless you with some new clothes. Pray about it." She answered.

"You always say that," I said abruptly cutting her off. It seemed as if every time a problem arose, she would always tell me to pray about it. I just wanted some simple solutions to my problems. There was nothing else to say to her, so I walked into the living room and sat on the couch.

While sitting, thoughts of the two guys earlier emerged. I had on my best outfit already, so I didn't have anything left to impress them with. *I guess I could pray,* I thought, but quickly dismissed the idea from my head. At that moment, my father walked through the front door and sat down on the couch opposite of me. I couldn't stand being in the same room with him for too long. I always felt awkward as if he was trying to find fault with me just so he could have a reason to gripe. I was already frustrated, so I leaped up and walked outside. I could feel his eyes on the back of my head as if he wanted to say something sarcastic. I didn't hesitate to give him an opportunity to do so.

It was beautiful outside. There were hardly any clouds in the sky. The air was cool and the temperature was nearly perfect. I was glad that the humidity had finally cooled off due to the rain we had gotten the previous day. I found an old chair on the side of the house and sat on it. For minutes, I sat there and watched as cars drove down the street. I didn't dare sit in front of the house to dismiss any notion from my father that I was trying to be fast in front of the new guys. Right now, I just wanted to be alone. I didn't even want to talk to the guy I had met earlier. I couldn't remember his name anyway.

I was still sitting in the same spot, looking clueless, when a short guy passed by our house. He looked like he was in his mid-thirties. When he did a double take in my direction, I could tell that he pondered on whether or not to say something to me. On the third glance, his gaze lingered a bit too long. I smiled and looked away politely. I guess that was his cue to talk.

"How are you today, missy?" He asked as if not getting the hint that I didn't want to be bothered.

"Fine, and you?" I replied lazily. I noticed then that he was chewing on something.

"Well, I'll be doing even better if I can get more of this good barbecue," he said as if he had known me for a long time. "My homeboy is barbecuing, and I'm going back over there to get some more." He continued now leaning on our fence.

"That sounds like fun," I said wishing he would leave and go to wherever he was going before my father saw him talking to me.

"Would you like to go with me?" he asked.

"No thanks, but you can bring me some barbecue back," I said playfully.

"I will," he said as he waved and resumed walking.

"I'm just kidding!" I screamed after him hoping he didn't take me seriously.

The front door opened, and my younger brother Ted came outside. "We'll be going back to school soon," I sighed trying to strike up a conversation.

"I'm glad, because I'm tired of staying around here with nothing to do," he monotonously responded.

"Will you ask Daddy if he'll take us shopping?" I asked getting straight to the point. I hoped he would be the brave one to ask.

"Are you crazy?" he said as he walked past me and into the front yard.

Actually, I was glad he had made that move because now it

was my opportunity to follow. In case my father saw me sitting out in the front, he would think I was just playing with Ted.

"Why are you following me? You just want to be seen," Ted said angrily when he saw me walk around the house to where he was playing with his big red dump truck. Although young, Ted was very observant.

"I'm not," I said chuckling at his wisdom.

"Then why did you wait until I came to the front to come around here?" he investigated. "Oh, be quiet," I said agitated with his probing.

At that moment, the new guy that had asked for my name came outdoors. He noticed me and immediately waved. I slyly waved back, so Ted wouldn't see. As he continued to unpack the U-Haul, his eyes kept making contact with mine. Each time our eyes met, we both smiled at one another.

The front door opened. Janet glimpsed in the direction of the guys next door. "Oh, so this is where you are," she said stepping outside. She looked at me knowingly as she brought a chair out beside mines on the front porch. She and I sat outside talking until darkness covered the sky and our new neighbors had gone inside their apartment. That night, I fell asleep thinking about my tall, dark, and handsome neighbor.

Early the next morning, Mom awakened each of us to prepare for a trip to the doctor for our physical exams. After eating breakfast, we loaded up in the van. First, my mother dropped my father off at the Labor Ready, so he could catch a ride to work; afterwards, we headed to the clinic.

It didn't take long for the doctors to examine each of us. When it was time for the results, it was discovered that I was slightly overweight. According to the doctor, I just needed to lose about ten pounds, but my brothers and sisters acted as if it were fifty pounds.

"You need to lose weight," Janet teased as she looked over my shoulder at the scale I was standing on.

"Maybe, she would if she stopped eating so much," Melvin chuckled.

At my previous school in Wynne, I was constantly teased because I was thicker and taller than most girls. Now, I had to put up with my siblings teasing me about the very same things. There wasn't any escape from the humiliation. The same spirit of low self- esteem once again began to descend upon me like a bandit. Due to the constant criticism about my weight, a struggle to fit the description of what society said was beautiful developed. Throughout the majority of my teenage and adult life, I went on countless yo-yo diets and tried to exercise regularly, but my addiction to food only grew stronger; and I sunk deeper into depression.

After everyone got their results at the clinic and had reloaded the van, my mother drove us to Janet's school first.

"This is where you'll be going to school," she said.

"Wow, it's huge!" I exclaimed as I pressed my face against the window to study the massive white and red brick building. Since Janet was going to the eighth grade, she would be attending a different school from Melvin and me.

After we had been there awhile, mom cranked up the van, and we proceeded to go see Ted's school. It was right down the street from Janet's, the same exact color but only smaller. Afterwards, we were on our way to see Melvin's and mine."

As we drove up to Howard Middle School, my mouth flew open. "Now this is what I call a school!" I exclaimed.

Before me, stood a colossal three-story building that covered half a block. Outside, on the basketball court, a movie was being filmed. Movie cameras and people overcrowded the area.

"What are they doing?" I asked to no one in particular.

"Looks like they're making a movie," Melvin breathed excitedly. It wasn't until later that we found out the movie, *White Men Can't Jump*, was being filmed.

My mother found a parking spot in front of the school. After exiting the vehicle, we entered the school. The hallways were quiet, only a few stragglers walked the long corridors. As we approached the front office, I noticed a police officer standing in the hallway talking to a student. When we walked in the office, I saw another officer sitting at the front desk next to an older lady. He was reading a newspaper.

The elderly lady's eyes raised from the work that sprawled before her as mom approached the desk. "Excuse me," she said cheerfully. "I want to register my kids for school." Next, she extended the results of our physicals and our identification requirements to the lady. The gray-headed lady retrieved the papers from my mother's hand and typed some information into the computer. Without a word, she stood and stepped out the office. A few seconds later, she returned followed by the officer that was in the hallway.

"These officers that you see here," she said, "are the school's patrol officers. Because of the school's size, we need these guys to help ensure all of the student's safety."

Each cop shook our hands as they introduced themselves. "Well, Crystal and Melvin, we're happy to have you both here with us at Howard Middle School," each of them said.

"Thank you," we both replied. The secretary then handed Melvin and I a folder full of information about the school along with our class schedules.

"If you'll wait right here," the officer said gesturing in my mother's direction, "I will show the two of them where their classes are located."

Melvin and I followed the officer out the office and into the still hallway. I was very nervous but tried to play it off. I had on a blue-jean outfit that looked fairly decent, and my jerry curl had plenty of activator in it.

"Let me see your schedule," Officer Brown told Melvin as he reached out his hand to retrieve it. "This is one of your classes right here," he said as we stopped outside one of the rooms.

The classroom was extremely quiet except for the sound of chalk hitting the board. I glanced over at Melvin. The expression on his face made it very visible that he was extremely nervous. I wanted to laugh, but because I was nervous as well, figured I had better wait until we got home to joke about it.

As they both went inside the room, I took it upon myself not to follow. I peeked through the miniature window as the officer interrupted the teacher and introduced Melvin to the class. *Oh, Lord. How will I be able to do that?* I panicked. Seconds later, they both walked back out. That was their routine with each of his classes. Just as soon as the introductions had begun, they had all ended.

The fact that I didn't know anyone at this school didn't bother me. I viewed it as an advantage because now I had the opportunity to change my whole identity. No one knew of my past, so they couldn't use it against me. No one would know of it unless I revealed it. Back home, my past labeled me as an outcast. I was nothing more than a poor, trashy, and ugly nerd as well as other negative jargons. Living here in Florida would be different. Determination on my part purposed to change those labels.

My time had arrived. Despite the eruption of anxiety, I tried my best to be brave. I walked into my first class with ease. I arched my back, straightened my poise, and displayed one of my best smiles. Everything got silent. All eyes were on me. *Okay. Crystal don't panic,* I muttered under my breath. *Inhale. Exhale. You can do this.* I continued to encourage myself. The officer then turned to me and introduced me to the class. Afterwards, I waved quickly and rushed for the door. By the time I had made it to my third classroom, my nerves had subsided substantially.

After Melvin and I had been introduced to our classes, the officer led us back to the office where the others were waiting. Once inside, the officer who had been sitting at the desk when we first arrived stood to address the two of us.

"We're looking forward to having you here. Do your best in

school and work hard. If you have any problems, come and see me." He smiled, revealing a mouth full of stained teeth.

"We sure will." Melvin and I both agreed. Next, after collecting all of our needed papers, we turned to leave and exited out the doors that we had come in.

"That was fun," I said once we were pulling off from the schoolyard. I looked down at my dingy blue-jean skirt with its matching jacket and stated, "We definitely have to get some new cloths. I refuse to go there looking like this."

The denim outfit had been passed down from my eldest sister Marsha then on to Janet, and now it finally rested in my hands. That was the same for most of the cloths I owned. I was sick of hand-me-downs. I couldn't even recall when I last had some new cloths.

"While being introduced to my classes, it seemed like everyone was looking at what I was wearing. I don't want everyone laughing at me," I said recalling how it was at my old school. I was the laughing stock of many.

"Did you ask your father about buying you some new cloths?" my mother asked, cutting into my parade of complaints.

"No, but I will. I'm desperate. He'll just have to fuss at me." I leaned back into the seat to conjure up a strategy to persuade him.

The Same Old Thing

When we made it back to the house, my father was already there. He was slouched over the kitchen counter talking to himself. I sat down on the couch and cut the television on. While glancing up at him, I could tell he had been drinking. His head bobbed as if an invisible string was attached to it pulling his head up and down over and over repetitively like a drunken puppet. Deviously, I hoped that he would get sloppy drunk. It would provide an excellent opportunity to ask him for some money to buy school clothes. Although at first, I might have to endure criticism and outbursts of profanity. But sooner or later, hopefully, he would give in.

I knew my dad very well. Occasionally, in his stupor, he'd leave his money lying around, and my siblings, along with myself, would sneak it from him. Whenever he sobered, he often asked where his money was. After no answers, he would assume he had lost it somewhere. Strangely, it seemed he was more pleasant when he was drunk than when he was sober unless he was sloppy drunk, and in that case, he was ready to fight. At least then, he had an excuse for being mean, but when he sobered, the look of detest could easily be detected in his eyes. And he couldn't blame that look on intoxication.

After I saw my father bob his head continuously, I jumped up and went into the bedroom with my sister, so I could tell her he was drunk. This was my last effort to try and get someone else to do the deed of asking him for some money. Someone had to do it, and I didn't want to be the one to do the dirty work.

"Janet," I said, causing her to look up from our bed she laid across.

"What do you want?" she asked sluggishly.

"Daddy's drunk. Will you ask him for some money, so we can buy clothes for school?" I hoped to persuade her.

"Why don't you ask him? He'll listen to you," she said, looking at me like I had lost my mind. I knew why. She and my father constantly fought with one another whether he had been drinking or not. He had met his match. Although Janet was about 5'7 with a medium build, she was awfully strong. She didn't let his tall stature or his outbreaks of anger intimidate her. She didn't like him either, and he knew it. She closed her eyes once more and resumed resting. I realized this was her signal that the conversation had ended. "Well, I might as well ask Ted," I sighed, thinking about my next plan of action.

I glanced out the living-room window and saw him playing in the backyard. Once outside, it dawned upon me that I hadn't seen our new neighbors in a few days. I sort of missed flirting with them. For some strange reason, there were new faces running in and out of their house all throughout the day and night.

"Ted," I said, once reaching him. "You might as well have fun now because you'll be starting school Monday." I wanted to ease my way into asking him to get money from Daddy. "I don't have anything to wear," I blurted out but quickly saw he was ignoring me, so I decided to jump right to the point. "Will you ask Daddy for some money to take us shopping? I know you don't want to start school all raggedly and trashy looking."

"Why is everyone always trying to get me to ask him for things?" Ted snapped. "I already told you no. If I ask, I'm going to ask for myself."

"That's fine," I said nonchalantly, knowing that if I saw Daddy give him some money, then I would run over and stick out my hands also.

I went back into the house and watched television for a while. Dad went to the store and bought more beer. By his third trip, he was staggering and bumping into almost everything. As the night progressed, the atmosphere in the house changed. He was no longer laughing to himself. I could tell by the tone of his voice that he was ready to start some trouble. I didn't want to be a part of it, so I went outside to breathe some fresh air. While sitting on the front porch, I could hear some arguing from within. I couldn't tell if the female's voice was coming from my sister or mother, but I knew that the male's voice was my dad's.

Suddenly, I heard a loud smacking sound. Without looking, I already knew my father had hit someone because the whole house was in an uproar. Everyone was screaming and yelling at him. Next, I could hear glass shattering against the door. I ran back into the house frantically to see what was going on. Just as I stepped through the door, my father grabbed Janet and hit her in the face. I was horrified. Enough anger was brewing inside me to kill him, but I knew enough of the Word of God to restrain me from acting on it. The depth of my anger frightened me. Soon, the anger I contained would be my fuel for survival.

"I'm sick of him!" Janet screamed. She jerked from his grasp and rushed into the bathroom. I could hardly believe my eyes when she walked back out. In her hands was the toilet tank.

"Janet, what are you doing?" I yelled after her. "Put that down now!" My mother screamed after seeing what was in her hands.

"I'm going to teach him to stop messing with me!" screamed Janet as tears streamed down her face. "I don't do anything to him, but he's always picking a fight with me!"

When my father saw what was happening, it was too late. My sister had already thrown the tank at him. It hit him on the shoulder and the back of his arm and then shattered into many pieces. Blood immediately trickled down his arm. The war had begun. It took both of my brothers as well as my mother to keep him off my sister. I ran and hid in a corner of the room as I rocked myself back and forth on my heels to calm the terror I was witnessing. "Why can't I be like other normal little girls?" I cried. I looked out of blinded eyes at my sister and father throw punches at one another.

Melvin and Ted weren't as panicky as I was. They refused to sit there and watch my father hit their sister. They started picking up items and hitting him with it. It seemed as if something had just clicked inside of Janet's head.

"I'm sick of this!" she screamed. She then walked towards the door, opened it, and slammed it behind her as she walked off into the humid night. Melvin and Ted followed behind her.

I refused to stay in there by myself and wrestle with the demons that hovered over the room. While trying to escape outdoors, Dad started yelling cruel obscenities at Mom. I wanted to defend her but rushed out the door and into the darkness instead. I hated myself for being so afraid of him.

Within minutes, I could hear the side door to the house slam shut, and the sound of the van crank up. I peered around the house. It was my father. I prayed that he would stay gone or that something would happen to him to prevent him from ever coming back. I silently reentered the house to check on my mother. She had wiped up the blood and was now sweeping the broken debris that had shattered on the floor.

"Where'd Daddy go?" I asked as she continued cleaning.

"I don't know. He probably went to buy some more beer," she said breathing heavily. "Where are Janet and the rest of the crew?" she questioned.

"I don't know. I think they went to the store," I said trying not to worry her. "I'm going to bed."

I jumped inside the bed with my clothes on. I wanted to go to sleep as fast as I could, so I wouldn't be awake when my father returned. Minutes after I had dozed off, I was awakened by the sound of the front door closing. My eyes flew open, sending my heart beating in an uproar. I heard my sister's voice. I was glad that despite the pain she was in, she decided to come back home anyway. I continued to lie upon the cold bed. It was a full moon outside. Its light shimmered through the blinds and illuminated everything in the room. Glancing at the clock, I could see that it was a few minutes after eleven. Suddenly, the front door slammed shut again. Thankfully, I recognized my brother's voices. I exhaled a sigh of relief knowing that we were all together. Even if they had run away, they didn't have anywhere to go. We were like aliens living in a foreign land.

My mom, along with my brothers and sisters, sat in the living room talking about the fight with my father for what seemed like hours. I didn't want them to tease me about how chicken I was, so I stayed in the bed, trying to strain my ears to hear what they were saying. I only grasped a few words here and there. Eventually they got tired of talking because the television came on.

After minutes of hearing the television's blast, my sister

came into the room and cut the light on. As quickly as it had come on, it was shut off. The bed sank down as Janet lied next to me. As I peeked out of one eye, I saw that she still had her tennis shoes on. I guess she wanted to be prepared for when my father returned.

I continued to lie there on my side as if I was asleep. I didn't say anything. I tuned in to the sound of nature. The grasshoppers had their own symposium, which was being orchestrated in a quiet, calming performance. Soon its melodic sounds relaxed me. It drowned out the thoughts that were racing through my head.

It wasn't until earlier the following morning when Dad returned. A hint of pink was starting to show in the gray sky, and all of the grasshoppers had retired for the night. Only silence filled the air. So when the living-room door opened, its sound echoed throughout the apartment. The noise jolted me from the realm of sleep, and immediately, my heart began to palpitate, causing me to brake out in a cold sweat.

I listened as my father's feet thudded down the hallway and inched closer to our room. Without a moment's hesitation, he entered his and my mom's bedroom and closed the door behind him. I waited for the sound of arguing to start, but the slight sound of mumbling was the only thing that could be heard. Shortly after, silence enveloped the small duplex for the remainder of dawn and stretched over into my sleep.

When I got up later that day, everyone was in his or her own world. We were all used to the fighting by now. Continuing on with our daily routines as fast as possible and acting as if nothing happened were the only things we could do.

My father was still asleep. Mother was up cooking breakfast, and my brothers and sister were lying around watching TV. Mom broke the silence.

"Your father said he'll take you all shopping to get some school clothes," she said. I guessed he felt bad about the previous night. Therefore to appease our anger, he'd take us shopping. I didn't say anything. No one else did either. "It won't be until next weekend though," she added while flipping sausages over.

For a few minutes, everything was quiet again. "Well, I'm sure I have something I could find to wear for the first week of school," I said breaking the cold and sullen silence. "I'm glad Janet goes to a different school than me. Maybe, she'll let me wear some of her clothes."

I waited for a smart remark to come from her, but it never came. I then walked over to the sink and ran some water to prepare for washing the dishes.

A Second Chance

The next day I awakened to the sound of pouring rain. I stayed in bed until late that evening. When I finally got up, everyone was in the living room watching a movie.

"Janet, do you have anything that I can wear to school tomorrow?" I asked hoping she was so caught up in the movie that she would give me her approval.

"Wear your own clothes," she snapped without diverting her eyes from the television screen.

I didn't feel like arguing, so I walked off to rumble through my things in hope of finding something decent to wear. After going through my closet, I decided on wearing my green and black outfit that I had worn when I met our new neighbors.

While laying it out neatly, I overheard my father talking to my mother in the kitchen. "I think our new neighbors are selling drugs next door. Cars run back and forth over there all throughout the night." The walls were thin, so it was easy to hear his deep voice seeping through them.

I pondered over his words momentarily and assumed he was right. I recalled sitting on the front porch a few days earlier and seeing an unrecognizable guy hide something on the side of my neighbor's apartment building behind a sheet of wood that lay propped up against their fence. He looked up as if perceiving he was being watched and looked directly into my eyes. I didn't pay it much attention though, but I could still remember the look the guy gave me as if daring me to say a word about what I saw.

By the time I finished laying out my school clothes, the sun was shining brightly through the window, and the rain had ceased from falling. I rapidly straightened our bedroom and joined my sister in the living room to see what she was watching.

As soon as my butt touched the stained and discolored fabrics of the couch, my mom bellowed from the kitchen, "You all might as well get up from that TV! Don't y'all see all of this work that needs to be done around the house? Now cut the television off, and start cleaning!" I didn't want to move, but I knew what I was in for if I got sassy and decided to rebel.

Disgustedly, I got up, grabbed the broom and started sweeping the living room floor. Cleaning had become a way of releasing some of my stress and venting some of my frustrations. After sweeping the living room floor, I dusted everything with a combination of Pine-Sol and water. Next, I moved into the hallway and swept it. Janet was slumped over the kitchen sink washing dishes. I glanced outside and saw mom hanging out clothes on the line while Melvin and Ted were busy raking the yard. In what seemed like only an hour, all the work was done. That was one advantage of having a big family and a small house.

The next morning, mother awakened us early for school. Lazily, I got up. Nervousness instantly seized me as I began dressing. After putting on my attire, I went into the bathroom to do my hair. Massaging handfuls of curl activator into it, I prayed my big Afro would transform back into a jerry curl.

"Hurry up, so someone else can use the bathroom!" Janet snarled from the other side of the door. "It's not like you're going to look any different from when you first went in there!"

"Be quiet!" I shot back. I finished doing my hair, briskly opened the door, and brushed past Janet. I walked into the kitchen and gulped down a glass of orange juice. While pouring a bowl of cereal, I could feel a presence behind me. I turned around. It was Mom.

"Hurry up. I don't want you all to be late," she said standing at the front door with her purse in her hand. "I'll be waiting out in the car."

After eating a few bites of cereal, I went to my room, grabbed my jacket and backpack, and then walked out the door into the cool air. A light shade of blue covered the sky. The bird's early chirping was a symphony to my ears, awakening my senses. I climbed into the van as I waited for the others to follow.

Within minutes, I was finally standing upon the steps of my new school. I took a deep breath and headed up the stairs. As Melvin walked ahead of me, I wondered if he was as nervous as I. He opened the heavy doors. The hallways were quiet. We were late. I looked at Melvin and exhaled, "Well, here goes nothing." Without a word, he departed, leaving me alone. I immediately went off in the other direction.

Standing outside my first class, I took a deep breath, conjured up a smile, opened the door, and entered. Everything went silent. All eyes were on me. I could feel them searching the whole length of my body as if trying to find anything out of place in regards to my wardrobe.

"Good morning," The teacher said. She was a short, blond-haired lady with a pleasant smile. She looked to be in her early forties. "We're glad to have you here with us, Crystal. Aren't we class?" There were a few muffled replies from the students. "I'm Mrs. Kraft. Would you please tell the class a little about yourself?"

I felt like a deer trapped in headlights. I silently prayed that my voice would come out nice and pleasant and not high and squeaky. "Hello," I began, "my name is Crystal McDaniel. I'm from a small town called Wynne, Arkansas." Laughter erupted from the back of the classroom. Nevertheless, I was determined to keep going.

"What do you like to do?" the teacher asked. "I love to sing and write poetry. That's about it."

After my brief introduction, I clumsily tripped on one of the student's backpack as I headed towards a seat at the back of the classroom. Embarrassed, I slumped into the nearest empty seat trying to tune out the circulated laughter.

By the third class, my stomach ached with hunger. I stared at the clock trying to will it to ring. Only mere seconds separated me from lunchtime. I gathered my belongings together as I anticipated what was about to happen. Expectantly, the bell's loud ring drowned out the sound of chalk hitting the black board. I waited until everyone had fled the room before I got up.

I walked slowly down the hallway while trying to let the overflow of students pass me. Apprehension about sitting at a table with people I didn't know set in. Students continued to stream down the stairs and out the doors to line up for lunch. I decided to freshen up and make sure my Jeri Curl had not turned into an Afro again.

"Where's the girl's bathroom?" I asked a stringy redheaded girl as she walked past me. "At the end of the hallway," she said barely glancing at me.

I ventured on towards the direction the girl had pointed. Both of the bathroom doors were ajar, so I couldn't tell which one belonged to the women or the men. Merely guessing, I chose the one on my right. Once inside, I looked around. There were funny looking sinks alongside each wall. Puzzled, I moved closer to take a better look. After seconds of investigating, I realized they weren't sinks but urinals.

"This must be the wrong bathroom," I concluded aloud shuddering at the thought.

Suddenly, I heard voices moving closer in my direction. The sound of the bathroom's wooden door slammed shut behind me.

Just as I turned to walk out the bathroom, a group of guys had entered. Upon noticing me, their eyes widened with surprise.

"Excuse me," I said trying to calmly pass through their mist and into the hallway.

Their look of astonishment didn't last long before one of the guys screamed out, "Hey, catch that girl," as they ran after me.

At that instant I decided that walking fast wasn't good enough. I took off running as fast as I could. *Just great*, I thought. *Now I'll definitely get a bad reputation. One day, I'll be able to joke with my kids about this, but now is not the time.*

When I came to the stairs, I didn't even waste time running down them individually. I jumped the whole flight and landed on my feet like I was starring in a Jackie Chan movie. Adrenaline edged me on. When I made it to the first floor, I spotted the dean of the school and ran in his direction. He stood at the end of the hallway reading a newspaper.

"Hey, catch that girl!" one of the guys yelled in his direction. "She was in our bathroom!"

The dean barely looked up from his paper. No trace of emotion crossed his face. He acted as if he were accustomed to seeing girls being chased around the school by a herd of guys.

By the time I made it to where he was standing, I was nearly out of breath. Before I could utter one word, the dean looked at the guys who had now made it to where we were standing and calmly stated, "Leave her alone. She's new here." That was it; nothing else.

After making that comment, he looked at me and simply said, "Go and enjoy your lunch." He didn't even try to make sense of what just happened. "They won't be bothering you again. Just stay out of trouble," he said dismissing me from his presence.

I didn't stay around to see the expressions on the guys' faces. I turned away and walked out the double doors that led to the cafeteria.

By now, there were only a few people standing in the lunch

line. I joined in behind the last one. Because I was the new girl, inquisitive eyes watched me. A surge of adrenaline yet lingered from being chased. I took a couple of deep breaths before retrieving my tray to subside the tremors of fear that yet rippled through my body. With downcast eyes, I sought an empty seat.

"Crystal!" someone yelled. I looked to my right and spotted some girls sitting together that were in my first class. "Come, and sit with us," they beckoned.

Happily, I sat down. To entertain them, I went into detail about walking into the boy's bathroom and being chased down the hall by them. Thankfully they found it hilarious.

After lunch and all throughout the remainder of the day, the incident about the boys chasing me spread throughout the entire school. It was that incident which made me become semipopular.

"Hey, aren't you the girl that was caught in the boy's bathroom?" students were constantly asking me.

"Yeah, that was me," I would say with a devious smile on my face as if I'd planned the whole ordeal.

Daily, I grew to marvel my new life, and before long, the hot days turned into months. It rained a lot, but despite that, I looked forward to going to school everyday. While there, oddly, I was drawn to a girl named Jackie Green. She was sort of a social reject because of some of the clothes she wore. Most of her attire composed of provocative pieces such as bra tops and skin-tight spandex that showed off everything including her panty lines. Habitually, the dean would ask her to put a long tee shirt on top of her attire. She eventually consented but not after giving him a good cussing out first. Although like most of the guys, I believed he really got a thrill from how she dressed. All of the attention she was getting from the opposite sex caused girls to envy her. This resulted in many confrontations between her and haters.

What drew me to Jackie wasn't her boldness. It was deeper than that. I saw myself in her. I saw the hurt and the pain that hid behind the masquerade of her made-up face and skin-tight clothing. Something was missing in her life. I was too young to understand the depth of my compassion for her, but I understood enough to know that she was crying out for help. I became curious to what that something was. After sharing long conversations with her, we became inseparable.

Over time, she started coming home with me after school and eventually started spending the night. Not long after, she began to grow on my family as well. Jackie and I became so close to one another that when anyone threw crude remarks her way; I became brave enough to take up for her. I dared anyone to touch her. I made people think I was tough. But inside, I prayed no one would take me up on the threats I issued out.

Surrounded by Greatness

The school year passed quickly, and it was time for final exams. I had gotten nominated by some of the staff to be a part of a Talent Search Program. It consisted of a group of students whom they thought were gifted. I was very surprised when I found out I was one of the chosen few from amongst the whole student body. Up until that point, I was so used to hearing how stupid I was that it was hard to digest that someone actually thought otherwise. This advancement in status made me excited about starting classes the following year. I would be placed in more advanced classes.

During those last days of school, all throughout the hallways hung flyers announcing that the Harlem Globetrotters were coming to our school to perform. The flyers also stated that all students who had maintained a perfect attendance throughout the semester would get a free pass to the NBA all-star game for the following week's game. It would be held at the Pepsi Arena.

Continuously, students chattered endlessly about the upcoming game. Because I knew I held a perfect attendance record and because I lived on the same street as the arena, I was thrilled. I was going to the game. I had earned it. Nothing could prevent me from going. At least that's what I thought.

The following week, after the Harlem Globetrotters performed for the student body, our principle stepped to the mike. "I'm going to call a list of names, and I want these students to remain in the auditorium. Everyone else may return to your classrooms."

My name was one of the many that were called. After everyone else left, I moved closer to the front. "All of you are the ones that have a record of perfect attendance. Form a single line, and you'll be given your NBA passes."

Afterwards, people started getting up from their seats. I could hardly contain myself from jumping up and down. I looked around. None of my friends were present.

After accepting my ticket, I burst out the auditorium doors. "I'm going to the NBA!" I yelled. A few stragglers smiled in my direction and continued to walk on. For a few seconds, I had a mental countdown of the remaining days left. There were only three days before school was out and only five more days for the NBA all-star game. After the brief pause, I walked on to class and fulfilled the remaining classes with daydreams of the celebrities I would see.

When I finally made it home after school, I could hardly put my books down before telling mom about my award. I knew that my sister and brothers would burn with envy, so wanting them to hear I jumped up and down yelling, "I'm going to the NBA! I'm going to the NBA!"

The words that came out of Mom's mouth pierced through my parade. "Ask your father first and see what he says."

I didn't like asking him for permission about anything. He seemed to take pride in saying no to anything we asked.

"You ask him, Mom," I pleaded. "You know he'll say no."

After seeing that she wouldn't bend in my favor, I went to my room and slammed the door.

Later that evening, when my father got off work, our family gathered around the dinning room table to eat. It was apparent that Mom had already discussed the NBA all-star game with him because over red-brimmed eyes he probed me for more details about how I was able to get the free tickets.

"I received the tickets because I didn't miss any days at school," I said. "As a matter of fact, the game will be held at the arena right down the street."

I hoped that by informing him of the game's close proximity that it would be enough to gain his stamp of approval. It wasn't. "Well..." he paused scratching his salt-and-pepper beard, "Stella and I will think it over."

I wanted to scream. *"What'd he mean he'll think about it? The arena was in walking distance. I stayed out of trouble. Both my sister and my brothers had been suspended from school for fighting. I never did,"* I objected silently. Without another word, I ravished the tasteless food and excused myself from the table to sulk in the privacy of my own room.

After impatiently waiting, two days later, he finally said yes. Sadness fled, and I was happy again. But unfortunately as usual, my happiness didn't last long. The night before the NBA game, I came down with the flu. I was so sick that Mom and Dad both declared I was too sick to attend the game. Although I knew they were right, I cried and pleaded with them. The answer remained the same, "No."

The morning of the game, gloominess filled the sky. I felt miserable not only because I was sick but because I couldn't go to the game.

"Get your clothes together," my mother stated as she stuck her head in Janet's and my room. "That includes you." She threw in my direction. "We're going to the Laundromat to wash today."

I was too weak to argue. I wanted to say, *"If I'm too sick to go to the game, then I'm too sick to go to the washer."* Before I could muster up enough strength to reply, she changed her mind.

"That's alright. Just put your dirty clothes in a pile. You can stay here." Her head disappeared back out the room. But because of my friend, Rebellion, I decided to go with them after all just so I could do opposite of what she said. I was angry with Dad and her for not letting me attend the game.

Each of us gathered our dirty laundry and loaded them into the van. From the distance, I noticed many cars lined up at the arena. Fancy limousines were already parked and others were yet arriving. After everything was loaded, we ventured on down the street. As we neared the arena, I noticed people jumping out of their cars and running in one direction.

"Hey, isn't that MC Hammer!" Melvin screamed.

I rammed my face to the window to get a better view. I could hardly believe it. There he was stepping from a limousine. Quickly, fans rushed to encircle him trying to break through his bodyguards.

While our vehicle was yet moving, to my amusement, Melvin opened the side door of the van and jumped out. Ted, Janet, and I followed in quick pursuit. We could have easily been auditioning for a part in a *Mission Impossible* movie. I chuckled at the thought.

Mom immediately slammed on the brakes as we leaped from the vehicle. Thankfully, she was driving slowly, and we didn't get hurt.

As my siblings and I neared the crowd, someone in the distance yelled, "Hey, there goes Penny Hardaway!"

The media went wild. TV newsmen littered the place as they snapped shots and threw questions in his direction. At that time, I didn't even know who he was, but since everyone else was running to see him, I did the same. As Penny took a basketball out of the trunk of his car, within minutes, he was completely surrounded by crazed fans. As some begged for his autograph, I stared up into his rich caramel face, mesmerized by his height. Our eyes connected. It was as if time had stood still. I wanted to melt into a puddle right at his feet. I finally conjured up the word, "Hi." He smiled revealing a set of pearly whites. Soon after, men in black suits surrounded him and escorted him indoors.

That day, I was surrounded by greatness. I was so glad that I had decided to go to the Laundromat after all. In fact, I probably was closer to the celebrities than most people in the arena would have been. That moment in history would always be held close to my heart.

After the episode died down and it was evident that the majority of the movie stars had made their entrance into the arena, Melvin, Ted, Janet, and I walked back to the van where mom was patiently waiting. I was relieved to see that she wasn't upset about us jumping out of the van. She was especially happy for me because I wouldn't be walking around with my lips poked out with a nasty attitude. She cranked the van up, and we resumed towards the Laundromat.

When we finally returned home, all of the day's excitement caught up with me. I fell extremely ill. For about three days I became bedridden with the flu mingled with bouts of asthma attacks. But since school was out and summer vacation had begun, I could sleep as long as I wanted to.

One morning over breakfast, Mom stated, "Your dad and I have been thinking about moving back to Arkansas. Madea has been getting sick lately, so we want to be close to her in case something happens."

Since we had only been living in Orlando for about two years, it was hard to digest moving back so soon. I was just starting to make new friends—Jackie and I had become inseparable. Without a doubt, I would miss our makeovers and our late-night chats. Although feeling defiant, I swallowed my pride and submitted to my parent's decree.

The Prophetic Dream

Sometime during summer vacation, we were packing to move back to Wynne, Arkansas. I didn't agree with the idea because at my new school, I was noted as popular, cute, and not just smart, but gifted. The short time in Florida had changed my life drastically. I wouldn't realize how great of a change until months later while back "home" in Wynne. Although I had missed our relatives back home and our occasional get-to-gathers over my grandmother's house, I wanted to cling to Florida. It seemed like my only hope for a better life. I knew that once back in Arkansas, I would resume being labeled as an ugly and stupid outcast.

The night before the move, I tossed and turned trying to find a comfortable position on the hard-carpeted floor. Everything had already been packed in our van, and we were destined to leave the first thing the following morning. When finally drifting off to sleep, I had a strange dream that my family and I were involved in a bad car accident. I saw our vehicle flipping off the road, over the side of a cliff, and into a lake. The dream was very disturbing, almost real-like. I awakened to sweat dripping down my arms and face. While asleep, I had shaken all of the covers loose from around my body to find them shriveled up at the bottom of my feet. I stayed awake for a few hours replaying the dream over and over until sleep finally came.

When I awakened, the sun was beaming through the blinds. Something out the corner of my eye caught my attention. I looked and saw a hairy tarantula scurry across the floor and into a corner of the room. For some strange reason, I didn't jump up and run. An ominous feeling crept over me, restraining me. From outside my bedroom door, I could hear the rest of my family stirring. I figured they were putting the last few items that my mom had used to cook breakfast with into the van. After moments of staring into space, I finally got up to help the others.

Knowing that we would be on the road for a long time, I decided to pack my shoes in the back of our vehicle and ride barefoot. When my dad saw me without any shoes on, he said something that sent chills racing down my body.

"Put your shoes on. We might have a wreck or something, and we might have to walk." The mention of the word wreck brought the memory of the dream rushing through my mind like electric jolts.

Somehow, I knew we were destined to have a car accident. After accepting the inevitable, I thought of a way I could prevent my uncertain death. I recalled watching on television how people had survived water accidents by clinging onto floating objects. That was exactly what I was going to do. When I got inside the van, I reached for the basketball from underneath the seat. *If we have a wreck and flip in a lake, then I'll just float in the water with this basketball,* I thought, concluding it was a logical plan. Mom decided to drive the first part of the trip since dad had been drinking and was slightly intoxicated. Once on the road, I clung tightly onto the basketball against my chest as if I was holding onto life itself.

After being on the road for many hours, darkness soon swallowed every hint of blue from the sky. Everyone appeared relaxed as if they were safe from harms way, but I knew better. I sat erect in the back seat of the vehicle, holding the ball in a deathlike grip. I wouldn't allow myself to drift asleep. I looked over to my side. Ted was already breathing heavily. He looked so at peace with the world. *"Please Lord, don't let us die,"* I prayed silently. *"We have been through a lot, just let us all survive."* Instantly, I felt his presence and knew that he was listening. It's amazing how hard situations or near death experiences provoke us to pray. Those that don't have a relationship with God occasionally develop one during those times.

A sign whizzed by and I noticed that we were a few miles outside of Nashville, TN. Just as I was about to rest my eyes from straining, the van jerked violently. By impulse, my eyes widened. I soon realized that we were driving in the wrong lane. It seemed as if traffic had stopped instantaneously by some Supreme Being. I clung tightly to the ball. I could see mother's hand tighten around the steering wheel. She managed to get back in the right lane. Dad jerked upright in his seat.

"Do you have it? Is everything under control?" he asked as his hands gripped the dashboard.

"Yes," Mom stammered. "I got it under control." Suddenly, as she finished that last word, it felt as if massive hands reached underneath our vehicle and pushed it so drastically that we were no longer on all fours but were flipping off the road and into a ditch at great speed. It was all happening so fast.

Somewhere during the flipping, I lost the ball. Actually, it was the farthest thing from my mind. My life flashed before me so quickly that I came to the realization that I was getting ready to die and go to hell. No byway stops but straight to hell. How did I know that? I knew about God. I was raised in holiness, but it was my fault that I wasn't saved. I didn't have any excuses to throw out. Simply, I knew better.

A moment of complete silence filled the air as my family, and I was being tossed around like a Caesar's Salad—those of us that weren't wearing seatbelts. A few seconds later Melvin abruptly cursed out loud. His words seemed to resonate from both sides of the van. This was the first time I had heard him curse, but this was not the time to be displaying my shock. In a moment like this, cursing should have been the last thing that any of us let slip from our mouths, but as the scripture says, "From the abundance of the heart, the mouth speaks."

As we flipped and the windows shattered, one of my legs flung through. Instantly it became numb. In my mind, it was inevitable that my leg had been amputated. When our vehicle finally became motionless, its wheels were in the air, and I was totally buried underneath heavy equipment that was in the back compartment of the van.

After taking a few gulps of air, I could barely make out Melvin loosening himself from his seat belt. Trying to flee as fast as possible, he stepped right on my face. The only light came from the illumination the moon provided.

Within minutes, everyone was out except me. I was still buried beneath the mass in shock.

"Is everyone out?" I heard dad ask his voice trembling.

"No. Where's Crystal?" another voice asked.

With a weak voice, I managed to squeak out, "I'm down here."

Without a moment's hesitation, I could see my mother climb back into the van to risk her life for mine. Sure enough, gasoline was leaking from the vehicle. We could've blown up at any second. As Mom began throwing items off me, the circulation came back to my leg that was hanging out the window. I breathed a breath of relief knowing my leg wasn't amputated. I slithered myself free from the remaining debris and followed mom out the demolished vehicle.

When I got out, I saw a few vehicles lined up on the side of the road. A tall man holding a flashlight walked towards us.

"Are you all alright?" he asked in genuine concern. "I called the paramedics, and they're on the way." As he drew closer, the moon's light sent silvery shimmers bouncing off his blond hair. He continued. "I saw when your vehicle flipped over."

I found his statement to be quite astonishing. God had allowed the traffic to cease while we swerved back and forth across the opposite lane, and then he allowed it to immediately pick back up as we begin to flip so that someone could see us go into the steep ditch.

The wreck allowed me to get a glimpse of God's love for me. Other than when I was born, that had been my first near-death experience—definitely not my last. Through a dream, God had prewarned me of what would happen. By actually seeing it come to pass, I knew I needed to pay more attention to my dreams.

It had started to rain, and quite ironically, I didn't have any shoes on. They had gotten thrown off my feet as our vehicle flipped repeatedly. After the ambulance arrived, everyone was checked for injuries. By the grace of God, none of us were seriously hurt. I came out the whole ordeal with only a small scratch on my leg. Everyone else was fine except my mother. It wasn't until we had caught a ride to the nearest hotel that she began to cough up black stuff. Whenever she coughed, she complained it felt as if glass was scratching her throat. Her guess was that she had swallowed glass, and the black stuff was old blood.

While each of us sat around in the comfort of the hotel room and replayed the accident over and over, Mom called her sister Gwendolyn and her husband Henry McNutt to come and get us. Later on that evening, they finally arrived. Once again, our family was headed to Arkansas; "The Natural State."

Back in Egypt

Flashbacks of the wreck hunted me many nights after returning back to Wynne. Occasionally, tears fell from my eyes as I contemplated on God's mercy in sparing my life. Without a doubt, I knew I had deserved to die, but obviously God yet had a plan for my life.

Not long after the move, my family and I resumed our daily activities that we had been participating in previously. Most of the activities involved school and church.

After being enrolled back into school, to my dismay, once again I was shunned by my peers. Despite my strong willpower,

I fell back into a deep state of depression. Since everything I said sounded dumb to my ears, I completely withdrew from talking and secluded myself from others. I stuck out like a "sore thumb." Once again my world was falling apart.

One day after many years of Dad's abuse, Mom realized that she couldn't take much more. After vocalizing that she wanted a divorce, the scene got nastier. One night after he had been banned from the property, he returned with a gun and demanded that Mom step outside to talk to him. We pleaded and begged her not to go because we honestly believed he would carry out his threats about killing us. I can recall another incident in which we had come home from church, and Dad had broken into our house. He literally demolished everything in sight. Food was thrown across the kitchen floor, tables were overturned and broken, and clothes were scattered throughout the house.

I was so afraid that he was going to kill us while we were asleep that I often laid restless through the night in preparation of his attack. During those devastating months of being chased in vehicles, enduring break-ins, and habitual threats, my family and I hung close together because all we had was each other.

Finally, the divorce came through. My father moved away, and the abuse stopped. After that, I never saw him again until I was viewing his body in a casket. On March 3, 2002, almost six years later, Dad was killed while crossing the street in Memphis, TN. The autopsy report discovered that he had been intoxicated.

Only months after the divorce process, Mom took Melvin, Ted, and me to a psychiatrist to help aid us through the healing process. I just wanted a "crazy check," so I consented on going. Once there, all the negative voices that people had told me for many years came flooding back. *"You'll never be anything." "You're stupid." "You're fat and ugly."* These were only a few comments that had once been uttered to me from relatives, peers, and unfortunately, my own Father.

When it was my turn to enter the psychiatrist's office accompanied by Mom, I began to anticipate all the questions that were going to be thrown in my direction. As mother adjusted herself in her seat, the discussion began.

"Crystal doesn't communicate well with people," she blatantly stated. "She usually stays to herself and writes. I try to talk to her, but she often explodes in an outburst of anger."

I sat in the cold, cherry-leather seat as mother and the lady discussed me as if I was not sitting there.

"Oh, by the way," mom continued as if remembering I had some good points, "she's an A and B student." Getting a crazy check was pushed to the farthest corner of my mind. Anger brewed in me like a volcano that was ready to erupt at any second.

When the accusations started to strike home, I looked the psychiatrist in her eyes and said as calmly as I could muster up, "I'm not crazy, and I won't be coming back to this place."

I could hardly believe what had just come out of my mouth. I refused to sit there any longer and be classified as a lunatic. The money didn't seem important to me anymore. I had to cling to my self-respect, the little I had left.

I glanced at Mom from the corner of my eye. Battling to stay composed, she stifled her amusement. The corners of her mouth twitched crazily as bouts of escaped laughter fought to break through. The lady looked from me to mom and stated, "Well...because of the fact that her grades are good...I do suppose that she could be a very intelligent child and just has an introverted personality. If she doesn't want to come back, then she shouldn't have to."

I exhaled rather loudly dissipating some of the steam from my wrath. I was disappointed that my last hopes of receiving "crazy checks" were gone, but simultaneously, I was relieved that I wouldn't be coming back.

When I went back to school the next semester, I was placed in lower advantage classes for reading and math. The Special Ed. classes were held in a pink trailer that was separated from the rest of the school. When it was time for class to start, I tried hiding so no one would see me enter the trailer. *Maybe, the psychiatrist was wrong,* I thought. *I can't be intelligent. I'm just stupid. Look at me. I'm taking "slow" classes.* I figured that since no one saw any potential in me, then maybe I should give up on myself as well.

After a few weeks of taking the Special Ed. classes, I went to the counselor and practically begged him to give me more advanced classes. I will never forget how he looked at me. He tilted his head to the side as the look of annoyance plastered his face.

"No, Crystal..." he said pausing briefly as if allowing me to catch up with what he was saying. "I think you're in the right classes."

"But I have a B grade point average," I pleaded frantically. As the images of being teased by some students for going into the trailer crept into my head, I continued to beg him. He didn't budge an inch.

Immediately, after his final no, I ran into the nearest bathroom and cried until my eyes were red and swollen. "Why does everyone think I'm so stupid?" I wailed loudly, not caring who heard. At that instance, something clicked within me. Caring about what people thought of me instantaneously vanished. From that moment on, I knew I was going to prove to the world that I could do anything that I put my mind to. I wasn't going to continue letting people dictate to me my worth. Although I had grown up with many negative things spoken over my life, I was going to wrestle with every curse in order to break free of their strongholds. Just like Jabez (I Chronicles 4:9–10), I was going to eradicate every negative seed that had been spoken over my life until God enlarged my territory!

The Free Gift

Eventually, my family and I started going back to my uncle's church. It was no longer located in Cherry Valley, Arkansas, but had been relocated to Wynne. During some of the services there, I could feel God beckoning me to come to him. Consistently, as I sat on those wooden pews as splinters scratched against my stockings, I observed those that were being "slain in the spirit." I felt compelled to rededicate my life to God, but fear restrained me.

During the last few weeks of school, I resumed carrying my Bible in my backpack and reading it every chance I could get. I was careful that no one saw me. Oftentimes, while on the playground or in class, I would end up totally immersed into Scriptures that I would lose track of the time.

When I first started reading the Bible, I couldn't comprehend some of its words, but after consistently praying that God would open up my understanding, slowly he honored my request. A deeper hunger to know him developed.

I don't have anything to lose, I thought one night while sitting in church. *I might as well give my life totally over to God.* Tears burned at my eyes. I felt so hopeless. I didn't have any friends, most of my relatives shunned me, and many of my peers classified me as weird. Contemplation about death entertained most of my thoughts. I longed for it like a jewel that was hard to find. For so many years, I cried out to God with my frustrations, and all he seemed to give me was dreams that I didn't understand. I just knew that in those dreams, I was clothed in confidence and exhibited success.

I reached a point where I ached for God. I became willing to do anything to receive him as my Lord and Savior. Daily, I petitioned him. I begged him to remove deep-rooted unforgiveness from my heart towards my mother for not protecting my siblings and me from our father. I was totally ready to release the grudge that I held against her.

As a means to purify myself, I went on a three day's fast without eating or drinking anything. All I could think about was the free gift that the Bible said was mine. I only had to ask for it and by faith receive it now that I was truly ready to receive Christ into my life.

On the third day of my fast, while at choir rehearsal, joy bubbled up inside me like a fountain of water. I had to muster up every ounce of strength to keep my mouth closed in fear of not being able to control my glee. I sat on the front row rocking back and forth trying to subdue some of the joy that was welling up inside. Ironically, the pastor and his wife decided to attend choir rehearsal that night. They rarely ever came.

Before rehearsal began, the pastor's wife stood up. "I just want to admonish everyone to keep their mind on Jesus throughout the day," she said resting her eyes on me. At the mention of Jesus' name, I couldn't contain myself any longer. I jumped up and went into the bathroom. By now, the anointing of God was sizzling inside me. As soon as the door was closed, I began pacing the floor. I knew that night I would come into contact with the Almighty Creator as never before. I looked at myself in the mirror. A glow covered my face. I couldn't wait any longer. I was ready to receive my free gift. I opened the bathroom door and made my way back to my seat.

As soon as I sat down on the front pew, the pastor's wife eyes fastened upon me. "You look so happy tonight," she said. "There's a glow upon you Crystal."

As I opened my mouth to speak, the power of God overtook me. I could hear my tongue begin to stammer in an unknown language as the spirit of God took over like in Acts 2:4. The peace of God transcended upon me as never before. I finally understood what Jesus meant when he offered the Samaritan lady at the well some water that would forever quench her thirst. His water would spring up from her belly as rivers of living water (John 4:5–30).

When I came to, I was on the floor and under a pew. Almost everyone in the congregation was shouting and praising God. The supernatural high I was experiencing was overpowering. I didn't have to worry about having a hangover or passing a drug test because this feeling I was experiencing didn't have any negative side effects.

By the second semester of high school, I no longer hid my Bible but witnessed to people that I came into contact with. I had such a passion for God that my zeal even caused me to share the gospel to some of my teachers. I, along with a few of my relatives that were filled with the Holy Ghost, started having prayer on campus.

God had completely changed my life. I wanted to do things for him. The quiet and secluded girl that I once was started transforming into a bold woman that stood up for righteousness. I continued to fast, pray, and read the Word of God habitually. My spirit was refreshed daily. God began to input wisdom and understanding concerning his word in me so rapidly that I quickly found favor with people.

After a few years of living saved, Pastor Davis (my pastor and uncle) asked if I would like to be the Youth Department's Sunday School Teacher. I did. God had anointed me to teach his Word. While being faithful to my new position, I walked in the vocation in which I was called.

A few years later, most of my cousins backslid. This "falling away" left me as the only young person saved in my uncle's church. Shortly after, I no longer just wore the title as Sunday School teacher, but also as the Youth Choir Director and the church secretary. Since I lived the life that I spoke of, most of my peers didn't invite me to their parties or social gatherings. I was totally shunned by them. The older saints were the only ones that accepted me and allowed me to tag along.

One day while coming from a prayer meeting over to one of

the sister's house from our church, the Holy Spirit spoke to me. "You were counted out, to be counted in." Those words came right when I needed them. This was the first time that I had ever heard the Spirit speak so clearly to me. I no longer was saddened by the fact that I was being neglected and ridiculed. The Spirit of God was letting me know that I was being counted out by the world to be adopted by him. It dawned on me that I had royal blood now; I was a King's kid.

Immediately after being filled with the Spirit of God, he started healing me of my past. I could've let the traumas of my past make me or break me. I decided to let it all go. God was housing something precious within me—jewels that were being sculpted through the refiner's fire. Afflictions of life made me feel tightly compacted, but even in the midst of them, God was producing a pearl of great wealth within me—sort of like an oyster. Just like our biblical Esther, this treasure would be revealed in God's appointed time when I would stand face to face with my kingdom assignment.

During the final years of high school, I worked hard to pull my grades up. Also during those years, many students approached me during class to ask questions concerning the Bible. I always responded. My heart went out to them.

It was in 11th grade when I got accepted in a program called Upward Bound sponsored by Harding University in Searcy, Arkansas. Its program was designed for low-income high school students that were interested in going to college.

Every weekend, other members and I would go to Harding's campus to be educated on different study techniques and career goals. My desire was to one day become a registered nurse. I didn't see any way to obtain this goal. My family was to poor, and I wasn't smart enough to get any academic scholarships—at least that's what I thought. All I knew was that God was absolutely capable of making a way. The Scripture, "Delight thyself also in the LORD: and he shall give thee the desires of thine heart" was inscribed in my heart (Psalms 37:4). I knew that if I continued to be faithful to God, he "[was] able to do exceeding abundantly above all that [I could] ask or think, according to the power that worketh in [me]" (Ephesians 3:20).

For the remaining years of high school, I attended the Upward Bound courses. I loved the university so much that I started daydreaming that I was a student there. I had already filled out a few college applications, and Harding was among those because it was a Christian school. It was one of the most expensive and prestigious universities in the state of Arkansas. But in faith, I filled out the application anyway knowing that God was capable of doing the impossible.

I continued to pull my grades up, while all around me, students bragged about scholarships they had obtained. At this point, the only scholarship I was aware that I had was worth five hundred dollars. It was given to me on the behalf of our Unity Bible Club. I was thankful for that, but knew that it would take more than five-hundred dollars to get me into college.

Graduation night finally arrived. I wanted to get the ceremony over with as quickly as possible. While waiting for my name to be announced to receive my diploma, I looked across the audience and recognized many of my relatives' faces. I was related to the majority of the town anyway, so I didn't find the vast recognition to be a big surprise. One by one, the principle called each of my classmates' names to receive their awards.

"Crystal McDaniel," the principal said. My turn had arrived. I stood up and slowly walked up the stairs. Everything went silent. After the principle announced the five hundred-dollar scholarships that I knew I was getting, I turned to walk off the stage. He caught my arm, and to my surprise, continued talking.

"Crystal. You have a thirty-five thousand dollar scholarship to attend Harding University."

I could hear the whole audience gasp for air. They were astonished, but not as much as I was. I could have literally fainted. I had a total of forty thousand dollars in scholarship money. I was so excited that I wanted to turn a flip and praise God all over the auditorium.

After the ceremony ended, I was the center of attention. I felt like a movie star. I was amongst the top five highest scholarship recipients in my entire class. What was so amazing was that I didn't even have the best grades in my class. I knew that it was nobody but God that had blessed me.

After all of my family had pressed their way through the crowd to congratulate me, I went to find my school counselor who had placed me in Special Ed classes in the beginning of my high school year. After locating him, instead of saying, *I knew you were going to choke on your words one day.* I just looked him in the eye and shook his hand. He gaped at me in total amazement. My victory spoke for itself. His look will stick with me forever, because on May 27, 1997, God allowed me to triumph over my enemies.

For weeks after graduation, gossip spread throughout the small town of Wynne concerning the number of scholarships I received. I was even featured in the *Wynne Progress,* our local newspaper. My few minutes of fame caused many to shower me with praise. "Keep up the good work," some would say. "I knew you were a smart girl."

"It was nobody but God who blessed me," I acknowledged gleefully. "After all, I am his baby girl." I didn't get the scholarships because I was so smart, but it was because God was faithful and true to his words. Because of him, now I had an opportunity to do something productive with my life.

CHAPTER THREE

The Trap

> "Be sober; be vigilant; because your adversary the devil, as a roaring lion, walketh about, seeking whom he may devour."
>
> 1 Peter 5:8

New Beginnings

Towards the end of August, I began packing for college. When the time of my departure had arrived, Mom dropped me off at Harding University. The campus was beautiful. It appeared livelier than when I was attending the Upward Bound program. White wooden swings decorated the campus's green lawn. Flowers were in full blossom, and they became the areas of play for quarrelsome squirrels.

After stepping out of the vehicle, I looked around. Students and parents rushed to their destination, totally absorbed with taking care of business and trying to buy time before they would have to say their salutations to one another. I silently prayed that I would be mentally prepared for the long day ahead. I had to wait in long lines to register for my classes, purchase my books, and unpack my belongings in my dorm room.

After finding out where my dorm room was located and being introduced to my roommate, Mom hugged me and departed for Wynne. The idea of independence delighted me. I was now officially an adult. And because God was with me, I felt a peace that was indescribable. He was my peace.

After unpacking all of my cloths, I set out to register for my classes. While walking, someone yelled from across campus, "Hey, Crystal!" I turned around. It was Mrs. Lilly Heart. She was one of the supervisors of the Upward Bound Program. I ran over to where she was standing and gave her a hug. My elongated arms covered her petite frame.

"You all surprised me with that scholarship," I said short of breath.

"Yeah, well, all of the staff was going to come to your graduation and present it to you, but an important business meeting came up," she disclosed.

"Now that would have really surprised me," I said. "Yet, I'm very grateful." I hugged her again to stress my appreciation. As I turned to leave, Mrs. Heart's next words froze me in my tracks.

"Crystal, I want to talk to you about a job." I turned around slowly. "How would you like to be an assistant for the Upward Bound program?" I was speechless.

Before she could finish, I blurted out, "Sure. I'd love to!"

She continued. "Come by the office when you get a chance, so we can talk about it further. You can tell me then if it sounds like something you'd be interested in." Afterwards, we separated, and I resumed going to register for my classes.

Later that evening after discussing the job procedures with

Mrs. Heart, I was hired on the spot. By the following week, I was working from my own desk as an administrative assistant for the Upward Bound Program. My job included typing business letters and memos, faxing and copying papers, and doing other general office duties. In a few incidents, I had the opportunity to make important decisions such as whether or not to hire certain applicants.

Not long after getting hired, I prayed and asked God for a car, so I could drive home on weekends to attend church services at my home church. A few weeks later, he did just that. A letter was sent by the business office, which notified me of money that was left in my school account from the scholarship money. Since all of my college expenses had already been deducted, the money was mine to spend at my discretion. It amazed me how everything in my life seemed to be finally falling into place.

During the first midterm of college my grades were good, the teacher's loved me, and I was starting to make new friends. But now with so many distractions in my life, I didn't realize that the enemy was setting up a trap for me.

Each Wednesday after classes, Stephens' Scholarship recipients gathered together to discuss issues that concerned us. Amongst the recipients was a girl named Rachel Nickson. A look of innocence covered her face, but at the same time, she seemed mysteriously sneaky. I found her to be quite intriguing. After numerous conversations together, we became best friends.

Many times, when I'd ask her what she was about to do after our scholarship meetings, her response was often the same, "Go shopping." And almost every day, I'd watch her model her latest outfit.

"It must be nice to shop till you drop," I said teasing her one afternoon. "Everybody doesn't have it like that."

"That's why I got a credit card, so I can have it like that," she tossed back while flashing her MasterCard before my face. "Why don't you get one? They come in handy."

"Girl, I don't have any extra money to be paying off a credit card," I retorted.

"That's fine," she interrupted," I'll help you pay it off. It's only ten dollars a month."

"Wow, that's all?" I exclaimed. "In that case, I might as well," I convinced myself.

As the friendship between Rachel and I grew, our love for shopping became the dominant factor that knitted us together. Rachel was a very pretty girl with big dark-brown, almond-shaped eyes and long lashes. Her small and petite frame was curvaceous. Her caramel complexion seemed flawless. Guys were constantly trying to flirt with her, but she seemed not to notice. She also loved to sing. Each time she'd do so, her voice reminded me of an angel. With her looks, along with her voice, who could blame the guys for being crazy about her?

Over time, I was eventually accepted for a Discover Card, a Master Card, and a Visa Card. Whenever I got frustrated or depressed about anything, I often spent lots of money shopping for clothes that made me feel good about myself. It became my quick fix. Spending money gave me a heightened sense of control. Not really aware then, but I was trying to make up for the years I spent in lack. I didn't realize that covering up my deep scars with addictive behaviors would only create more chaos for my life. I lived for the here and now by seeking instant gratification. As a result, by the age of 23, I was reaching $10,000 in debt.

Perhaps because of my physical upkeep, I started becoming very popular around campus. I had African friends, Caucasian friends, Italian friends as well as other nationalities. I knew the majority of the track team and the football team and was active in my scholarship club. I eventually got used to hugs that many of my teachers tried to force upon me. Due to the friendly atmosphere of the university, I eventually began to loosen up.

I became so engrossed in my education and fitting in with the "in-crowd" that I slowly started pushing God further to the back of my priority list. Sadly, the only time I picked up my Bible was in Bible Class at school, which was only twice a week. As I neglected my "soul cleanser," spiritual stagnation was inevitable.

The words my Bible instructor spoke oftentimes agreed with my spirit. Then there were those times when I felt like the professor should've sat down because he didn't know what he was talking about. He would say things like: "God used miracles in ancient times only, so people could have faith in Jesus as the Messiah," and that, "instantaneous miracles don't happen in this day and time." He also felt like believers that spoke in tongues were just emotional people who were eccentric. In other words, "it didn't take all that."

I would sit in the back of the class trying my hardest not to debate, but many times I ended up doing it anyway. "My Bible says that Jesus Christ is the same yesterday, today, and forevermore," I pointed out to him struggling to keep the tone of my voice in a suitable range. "That means the same things he did back in the old days, he still does today. The only difference is that people don't have as much faith as they did back then. Therefore, manifestation is limited."

Anyway, I got through those difficult moments, and despite all of the Word I was getting inside the classroom, spiritually I was dying because I neglected the personal relationship that I once had with God outside of it.

The Opened Door

One night, Justin Price, one of my good college buddies, stayed up all night conversing on the phone with me. Deep down, I knew he liked me, but I chose not to acknowledge it, because I was not attracted to him. He towered over me at about 6'5 and weighed approximately three hundred and fifty pounds.

Because of his appearance, I didn't even consider the fact that he was very nice.

That night, I ended up engaging in phone sex with him. I justified it since there were no physical acts of sex being done. I tried to convince myself that what I was doing wasn't wrong. I failed to acknowledge my behavior as sin because I had slowly slipped into a spiritual coma. Of course Satan was luring me in like trout getting ready to chomp on a baited worm. He made phone sex seem so harmless, but the end result was deadly.

Although I was still a virgin, I talked about sex so explicitly that night that Justin assumed I was promiscuous. What he didn't know was that my young mind had been saturated with pornography from romance novels that fed me on a consistent basis. In my mind, I was simply role playing characters that I had read about. I was their novice. Like many of them, I craved for adventure and desired to stare passion in the face as it ached for me. As I continued to open my mind to illegal images of sex, I didn't realize that I had opened the door to sexual perversion. What I considered as innocent then became a snare that captured me in a web of deception in which only the Breaker's Anointing could break me free.

Sidebar: Parents please pay attention to what your children read and look at! The Scripture says, "Be not ignorant of the enemies' devices," and to "be careful for nothing (2 Corinthians 2:11 and Philippians 4:6)." Sexual perversion is one of Satan's greatest tactics. The media is making it even easier to penetrate peoples' minds, creating emotional and physical strongholds by sexual garbage that it injects in innocent children.

To sum my life up at this point, I no longer read my Bible everyday, and because I stopped going to church, I rarely prayed unless I was having a rough day. The scriptures let us know in Romans 8:14 that "For as many as are led by the Spirit of God, they are the sons of God." I was still saved, because the Spirit of God was clearly letting me know that I was going in the wrong direction, but I refused to obey its unction. I became so engrossed with the cares of this world that it began to choke the Word out of me (Matthew 13:22).

One night, while sitting in a good friend's dorm room, a brilliant idea crossed my mind. "Tracy, I'm ready for a new look." Tracy Goodwin and I had become friends right off since we first had met. Rachel had introduced the two of us. Shortly after, we became the Three Amigos. Tracy was on the plush side with short hair and masculine features. She even dressed sort of tomboyish. Tracy looked at me sideways waiting to hear the rest of my so-called brilliant idea.

"I'm ready to start wearing pants. Can I wear a pair of yours tomorrow?" Since her mother had just bought her lots of new cloths the previous weekend, I figured she wouldn't mind.

"What!" she shrieked. "You don't wear pants, remember?" Most of my friends knew I didn't wear pants because of my Pentecostal upbringing. I was Apostolic to the core.

"You heard me right," I said. "I'm ready for a change."

After Tracy finally agreed, I grabbed a pair of her pants and ran to my room to try them on. For over twenty years, I wore nothing but skirts, so naturally I felt awkward stepping into my first pair of black Wranglers. I was determined that I was going to go through with it. Once on, I admired myself in the full-length mirror.

"You go girl!" I said snapping my fingers at the mirror while observing the curvature of my body. Within minutes I had transformed from a sanctified geek into a thick diva.

After a few minutes of prancing in front of the mirror, I ran to Tracy's room and tapped repetitiously on her door. When she opened, she gawked at me in total shock.

"You look really nice!" she exclaimed.

"Really?" I asked as I searched her face for any signs of disapproval.

"Yeah, pants really become you."

"Do you have a shirt I can wear with it?" I asked walking past her and into the room.

"Look in my closet," she said sitting down on the bed while yet watching me admiringly.

"I'm so excited! Everyone will be totally baffled to see me in pants," I rambled breathlessly.

"Yeah, they will," she agreed, "but you look good in them."

After rummaging through her things, I finally found the perfect shirt that went with the pants.

"Girl, with my black boots, I'll be some hot stuff," I said. I then thanked her and ran back off to my room.

Once in the privacy of my room, I took off Tracy's pants, ironed them nicely, and hung them on a hanger. Next, before going to bed, I took a hot bath to dissolve some of the day's excitement.

The next morning after awakening, I reached over to my radio and pushed play. Soon after, "Waiting to Exhale" filled the room and stirred up the monster of seduction inside of me. When I finished showering, I massaged my skin with some Elizabeth Taylor's *White Diamond* lotion I had purchased the previous day. On top of that, I sprayed some of its matching perfume onto my palms and behind my ears. Afterwards, I picked out a pair of satin black underwear and put them on.

The moment I was so excited about finally came. I put the pants on then the shirt. After tucking it in, I put on a black Tommy Hilfiger's belt. I looked down at myself.

"I know I look good!" I said out loud as the smile widened on my face. I glanced at the clock. It was already time for breakfast—the moment I would make my grand entrance. I looked in the mirror. The pants were firmly shaping my wide hips and slim waist. I walked into the bathroom, brushed my teeth, and washed my face. My hair was neatly done thanks to the Shirley Temple ponytail weave I had in. I stepped back inside the room and found my makeup bag. I located a black eye liner, lined it around my lips, and then applied some lip-gloss on top of them. Next I took some black mascara and teased my eyelashes. I was finally ready to go. After another quick glance in the full mirror, I grabbed my backpack and headed out the door.

As soon as I stepped into the cool air, people threw admiring looks in my direction. Due to the fact that by now I was pretty popular, most people noticed my new appearance right away. All the way to the cafeteria, I received comments on how nice I looked. Their compliments caused my self-esteem to soar. I felt confidence like never before. I was ready to conquer the world.

Underneath the makeup and the nice wardrobe, the Spirit of God was warning me to be cautious. But I was so focused on looking good and trying to conform to the world's standards that God's voice was beginning to grow fainter and fainter. It was being suppressed by all of the garbage that I was allowing to contaminate the anointing that was upon my life. As a result of all the attention I was getting, I became obsessed with trying to keep up with the world's image of sex appeal that resulted in approval addiction.

Once inside the cafeteria, I looked around for familiar faces. None of my friends had arrived yet. After grabbing a few items to eat, I walked over to our table and sat down. Soon after, Jason, a track athlete from Kenya, Africa, whom I had met earlier in the semester, came over to where I was and sat down next to me.

"Wow!" he said looking at me ravishingly as if wanting to gobble me up in one bite. "You look stunning."

Although he occasionally complimented me in passing, I was pleased with his flattering remark. He had made it quite obvious on previous encounters that he liked me. Since he was about the size of my arm, dark, and had a wide gap in the center of his mouth, I didn't entertain his pursuits. Since I was moving further away from my first love—God—a void developed. Therefore, when Jason asked me if I would go out with him that night, I said yes. I had never been on a date before, so I was very anxious to see what it would be like simply as a teaching tool.

Throughout the remainder of the day, I watched guys turn their heads to glance after me, and for once, I felt like I was somebody. I was important. I felt seductive. For some strange reason, the idea of being provocative excited me.

As I look back at the cycles in my life, it amazes me at how blind I was to the fact that the enemy gave me exactly what I so desperately craved—love and attention. He brought men that made me feel attractive and in turn gave me a superficial sense of power. Each of them became bait to lure me from purpose and destiny. I was so engrossed in seeking their attention that the Word of God that was in me began to "get choked by the cares of this life." Chasing after the high of being loved, I found myself doing whatever necessary to keep their attention regardless of the cost.

When I finally made it back to the dorm after my classes, I cleaned up then decided to take a nap before dinner. I needed time to process everything that had happened throughout the course of the day. Just as I lied down and was starting to relax, the telephone rang.

"Hello?" I said rather lazily. "Hey girl, what's up with you?" A male's deep and raspy voice replied.

"Not much," I said stalling to figure out who I was speaking to. I gave up. "Who's this?"

"This is your secret admirer," the reply returned with a hint of amusement.

"Is that so?" I asked tiring quickly of the foolish game by whoever was on the other end.

"This is Rashad," he finally revealed with a hint of a smile.

"Boy, I didn't know who you was," I chuckled. "You almost got hung up on."

Rashad, also a Stephens' Scholar, was a very handsome guy that I had a secret crush on. He was in the military, and I must admit I had many impure thoughts about him that I fought to suppress. I was shocked he had called. We were cool and everything, but we never really hung out together on a personal level.

"What's up?" I asked. "What made you decide to call me?"

"I was just thinking about you, so I decided to call," he responded in a Rico-suave sort of way.

"That was sweet of you," I said trying to think of something else to say fast. I wanted to keep him on the phone as long as possible.

He continued. "You looked very nice today. I didn't know you wore pants. I always saw you in skirts or dresses."

"First, thank you for your compliment. Now about the pants, well..." I said hesitating slightly, "I didn't wear them at first, but I've decided to do something new. It feels strange wearing them now, but I'll eventually get used to them."

I briefly revealed to him about my strict Pentecostal upbringing and how it was my first time to wear pants publicly.

"I think they look good on you," he said pausing. "You're a very beautiful woman."

His startling remark caused me to smile from ear to ear. "Why thank you Rashad," I exclaimed.

"I really wanted to call just to say hi, but I have to go now," he interrupted before I could continue. "I have to study for a test. I'll see you later at dinner."

There was a brief pause. "Alright," I replied wanting so badly to continue the conversation. "I'm glad you called." With that, we both hung up.

Soon as I rolled over onto my back, the phone rang again. I picked it up on the first ring, "Hello," I said rather abruptly.

"Hi. How are you," the reply came. Due to the strong African accent, I knew right away that it was Jason. "I was calling to see if you would be ready at 6:00 for our date?"

"Yes, I will. Where will we be going?" I questioned.

"I thought maybe we could go see a movie or something. Is that okay?" he asked. "Sure, that's fine with me," I said not really caring one way or the other. I was tired. I just wanted to take a nap. I glanced at the clock. There was only an hour left before dinnertime. "I'll see you tonight," I said hoping he would get the clue that I was ready to hang up the phone. He did. We said our good-byes and concluded talking.

Afterwards, I plumped my pillows up and lie back onto them vowing that if the phone were to ring again, I wouldn't answer it. I didn't want to think about anything, I just wanted to sleep. I reached over and turned my ringer off and then set the clock's alarm for 4:50 p.m. I turned onto my side and drifted off to sleep.

Warning: Destruction Ahead!

The alarm's shrilling howl startled me to consciousness. After cutting it off, I walked into the bathroom to freshen up for dinner. Before leaving, I sprayed a fresh application of my favorite White Diamonds on, rechecked myself in the mirror, and was soon ready to go.

When I arrived at the cafeteria, I instantly spotted Rashad standing by the salad bar with a tray in his hands. He looked up. Our eyes locked. He smiled. My heart thudded in my ears. I held my composure wanting him to think I was used to getting attention from guys. With the corners of my mouth raised slightly, I lowered my eyes, picked up a tray, and turned to walk away. I strutted with my head held high, making sure my hips swayed seductively in case he was watching. I turned around. Sure enough, he was. He smiled embarrassingly then mouthed the words, "You got it going on." I laughed playfully, and resumed walking.

After I had gathered all of my food, I joined the rest of my clique at the back table. A few of the guys looked at me with desire beaming in their eyes.

"Crystal!" Rachel shrilled with her baby-like voice as she came up behind me. "You look so cute!"

I stood up and gave her a hug. "I haven't seen you all day, but I heard how good you looked," she said.

"Girl, I have a lot to fill you in on," I said winking, signaling that it was going to be some juicy information.

She interrupted before I could continue. "Let me go and get some food first. I'll be right back." With that, she turned and walked away.

When she came back to the table, I quietly filled her in on the date, which was planned that night with Jason. She was so thrilled that she let out a loud shriek. Everyone at the table looked at us curiously hoping to be included in on the joke. We both continued to laugh hysterically. Neither one of us thought that Jason was cute. I made it clear to Rachel that I was using him to practice my dating skills. There weren't any attractions on my part.

When we finally calmed down from giggling, I decided to make some of the guys at the table jealous—especially Rashad. "We were laughing because I have a date tonight," I said slowly eyeing each guy at the table and finally resting my gaze on Rashad. Rashad almost choked on his pizza.

"With who?" He blurted out.

"I'm not going to say. It's Rachel and my little secret." He and the other guys at the table consistently probed me to tell them who it was, but I refused to release the information. I could tell that Justin was getting upset.

"You better be careful Crystal," he said looking straight into my eyes without a trace of a smile. It was as if he was warning me of some unseen danger. I looked over at Rachel.

"You better not tell anybody who it is," I threatened as we both burst out laughing again. I got up and excused myself so that I could get ready for my date.

When Jason arrived at 6:05, he called me from the down stairs lobby. I was ready to go. My stomach churned as I went to meet him. When we made it to his car, he held the door opened for me. After both of us settled in, he drove off. While riding, nervousness seized me, tightening my stomach. As usual, I simply dismissed it.

After we had been driving for a few minutes, Jason said, "Let's stop by my house first, so I can pick up some extra cash." By now, warning signals were going off like fireworks on the Fourth of July.

"Sure," I said ignoring them. "I'll just stay in the car."

When we pulled up outside of his apartment building, he looked at me so tenderly and said, "You can get out. I won't bite. I promise. I just want you to see my apartment."

I hesitated before responding. I felt I had to act mature since after all, I was dressing very maturely. *If the situation get out of hand, I can handle it,* I lied to myself. *But why do I feel so nervous?* My hands trembled as I reached for the car door.

"Come on," I said opening it and stepping out. There wasn't any harm in just looking around, I concluded. I had waited this long before having sex. Surely I wouldn't get deceived now. After all, I was saved and spoke in tongues. God wouldn't let anything bad happen to me, right?

I followed Jason into the tiny apartment. He flipped on the lights and began to take me on a tour of each room. Afterwards, he motioned me to a couch in the living room.

As if coming up with a brilliant idea, Jason turned to me. "How about we watch a movie here?" he asked flipping on the television with the remote control. Despite my gut feelings, I was to naive to tell him that I was ready to go, to afraid of what he would think of me.

"That's fine with me," I heard myself say. "I have a lot of tapes down here," Jason said rummaging through his collection. "Pick one that you want to watch."

Movies were the farthest thing on my mind at that particular moment. I wanted to leave, but was afraid of being thought of as childish, so I refrained from expressing this desire.

"Surprise me," I heard myself saying, settling in my mind

that I was going to stay. "Pick out something good that you think I might like to watch."

I don't even recall the movie that he put in, because as soon as he put it in, he turned the lights off. The only remaining light came from the glow of the television.

After sitting down on the couch opposite of me, he looked across the room, patted the seat next to him, and said "Come sit over here by me."

My heart began beating rapidly as I got up and obeyed his request. As soon as I sat down, he scooted closer to my side. "I won't bite," he whispered as his hot breath with the scent of Big Red caressed my neck.

I acted as if I was absorbed into the TV. He reached for the remote control, pushed the mute button, and with the flick of a button, the radio came on. A familiar love song flowed from the stereos' speakers.

Before even recognizing what was happening, I was snapping my fingers, swaying my head, and blurting out, "Ooh! That's my song!"

Before I had converted to holiness, music—especially slow jams, was my weakness.

Instantaneously, as if my outburst was his cue, Jason stood up and pulled me up alongside him. "Let's dance!" he exclaimed.

Because I was so spiritually weak, I easily gave in. At first I felt guilty for dancing so close to him, but after a while, I got into the rhythm. Song after song, we continued to dance as our bodies rubbed against one another. I could tell by the way his pants rose up in the front that he was getting aroused. Although I had no intentions of having sex with him, his arousal excited me. We continued to dance. His hands slowly began to trace the frame of my body. The voice of the Holy Spirit was drawing fainter, but nevertheless, it was heard. I continued to move to the groove.

At first, every time his hands reached out to stroke a breast or grip my buttocks, I "politely" removed them. As he continued to persist, I begin to compromise in my head that maybe it was alright if he only touched as long as we didn't take it any further than that. After all, I wasn't fornicating. As I tried to justify the situation, the scripture, "How can a man put fire into his bosom and not be burned?" became audible in my spirit (Proverbs 6:27).

I had read enough books to know what generally happened in instances like this. Someone ended up walking away mad or either giving in to their desires. Nevertheless I continued to enjoy the exploration of his hands over my body. *I won't go any further*, I reminded myself again.

Shortly after compromising, everything started to move fast. Jason started backing me towards the bedroom's door, which was only a couple of feet away. The television's glare revealed the silhouette of the bed.

Things started moving even faster. His hands were all over my body, grabbing and peeling away my cloths. Politely, I finally mustered up enough courage to say no. The sound of fear was resonated with that one word. I hoped he understood that I wanted to stop at the petting part. He continued seizing. My shirt came off, next my pants.

Within minutes, I stood naked and ashamed standing in Jason's bedroom. My adjusted eyes could see in the darkness that now he was yanking his own clothes off as well. I could hardly believe that all of this was happening. It was too much to digest.

The next thing I knew, we were both lying on the bed.

"Wait!" I shouted panicking. "I don't want to do this! I don't want to go any further!"

Quite roughly, he continued to pull my body closer to his own slim and lengthy one.

"No!" I yelled again as he wrestled to pry my legs apart.

I could feel his mouth moving ravishingly all over me kissing, gnawing, and licking my burning flesh. My body was screaming yes, but the God part of me knew that our lust was wrong.

"No!" I said rather sternly now that he was on top of me. His arms tightened around my wrist. I struggled to loosen his grip, but he was too strong. All of my morals and remaining purity were being aborted.

"No!" I screamed as he robbed me of my virginity. "I'm ready to go now. I mean it!" I was furious. I was mad at the fact that I had let it go so far and mad at him for not understanding the word *no*. All sorts of accusations started racing through my head.

Jason knew I was a virgin. We talked on the phone occasionally for hours about our future dreams and goals. I had high values for myself. I wanted to save my virginity until I was married and was able to offer it to my future husband. Jason knew all of that.

From somewhere within, I mustered up enough strength to push him off of me. There was no time for being cute. I had just committed the ultimate act of sin—fornication … or was it rape? I was so confused. All I knew was that I had to leave. I seized my clothing and frantically put them on. Next, I grabbed my soiled undergarments, shoved them into my pants pocket, and threw an abhorrent glare in Jason's direction. It was one that prophesied of ultimate destruction if he even attempted to touch me again.

He finally accepted the fact that our "so-called date" was over. After putting his cloths on, he retrieved his keys from the kitchen table and motioned me to follow him out the door.

"What's wrong?" he questioned as we walked towards his car. "I thought we were having a good time." He seemed so innocent.

"I'm not ready for this," I stammered on the brink of tears, "I just want to go back to campus."

The ride back to campus was quiet. I felt nasty and ashamed. I was totally disgusted with myself. *How could I have failed*

God? This question replayed repetitively within my head like a blues song on a scratched record. When we pulled up outside my dorm, I jumped out the car without even saying goodbye, slammed the door, and ran up the steps.

As soon as I made it inside the privacy of my room, I fell on my bed and begin to cry hysterically. I cried until not even a trickle of moisture gathered at the corners of my eyes. I sensed demons sneering at me because of my failure. I had let God down. He would never be able to use me again. I quaked with humiliation until I became nauseated. I rushed into the bathroom, ripping my clothes off as I went. After turning the shower on as hot as it could get, I climbed in. I wanted to rid myself of the disgust I felt.

That night, I was restless. I replayed the incident between Jason and me over and over. The fact that I could no longer tell my future husband that I saved myself for him tore me to pieces. I really wanted to die, to decompose into a mass of nothingness.

Satan's Bait

Many weeks after my incident with Jason, I constantly felt nauseated. I sincerely suspected I was pregnant. And if I were, I concluded that my life would be ruined. One of Harding's many regulations prohibited sex outside of marriage. Without a doubt, I would lose my scholarship. "*What would everyone think about me?*" I tossed the probing question over and over. If I were pregnant, in order to protect my name, I decided I would have an abortion. And with that acceptance, there was no way, I could continue to go before the Lord in praise and worship with premeditated sin in my heart. Before long, monstrous guilt and shame imprisoned me.

I tried to go to church a few more times after that horrible night with Jason, but condemnation soon stopped me altogether. My mother often called to ask about my missing church services, but I always used the excuse that I was taking exams or something else that was justifiable.

For the next couple of months, I silently withdrew myself from everyone. I avoided Jason every chance I could. I loathed him. I hid my secret pain from everyone. No one was allowed to know what had happened especially not my mother or pastor.

As a youth Sunday school teacher, I taught on repentance so many times, but somehow now that I was in a dilemma, I felt like repentance alone wasn't enough to rid me of my filth. It was hard to accept the fact that God's grace was powerful enough when it came down to forgiving my own sins.

After reflecting back on those initial months of having my virginity taken, I realized that the Holy Spirit had been warning me all along that I was going down the wrong path. It was my rebelliousness and disobedience that caused me to get stuck in the mess I was in.

Any glimpse of recuperating from my present distraction seemed gone. I fell so deep into a state of depression that I knew I had to find something that would pacify my pain, or if not, suicide would be the ultimate outlet.

***

One afternoon after I had eaten dinner, I wanted to get as far away from campus as possible. After spotting Rachel walking from the student center, I ran to catch up with her.

"Hey, let's go walking," I suggested.

"Walking?" she asked looking startled. "Where to?"

"I don't know," I said. "I just need to get off campus for a while."

As if sensing my desperation, she replied. "Let me go change clothes, and I'll meet you at your room."

"Great," I said as I walked away to find something to wear as well. I went back to my room and rummaged through the closet. I found a pair of white jeans, white sandals, and a multicolored-tie shirt.

While applying finishing accessories to my wardrobe, a light thud was heard from the door. I assumed it was Rachel, so I yelled from the bathroom, "Come in!" Seconds later, she appeared from behind the closed door looking pretty in a pair of blue jeans and a sleeveless blue shirt. Her hair fitted her face splendidly. She had a cut that was short in the front, and long in the back.

"You look so pretty," she exclaimed standing outside my bathroom watching me re-examine myself in the mirror.

"So do you," I replied. "Are you ready to go?"

On my way out the door, I walked over to my dresser and retrieved a pair of gold-rimmed Ray Bans that my oldest brother had given me as a gift.

"Let's do this thang!" Rachel jokingly yelled as we headed out the door.

While walking further away from the college, we noticed guys glancing back at us from their cars. I inhaled then slowly exhaled. It felt so good to be off campus. I felt free.

After walking for about ten minutes, it seemed as if Rachel and I had stepped into another world. There was no doubt in our minds that we had stepped in the hood. Everywhere we turned stood brothers on every corner. We were totally surrounded by Afros, braided hair, tattoos, and gold grills (teeth). Cars zoomed by with glistening rims and blaring music.

"This is what I'm talking about," I said with pleasure. This picture was more realistic than the plastered smiles and the "everything is just peachy" attitudes I saw on campus everyday. My world had fallen apart fast. I had enough masquerades of my own. I was happy to be around some "real" people for a change.

A long brown car with gold rims on each tire passed Rachel and me. Its music was so loud that the car vibrated from the intensity of the bass. While passing, the driver, a dark-skinned brother with cornrows, looked back at us. He smiled revealing a mouth full of gold teeth before disappearing down the street.

"He was checking you out girl," I teased nudging Rachel in the side.

She smiled. "I think he was checking you out," she shot back. We both laughed.

After about forty-five minutes of strolling, we decided to head back towards the campus. Suddenly the sound of sirens followed by tires squealing to a halt could be heard from the next street over. After running to see what the commotion was, we spotted five police cars surrounding an apartment complex. A crowd of people was already accumulating at the scene. Rachel and I both wanted to be nosy, so we joined them.

To my astonishment, two guys were handcuffed and were being shoved face down on the ground as police officers yelled at them. When one of the guys looked up, recognition set in for the both of us concurrently.

"What's up, cuz?" he said with a wide grin.

"Oh, my goodness!" I exclaimed in shock, bursting into a fit of laughter.

People in the crowd looked from him to me as if hoping to get some juicy gossip that they could spread around town.

"Girl, that's my cousin!" I said proudly to Rachel not caring who heard. "We grew up on the same street in Wynne, and I haven't seen him in years since we were kids."

"What's his name?" she asked, continuing to watch the police officers wrestle him and the other guy down on the damp grass.

After pondering for a second, I said, "People call him, Tiger."

Under the current circumstances, I figured he wouldn't appreciate me giving out his real name, so I decided to stick with that.

"What kind of name is Tiger?" she said turning her puzzled brown eyes towards me.

"That's the name he goes by." I hoped she got the hint that

I didn't want to discuss it any further, especially in the presence of lots of strange ears.

Immediately, three officers jerked the other guy upright. It happened so rapidly, that I didn't get a chance to look at his face. He and they exchanged harsh words between one another as they flung him into the back seat of the patrol car.

As two other officers were getting Tiger off the ground and escorting him to a nearby car, he yelled out in my direction "Cuz, I'll be getting out in a few days. Come and see me. I live in Skyline Apartments."

"Alright," I said, embarrassed. I wasn't sure if he heard me or not, but I knew that he understood my nod.

After the police cars left with Tiger and the other guy in the back seats, a few people questioned me about whether or not Tiger really was my cousin. After assuring them that I was, Rachel and I lingered on for a few moments before leaving.

When arriving back on campus, Rachel and I said our goodbyes and went our own separate ways.

"Whew, I'm exhausted!" I exhaled as I unlocked the door of my room and flicked on the light. I froze. I had clothes all over the place from trying to decide what I was going to wear earlier. It looked as if I had thrown everything out of my closet and my drawers combined. I took a deep breath, rolled up my sleeves, and literally dived into work. It took me almost an hour to make my room spotless. When I was finished, I was too tired to study for my Bible test that was the following day. I pretty much knew my material anyway. I decided I would skip lunch the next day and study for it then. After putting on my pajamas, I was out before I knew it.

The Rapid Decline

In one night I had lost the two most precious things in the world to me—my relationship with God and my virginity. The void that had resulted because of their loss grew larger each day. I didn't realize that I was in search of fulfillment. The next few weeks I made a habit of walking to the hood daily because staying in the four walls of my room gave me too much free time to think about the rape—I still wasn't sure if that's what it was.

One day while out walking, I decided to find the Skyline Apartments. Since the first person I asked gave explicit directions, it didn't take me long to find it. Within minutes, I was there. I spotted Tiger outside talking to some guys.

As I headed in his direction, he looked up. Upon seeing me, his mouth curved into a huge grin.

"Cuz, I didn't mean for you to see me like you did a few weeks ago. I got caught up in some stuff." Yet smiling, he resumed. "I heard you were going to school at Harding, but I didn't expect to look up while being arrested and see you standing there."

"I wasn't expecting to see you either," I chuckled.

"Hey guys, this is my cousin," he announced proudly to the guys that were sitting with him. After the brief introductions, the guys soon stood to depart.

Tiger turned to face me. "Come with me. I want you to meet my lady." Afterwards, he motioned me to follow him as he turned to walk away.

As he led me to his apartment, I could hear a baby crying from behind the closed door. Without much effort, Tiger opened the door and yelled towards the back room.

"Brandy, I want you to meet my cousin! She goes to the college up the street!" He soon left me and disappeared into the darkness.

Shortly after, a short stocky girl with shoulder length hair appeared from the shadows holding a baby.

"Hello, I'm Brandy," she said extending her hand.

"I'm Crystal," I returned.

"Tiger told me that he had a cousin that went to Harding," she said motioning for me to take a seat. She continued. "I'm planning on going to Harding next semester. How do you like it?"

After getting positioned, I replied. "I love Harding. Since it is a Christian university and because it is predominately white, it challenges me to work hard."

Brandy continued to pat the infant's back. "You'll love it," I reassured her. Tiger walked over to where Brandy and I were sitting, retrieved the baby, and then disappeared again. I continued.

We continued talking for a few more minutes. "Just yesterday, Harding awarded me a full scholarship to study in Europe next semester," I said.

"Wow! They did?" She asked her eyes widening with surprise.

"Yeah, it was the grace of God!" I declared humorously. "They allowed me to pick from a number of different countries that I wanted to study in. I chose Florence, Italy."

As she gloried in my accomplishments, no satisfaction could come. I knew that despite my spiritual digression, it was God who had given me unmerited favor to obtain another scholarship.

Soon, she became engrossed in every detail of how I got the scholarship. I briefly explained the qualifications of getting accepted: a high G.P.A., a well-written essay, and good references. I had them all. Therefore, I became one of the recipients.

Tiger reappeared in the living room wearing a different wardrobe, still holding the infant. "Hey, cuz, I'm throwing a barbecue cookout here this weekend. I want you to come."

"That sounds fun," I said. "I'll let you know something before then." After a few hours of playing catch up, I decided to leave and go back to campus.

The visit over Tiger and Brandy's apartment was the first

of many. The rest of that week after finishing my last class, I went over to their apartment to escape the bustle of campus life. While there, on many occasions, I met a few of Tigers' acquaintances. All of them seemed thuggish. It wasn't long before I saw a trend. He as well as they wore expensive cloths and carried large bundles of money. Day in and day out, people knocked on his door, and in hushed tones, he'd stuff money into his pockets but not before handing the visitors something first. I easily put two and two together; Tiger was a drug dealer and most of his friends were to.

Thursday evening, while Tiger and I played Nintendo, he practically begged me to spend the night over his apartment that weekend, so I could help out. Finally, I accepted his plea. After a few hours of playing, I glanced at the wall and realized how late it was.

"I guess I'll get ready to go back to campus. I have some studying to do."

Tiger paused the game, stood up, and stretched before sitting back down. "You always were smart. Keep your head on straight, cuz. Remember, books come before fun."

The advice sounded kind of funny coming from him. I gathered my things and walked back to school where I spent most of the night at the library.

Somehow over time, I had entirely cut off all my associates at school including Rachel and Tracy who were pretty much the only two I hung out with on a regular basis. That Friday, to include her in my whereabouts, I told Rachel that I was going to sign out to spend the night over Tiger's house.

"Be careful," she said sincerely concerned.

"I will," I returned. "He's having a cookout tomorrow. I'm going to stay at his place tonight, so I can get up early and help him and his girlfriend out in the morning," I added.

"Ooh, can I come to the cookout?" she begged enthusiastically.

"Sure, I don't see why not," I said suspicious of her new burst of energy.

She resumed. "I can meet you over his house tomorrow. First tell me how to get there."

"We are going to have some fun," I said with excitement. I proceeded with giving her the directions along with his phone number.

"Hey, wait a minute," I said, stopping her in her tracks as she turned to walk away. "I can pick you up if you need me to."

"Thank you, Crystal. Are you sure you don't mind?" she asked as her almond-shaped eyes sparkled up at me.

"Of course, I don't mind. When I find out the exact time it starts, I'll call you and let you know."

"Thank you!" she practically yelped. Afterwards, we both hugged and left to go our separate ways.

While deciding what to bring with me for the weekend, I selected some of my shortest and tightest clothing, dumped them into my backpack, and then headed for the door. Suddenly with a hand on the doorknob, I came to a complete halt. I was struck with the realization of how much I had changed. Only a few months ago, I was practicing modesty and was busy doing things for the Lord. Now, I had little time for anything that pertained to him. I slowly exhaled. "I've done too much to be forgiven for anyway." I shrugged and walked out the door, pushing the ominous feeling of doom away. I threw my luggage inside the trunk, jumped in my car, and drove away down the road.

When I arrived over Tiger's apartment, I noticed a few people in the front of his complex sitting on top of a car drinking beer and passing a cigar around. The scent of the stuff they were smoking filled the air.

I stepped outside the car and was immediately greeted with the look of admiration from the group that was sitting on the car—from the guys anyway. Amongst the admirers, I spotted a handsome guy Tiger had introduced me to the first time I came over to his apartment.

As I neared them, a girl blurted out, "If you're looking for your cousin, he's in the house."

"Thanks," I said wondering how she knew who I was.

Before I could knock on the apartment door, it opened and out stepped Tiger. "What's up, cuz?" he asked sluggishly while doing our ritual handshake.

"What's wrong with you?" I asked sensing his sour mood.

"I just woke up."

I followed him as he began making his way towards the group of people that were posted on the vehicles.

"Hey, y'all bums get out of the front of my house!" He erupted. Everyone ignored his outburst as a tall slender guy turned the music up louder. "Hey, don't make me come over there!" Tiger yelled continuing to walk in their direction.

After finally approaching the small mob, to my surprise, Tiger's tone completely changed. "I smell that green...I smell that green... and it smells like some fire," he chanted amusingly in reference to what they were smoking.

A tall, dark-skinned guy reached over inside his car, pulled out a 40oz. of Old English, and chugged down most of its contents.

After coming up for air, Tiger reached for the guy's drink. "Let me get some of that beer." The guy swatted at his outstretched hand and said, "I kept one for you in the car."

After locating the beer and taking a few sips, Tiger handed the bottle in my direction. "Here, take a sip of this, cuz."

"No thanks," I said.

He unscrewed the top again, and took a big gulp. "Yum, yum," he said deviously, licking his lips afterwards.

At that moment one of the girls that sat on the top of the car handed him the funny-smelling cigar. "Hey don't mess up the rotation!" one of the guys snapped angrily at her. "He can take his turn after me." The guy took two puffs from the blunt and then passed it to Tiger. For a few seconds, it seemed like everyone was unified.

After only a few minutes of smoking, I could sense that Tiger was in a different "zone" (spaced out). He no longer acted sluggish but was now bouncing to the music that was blasting from the car's system. "Cut that up!" he yelled as he danced in front of the car." Everyone appeared to be in his or her own little world. Some guys were off in a corner free-styling while the girls on the car were busy talking amongst themselves. I stood aloft and took it all in.

After about forty-five minutes, everyone began to slowly disperse into different directions. It wasn't long before the street was filled with silence.

"Let's go in the house," Tiger said.

"You go ahead. I'll be there in a few minutes." I responded. "Let me lock my car doors."

So this is how he party, I said to myself while checking each door. *It'll take me a while to get used to this.* After making sure all the doors were locked, I opened my trunk and took out my packed belongings.

When I walked into the house, Tiger and Brandy were snuggled up on the couch watching television. "Cuz, you can sleep in that room," he said as he pointed to the backroom straight ahead. The door to the room was ajar. I noticed a cot lying on the floor.

I went into the room and closed the door behind me. After laying out my cloths on the cot, I cut the light off and joined the others in the living room. The excitement of staying off campus became a distraction from paying attention to what was happening on the television.

Tiger interrupted my thoughts. "Cuz, you should stay here on weekends more often. By the way, what are your plans for Christmas break?" He semi-rose to see my face.

"I haven't made any yet. I know I don't want to stay home for the entire Christmas break. I only want to spend Christmas Eve and Christmas Day with my family."

"Well, if you decide to stay here in Searcy, you can stay with us," he said patting Brandy on the leg.

"Yeah, it'll be fun," she said. "I might have to take you up on your offer. I'll see," I responded.

After yawning a few times, I excused myself to go to bed. Only minutes after putting on my pajamas and lying upon the cot, there was a knock on the room door.

"Come in," I said, quickly looking down to make sure I was presentable. Brandy stuck her head inside the room and pointed towards the closet. "

Crystal, there's some more cover in the closet over there." I glanced where she pointed.

"Thanks. If I get colder later on, I'll get some," I said.

"Goodnight," she added before closing the door behind her. I lie restless for hours daydreaming about the success of the cookout.

The Antidote

The next morning, I awoke around nine o'clock. I opened the bedroom door. Brandy was sitting on the couch, putting some things in the baby's diaper bag.

"There's some clean towels in the bathroom if you want to take a shower," she said acknowledging my presence. "If you're hungry, you can also help yourself to some breakfast. I have to hurry and take the baby over to my mother's house before she leaves. Occasionally the baby stays with her." I simply responded by saying okay.

After she left, I took a quick shower and put on my clothes. When I came out the bathroom, Tiger was in the kitchen taking meat out of the refrigerator.

"Good morning. How'd you sleep?" he asked as I walked towards him.

"Oh, wonderful," I responded enthusiastically.

He continued. "I'm trying to get some of this meat together. A few people are coming to help me get everything together. The cookout probably won't start until later on in the evening when it's cooler outside."

"That's good. It looks hot out there," I said glancing out the window.

I grabbed a juicy red apple from the table and bit into it. Remembering Rachel, I said, "One of my friend girls from college wants to come to the barbecue. Will it be alright if I invite her?" I watched his eyes light up.

"Is she a cutie?" he asked excitedly.

"Yes. She's cute." I chuckled rolling my eyes upward.

"Then you can definitely invite her," he said.

Later that evening, when all of the food was done, I went back to the campus to pick up Rachel. When she and I made it back, the party was in full blast. There were beer cans all over the place. People were up dancing around the picnic tables to the loud music that was blaring. Somebody nearby was smoking weed. Its pungent smell filled the air and traveled with the humid breeze. After parking the car, Rachel and I got out and soon became enraptured by all of the commotion around us.

Most of the evening, I kept glancing up to find Rachel engrossed in conversation with the same tall caramel-skinned brother. I could tell how she cocked her head to the side and playfully twirled her hair that she had a crush on him. Before the day had ended, Tiger had introduced me to nearly everyone that was there. The cookout turned out to be a total blast after all.

Around 8 o'clock that night, Tiger, Brandy, Rachel, and I went in for the night. We sat up and chatted for a while, but around eleven thirty, everyone retired. Not long after, snores penetrated the quietness around me, and before long, mines were mingled with everyone else's.

Weekend after weekend, I began to stay over my cousin's apartment. Many times I would awaken to find him blowing marijuana smoke up my nose. While gasping for air, his demonic laugh taunted me until I laughed with him.

One morning in particular, after he had followed the routine of blowing smoke up my nose, I started feeling the effect of the weed.

"I might as well smoke," I said rolling over to reach for the blunt.

"Are you sure, cuz?" he asked slightly hesitating.

"Yeah, let me have it," I insisted. I took the blunt in my hand and slowly inhaled. After watching some of the smoke escape through my nose, I released the remainder through my mouth as I had seen him do so many times.

"You sure you've never smoked before?" he asked looking at me with his head tilted to one side.

"No, I'm for real," I said as I took another puff and passed it to him.

A few minutes after smoking the blunt, a loud knock pounded at the living room door. I was so high that I jumped up in a paranoid frenzy. The first thought that crossed my mind was that Harding Security had found out I was doing something illegal, and they were coming to take me back to campus. My heart thudded in my ear like a machine gun firing furiously with one mission in mind—to kill. Tiger leaped up and peered through the peephole for what seemed like minutes. Finally, he opened the door.

A nicely-toned, older gentleman accompanied by a tall, light-skinned guy that resembled Big Bird walked in. I continued to peer behind the half-cracked bedroom door. They couldn't see me, but I saw them. I was relieved to see that it wasn't campus security.

After watching them head in my direction, I hurriedly ran my fingers through my hair, sat down on the cot, and pretended I had been in that position for a while.

"Crystal," Tiger said stepping into the room with the other two guys trailing behind.

"This is your cousin," he said pointing to the tall guy that looked like Sesame Street's very own Big Bird.

Then again, he looks like a hawk, I thought as I held back the giggles that were ready to erupt.

I tried to focus back on what Tiger was saying. "They call me Tree," the tall guy announced.

"What's up?" I asked continuing to lean against the wall.

"Yeah this is definitely Stella McDaniel's daughter," he said studying my face. "She looks just like her mother."

I still didn't recognize him, but I took his word that we were related. After all, he knew who my mother was. My eyes were so tight that I could barely keep them open while talking to him.

"Look at her. She's high, isn't she?" Tree asked smiling at Tiger. "I didn't know she smoked. Her family always went to church when I knew them." I remained quiet, hoping he would shut up because he was starting to blow my high.

"Let's fire up another blunt," Tree said. "Let's get her as high as she can." That sounded like a good plan to me.

The guy that had come in with them had been quiet. Until he smiled, he was totally unnoticed. He had the cutest smile. Two gold teeth were revealed. Diamonds were engraved in each one.

"My name is Sweets," he said in a southern slur while extending his hand for me to take. I returned the gesture a little too eagerly. After noticing how he was dressed—in snake-skinned boots and a silk pants suit, I concluded that he had some "mad dough" (lot's of money). He looked like a sophisticated thug. It would be only a matter of time before I found out that he was one of the biggest drug dealers in the area.

Our eyes met. "Now that's what I call high," he chuckled, "she can barely open her eyes. Maybe I can come back over here later on and get you even higher," he said winking at me.

"This is cuz's first day smoking weed," Tiger said enthusiastically. "I usually come in here in the morning and blow smoke up her nose. This morning she woke up and said, 'Let me hit the blunt!'" They all roared with laughter.

Sweets took my hand and placed it in his. "I'm sure you'll

be seeing me again." Afterwards he looked at Tiger and then at Tree. "Come on. We have some business to take care of."

They both followed behind Sweets out the door. After they left, I continued to sit in the same spot until I dozed off.

Hours later, I awakened to the sound of knocking on the bedroom door. "It's open," I said running my fingers through my hair. It was Tree.

"Here, roll this up," he said, pulling out a bag of marijuana and two Swisher Sweet cigars. He handed them to me.

"I don't know how to roll a blunt," I said yawning dismissing the contents in his hands.

"Well, if you stick around long enough, you will. I guarantee that."

Minutes later, Tiger walked in. "Get your butt up!" He yelled snatching the covers off of me. "We are getting ready to get smoked out up in here!"

We all laughed as I sluggishly stood and folded the covers I was lying on. Tree sat down next to me on the cot, took the weed, and began to break it up into tiny fragments. Next he opened the cigars, emptied them of their contents, and filled them with some of the marijuana. I continued to watch as he strategically rolled each blunt.

For the remainder of that day, Tree, Tiger, and I got high while "free styling" about our pasts. This was the first time that I had ever tried to free-style, and might I add, I was very good at it. Rapping was nothing more than poetry with a beat. It provided me with an outlet of release—an opportunity to express my inner thoughts and conflicts. This exit allowed pain to pour out of me without any restrictions. Amazingly, I felt empowered.

Many nights thereafter, I would experience free styling with various guys that hung out in the streets. When they free styled, I had access to their souls. I was able to see how they viewed life from their deepest perspectives. I was able to feel their pain and hear their secrets without any reluctance. There weren't any critics among us. Caught in the web of heart-throbbing lyrics, we became each other's family. For a few seconds, they allowed me into their "real" worlds. Most of the beats were good, but I thrived to listen to their lyrics. I was hungry for knowledge. For some reason, I craved to know these people better. I almost felt as if I was a reporter covering a top story, hanging on to their every word.

Some nights while leaving my cousin's house, I barely made it back to the dorm by curfew, and when I did, I usually ended up so high I couldn't walk straight. One night in particular, after bursting through the entrance of my dorm, reeking with the fragrance of marijuana, it appeared as if everyone knew my secret. Those sitting in the lobby whispered amongst themselves and fanned the air as I rushed towards my dorm room. My dorm mother stared at me with discerning eyes. It didn't do me any good to have sprayed perfume over myself to rid the smell of marijuana on my clothes. It only made it worst. When I finally made it inside my room safely, I leaned against the door and exhaled. That had been a close call. I knew if I was given a random drug test, I would have immediately lost my scholarship.

Although I managed to keep my grades up, my social life digressed tremendously. Despite my good grades, suspicion arose from the director of the Steven's Scholarship Program who had awarded me $35,000 to attend Harding. Ray Shields was his name. He was known for going the extra mile to help reach people who were going down the wrong path.

One day, after our weekly scholarship meeting, he called me off to the side. "Are you okay, Crystal?" he asked as his gray eyes searched my face for clues.

"I'm fine," I lied trying to convince him.

"Well..." he said, pausing a moment. "I've looked over your grades. They still seem to be pretty good, but I've been noticing that you're not your usual, bubbly self. In fact, lately you seem rather distanced."

I took a breath, not at all prepared for the truth to slap me in the face. I was shocked to find out he actually cared about my life outside of making good grades.

"I've just been a little exhausted from studying for my finals," I said staring back at him without any trace of emotions.

Inside, I yearned for him to reach over and hug me. I wanted to lay my head against his broad chest and bawl away all of my frustrations. I yearned for him to read the signs of my depression and to make all of my hurt go away. I didn't know how to reveal this to him, so this urge remained buried underneath the masquerade of, "Everything is fine."

He placed a warm hand on my shoulder. "If you need anything or have any concerns at all, you can always talk to me, Crystal," he said with concern evident in his voice.

"Thank you," I said politely, overwhelmed by the display of his heart.

After I got back to my dorm room, I stretched out across the bed and stared at the ceiling. It bothered me that I had lied to Mr. Shields. In a strange way, I knew I was letting him down simply because he believed in me. He revealed it the day he granted me with the scholarship to come to Harding.

Around four o'clock that evening, Tiger called. "Cuz, you know the high school graduation is tonight, right?" he asked.

"I totally forgot about it," I replied nonchalantly.

"I know it's going to be a lot of parties this weekend," he resumed. "Are you coming over here this evening?"

After hesitating for a moment, I finally replied. "I'll be over shortly. I could use a fat blunt right about now."

I didn't want to sit around and sulk about the meeting with Mr. Shields; so once again, instead of dealing with my feelings, I searched for an escape route to avoid them.

After hanging up the phone with him, I went into the bathroom to take a quick shower. When done, I stepped back into the room with my towel wrapped snuggly around me. There was a knock on the door.

"Who is it?" I yelled in the door's direction while frantically drying myself off.

"Rachel," came the reply.

"Hold on one minute!" I screamed remembering that my door was unlocked.

I quickly pulled on a pair of blue jeans and threw on a black silk shirt. I managed to get one foot in my black sandal heels before she knocked again. I went to the door and opened it.

"Um, where are you going?" she asked walking past me to examine my attire.

"I figured it's going to be hype tonight because of the high school graduation. Therefore, I'm getting ready, so I won't miss out on any of the after parties."

"That's exactly why I came by," she said. "I wanted to know if you would ask your cousin if I could spend the night with you, over at his house tonight."

I looked at her sideways. "Am I hearing correctly?"

I knew Rachel very well. She was a good girl. She didn't drink or smoke, so I wondered why she wanted to hang out with me more frequently.

"You remember that guy I met at the barbecue?" she asked smiling.

"Yeah, he's cute," I said.

"Well..." Rachel said, her eyes glistening.

"What?" I questioned anticipating the real reason she wanted to stay. "He's a twin, and we're supposed to be hooking up tonight."

"For real?" I exclaimed thrilled with the news. I knew that twins fascinated Rachel because she was a twin herself.

"Girl, we'll have so much fun together. Let me call Tiger now."

I rushed over to the phone and dialed Tiger's number. On the first ring, he answered. After getting his reply, I turned towards Rachel. "He said 'yes.' Now go and get your clothes together. My car will be parked behind the cafeteria after dinner, so we could leave from there." When she left, I finished getting dressed.

After the graduation that night, a street party was held in the hood. While there, I drank some Courvoisier, which is some very potent liquor. It was the first alcoholic beverage I had ever drunk. Despite the fact that it made me sick for about three days afterwards and I had promised myself never to drink again as soon as I felt better, I found myself buying some more liquor.

Outside of the safety of God's presence, I found myself vulnerable to all sorts of sinful practices. The very things I once shunned were the very things I found myself entertaining.

The Escape

Within months of my virginity being taken, I went from being a quiet and gentle Christian to becoming a riotous weed and alcohol addict. I found myself smoking up to ten blunts a day—sometimes more. Even when I didn't smoke, I felt high. This was the result of a surplus of PCP in my blood. During my undercover digression, an "I don't care" attitude developed. All I wanted to do was party and get high.

Narcotics Anonymous and Alcohol Anonymous classify these two addictions as diseases, but I knew better. They weren't diseases. Alcoholism and drug addiction are the results of a lack of self-control. I agree that genetics predispose some to various forms of addiction more than others, but a lack of moral restraints plus continuous over-indulgence will lead anyone down a road of addiction. Regardless if the addiction is food, sodas, shopping, sex, relationships, alcohol or drugs—overriding one's conscience for a long period of time and not practicing moderation causes one's flesh to crave after its drug of choice. Sadly, some people start believing that their frequent voyage into addictive behaviors or impulses are normal and start to accept it as a way of life. After overriding one's conscience for so long, a reprobated mind develops (Romans 1:28). This is when someone starts calling right wrong and wrong right. This mindset is running rampant in churches today and is sweeping across our nation at an alarming rate.

I knew my behaviors were wrong. There was no way I could justify them. Everyday when I looked in the mirror, I saw the monster that I had become. Once in my life, I looked down on people that lived riotous. Then, bound by a religious mindset, it never dawned on me that maybe there was a "defining moment" that lead people to act in such bizarre ways. Being raped was mine. I was left feeling dirty and unworthy of God's forgiveness. Although I once spoke in tongues and shouted all over the church, I didn't grasp the knowledge that God could still love me despite my failures. I felt like he only loved me when I prayed, fasted, or did "good works." The scripture, "For by grace are you saved through faith; and that not of yourselves: it is the gift of God" could not be comprehended by me before I fell from grace (Ephesians 2:8). It first had to be tried and proven. Although I knew that scripture quite well, I really didn't believe that that type of love was possible when it came to myself. The only way I figured I could be loved was if I had earned it. The scripture says that, if we love God, we would keep his commandments, but it never says that if we don't keep his commandments, he wouldn't love us. Only years of God's grace and mercy could convince me of this.

Lost in my pain, the whole idea of going to Italy for the next semester didn't seem real. My enthusiasm as well as my ambition to succeed was slowly digressing. I realized that without God's peace there was no such thing as success. Nothing excited me anymore.

Once a week, a meeting was held for those who would be traveling to Europe. I sat lifeless in these meetings as the speaker informed us of issues that was happening overseas, best ways of overcoming culture shock, and the important documents we would need for traveling. I was physically present at these mandatory meetings, but my heart wasn't in them. Burying myself with details of the trip, I suppressed the fear of leaving America to live amongst strange people with strange customs.

The summer was soon approaching. With only a few weeks of school left, I spent many hours preparing for my final exams. One afternoon, while studying, my phone began ringing. My roommate answered it.

"Crystal, it's for you," she said as she handed the receiver to me.

"Hello?" I said. "What's up girl!" responded the voice on the other end. Immediately, I recognized Tamar Shelt's voice. She was a close relative that lived back in Wynne. Somehow over the last few years, she and I had become very close.

A few weeks earlier, I had told her all about me getting high and camping out over Tiger's house whenever I wanted to get away. I felt kind of embarrassed revealing that to her because when I first came to Harding she knew that I had a deep spiritual life. She had shown me the utmost respect. For the longest, Tamar had been the wild one. In a way, she was happy that I had started partying because now she had another female to do it with.

"What's up, girl? How are you doing?" I asked.

"You know I had to call my homie," she said excitedly. "Have you been over Tiger's house lately?"

"Yes. I go over there almost every day," I replied. She paused briefly then continued. "I miss hanging out with you. I've been thinking about coming up there and staying over Tiger's house until you're out of school for the summer. You only have two more weeks don't you?"

"Yeah," I replied. "I think that's a great idea! Just tell me when, and I'll come and get you," I said. "So what have you been up to lately anyway?" I wanted to know.

"The same ole thing: hanging out with our male cousins," she answered sarcastically. "I feel kind of awkward being the only girl in the group. When we go out to clubs, my brothers are always keeping their eyes on me while I'm trying to get my 'groove' on."

"Well, in that case," I said laughing at the tone of her voice, "I'll come and pick you up tomorrow after my last class."

For some reason, I had a genuine love for Tamar. I felt closer to her than any of my other relatives, although all of us were really close to one another. It was rare that any of us hung out with outsiders. Tamar and my bond weren't joined by blood alone, but over time we became bonded by experience.

After making arrangements to pick her up the following day, I resumed studying until it was time for dinner.

After dinner, I wanted to enjoy the cool air without being bothered by anyone. I picked an empty swing in the middle of campus and sat on it. Everything looked lovely. All across the lawn, lovers sat on blankets and held one another's hand as they whispered sweet promises in each other's ear. Laughter traveled through the humid air. Even the squirrels seemed to be having fun chasing one another across the green grass and up into the full budded Sycamore Trees. Everyone looked so peaceful. I missed that—the feeling of complete serenity.

My heart ached for the peace of God. I understood that outside the realm of God's perfect will was the devil's territory. There was no doubt in my mind that not only was I treading on it, but I had pitched up tent to dwell there also. Every where I went, I could feel his presence slowly sucking the life out of me.

I continued observing my surroundings while slipping into a state of despair. I stayed there sitting in the same seat until night fell. For some vague reason, I was afraid to leave. It almost was as if the oneness I was experiencing with God through the beauty of nature would be forever lost. I was looking at his love in action. I figured that if I couldn't enter into his presence because of my sinful lifestyle, then I could at least watch him bring pleasure to the lives of others. Simply put, I was miserable.

The following day, after I had finished my last class, I went to my room and grabbed my purse. "I'm getting ready to go to Wynne, to pick up my cousin," I told my roommate. Absorbed in the book that she was reading, she just nodded her head. I hurriedly went down the stairs and exited out the double doors. I wanted to get back before dark so that I could resume studying for my finals that were coming up in three days. After finding my car in the parking lot, I got in and drove off.

I made it to Wynne in forty-five minutes; it usually takes an hour. I found Tamar over to her mother's house. She was packed and ready to go. As soon as her things were loaded in my car, I headed straight back to Searcy.

"I'm glad you came to pick me up," she said. "My mother was starting to get on my last nerve. I'll stay over to Tiger's house so that you can study. I don't want to bother you."

Glancing over at her, I realized that she was just as broken as I was. It looked as if she was fighting back tears. "Everyday, when I get through with my exams, I'll come over there with you," I promised. "I might even bring my books with me and study over there sometimes." We talked for a few more minutes then I cut the radio up loud, blasting it all the way back to Searcy.

I drove straight over to Tiger's house when we arrived back in town. The door was halfway opened, so I walked in with Tamar trailing behind. Tiger and a few other guys were brutishly playing the Playstation. The scent of reefer was in the air.

"What's up y'all!" he said barely glancing up from the screen.

After their game ended, he got up and hugged Tamar and me. "Ya'll want to smoke some hay?" he asked.

"That sounds like a plan to me," one of the guys exclaimed. I could tell by everyone's' demeanor that they were already high. I was tired from the ride, so I took a seat on the couch.

"Can you roll a blunt?" Tiger asked Tamar.

"Watch me and see. I can roll like a pro," she bragged as he handed her the weed and cigar.

It looked like she was dissecting a frog or something—with such skill and precision. As she cut the cigar in a straight line, everything went silent. Each move she made was severely scrutinized by each occupant in the room. Everyone waited for her to falter in her attempt in cutting the blunt. She cut the cigar into a perfect line and produced a perfect blunt. I was impressed. I wasn't aware that she knew how to do it.

"That almost looks too pretty to smoke," Tiger said breaking the silence. He reached over, took the blunt out of her hand, and without a second thought, lit it up. I ended up staying over at his apartment getting high instead of studying like I should've been doing.

As usual, I made it back to the dorm a few minutes before curfew. Just as I was getting ready to turn the corner to my room, the dorm mother stopped me. I was so high that I could barely keep my bloodshot eyes opened. I became paranoid. *She's going to smell me*, I thought. *Maybe I should run.* While trying to debate what I should do, she was rapidly approaching.

"You seem to be pretty strong," she said. "I want you to help me move this table to a different spot," she said pointing to a glass table in the middle of the floor. *There has to be a catch to this*, I thought. *Maybe, she's trying to observe me up close to see if I really am high?* With caution, I helped her move the table.

Afterwards, she thanked me and didn't say anything else. I excused myself rather quickly and ran to my room to take a shower. *Whew, that was another close one*, I said out loud. After I had scrubbed the scent off of my skin, I tried to study, but my mind kept drifting off to other things. I finally gave up and fell asleep.

After staying on campus and studying the whole weekend, I was ready to take my finals. After finishing my last exam, I bid farewell to my professors along with some of my friends. I found Rachel in the Student Center engaged in conversation. I tiptoed quietly behind her.

"I'm going to miss you," I said grabbing her in a bear hug. For a split second, she became stiff as a board.

"Oh, girl you scared me," she said as she turned around and saw that it was me.

"I'm getting ready to go home!" I exclaimed victoriously.

"Oh, you're lucky. You get to spend next semester in Europe. Bring me a nice looking guy back," she said flashing her pearly whites.

"Alright. I'll bring one back for the both of us," I said with a serious expression on my face.

"I have one more exam to take tomorrow, and then I can go home," she added.

"I hope you do well," I said as we hugged once again.

"Goodbye and be careful," I said as I straddled out the door carrying my book bag.

A few hours later, when I found out my grades, I was totally amazed. I had aced every one of my exams. Although I didn't make it on the Dean's List again that semester, I had maintained a B+ cumulative G.P.A.

Summer had finally arrived. I was free! I had already packed and loaded up my belongings in my car to take home with me. My dorm room was totally empty. I was finally ready to check out. I turned in my keys and collected my room and key deposits. The only thing left to do was turn in my books so that I could get reimbursed for them.

After getting over two hundred dollars back for my books, I leaped up in excitement. Since my scholarship had paid for the books in the first place, I wasn't expecting anything back. "It's time to party!" I sang out loud. I had totally forgotten that I was in a Christian setting, but remembered quickly as I began getting a few sideward glances from students that were also in line for reimbursement for their books. I rushed to my car and sped over to Tiger's house.

When I made it there, Tamar and Tiger were both sitting outdoors. After parking my car, I jumped out. "I'm rich! We're going to party!" I yelled. When I was able to get Tamar off by herself, I whispered to her how much money I had gotten back for the books. She was just as excited as I.

"Let's get a sack of weed, a few beers, and be on our way," I said feeling proud of myself.

While I was yet talking, Sweets drove up next to us in a nice Ford truck. Each tire had gold rims. He pulled down his shades and smiled as his gold diamond-studded teeth glistened in the sun's light.

"What're you girls up to?" he asked looking sexier than I had remembered.

"I'm trying to buy a fat sack of weed. Do you know where I can get one from?" I asked, trying to show him that I could support my own habit.

"Sure I do," he replied. "If you girls kick it with me, you can have anything you want. Exactly how much are you looking to buy?" he wanted to know.

"I want a quarter bag," I declared, handing him a crisp fifty-dollar bill.

"Does one of you girls want to ride with me to go get it?"

"Tamar, you can ride with him." I volunteered. Without any feedback, she climbed in.

Within minutes, they returned. Tamar was smiling from ear to ear. After Sweets drove off, she handed me the bag of marijuana and said, "He gave me his business card and said that if we ever wanted to make a lot of money, we should get in contact with him."

"How will we make some money?" I questioned. "I'm not about to sell drugs!"

"No," she interrupted, "all we have to do is dance for some of his clients, and we can get paid!"

"So I guess the rumors I've heard about him being a pimp were true.

"Keep up with that card. It might come in handy," I said, not really taking it seriously.

"Y'all need to hook up with him," Tiger said, walking over to where Tamar and I were standing. "He got money and doesn't mind spending it. He's one of the biggest drug dealers from this area on towards North Little Rock." I didn't like the feeling of being "pimped" by my own cousin. That's exactly what it sounded like to me.

"Well...we better get going," I said interrupting him. "We'll come back to visit you sometime during the summer." We both exchanged hugs with him and left.

Marked by God

After being in Wynne a few weeks, I soon tired of my mother nagging me about going to church. By now, it was pretty obvious to her that I had backslid. Never before did she have to beg me to go to church. I usually was the first one ready to leave out the door for Sunday or weekly services.

While Tamar and I did our usual routine of watching television and perhaps drinking a few beers (of course not in my mother's presence), we both decided that it was time for a little excitement in our lives. We eventually started going to nightclubs in Forrest City, Arkansas, which was located only fifteen minutes away from Wynne.

When at these clubs, I oftentimes ended up getting so drunk that I would stagger up to any guy that appeared to be checking me out and breathe my hot breath down his neck, trying to persuade him to dance with me. They often agreed. In their eyes, I probably was nothing more than a freak or some tired "hoochie momma." Little did they know (little did I know for that matter), that like Esther, God was going to use me as a vehicle of deliverance to help his people for such a time as this. It was the same calling as hers, but a different task—to help dispel people's myths that God can't use them because of their past and to introduce them to the grace of God, which in turn nullifies the enemies plans of utter destruction.

One night, while shaking my stuff on the dance floor, a tall blue-black brother walked in my direction, eyeing me as he approached. I danced my way towards him assuming that he was trying to dance with me. He motioned for me to tilt my head, so he could whisper in my ear. I smiled as I obeyed preparing for the mental foreplay I was sure to follow.

"You look like a sanctified church girl," he accused. "What is a girl like you doing in a place like this? You stick out like a sore thumb."

I was completely taken by surprise. *How dare he mess up my buzz like that!* I fumed internally. I tried to play my embarrassment off by dancing my way to the other side of the club, but not before throwing a few choice words in his direction. Once out of his sight, I found a nearby seat and sat down. It seemed as if God had marked me. No matter what I did to persuade people that "I never knew him" (just like when Peter denied Jesus), they often saw through my facade and saw the anointing that was upon me. The masquerades of drinking, dressing hoochified, using explicit profanity—all proved themselves worthless.

I even caught myself a few times giving people Scriptures as they brooded depressingly at the bar. I would tell them rather bluntly, "I'm not doing the right things, but I do know what is right." Afterwards, I would offer scriptural solutions to their problems.

Somewhere during my adventures of clubbing, a genuine love for people—worldly people in particular—developed. For hours, I often sat in the dim nightclubs and observed them. It was easy seeing straight through their pretense that everything was great in their life. I often could see the pain in their eyes that they tried to drown with liquor. It was easy for me to see pass the front because I was so accustomed to doing it myself.

One night, while at the Blue Flame Lounge, one of the more sophisticated nightclubs in Forrest City, someone tapped me on the shoulder. I turned around thinking it was Tamar returning from the bathroom. To my surprise, it was April Dawson, a distant cousin whom I hadn't seen in a long time.

"Hey girl, what're you doing here?" she asked as a look of puzzlement crept over her face.

I was sort of embarrassed because she had never seen me wear pants or seen me inside of a nightclub for that matter. I had always been classified as a "good church girl."

"Well, I just grew up," I said hoping that was a good enough answer for her. It was.

At that instance, a loud shriek erupted from behind me. April and I both spun around. It was Tamar. She ran and threw her arms around April's neck. Apparently, they had been closer than her and I had been.

"Girl, you nearly scared me half to death," I said clutching my chest. "I thought somebody was getting ready to fight or something." After a few minutes of laughing and hugging, we all ordered drinks and took a round table to catch up on the last few years of April's life and she with ours.

As if remembering how boring my life had become, I sighed heavily. "Wynne is so boring. There is absolutely nothing to do there."

"Then you should come and stay up here with me for the summer. We'll have some fun," April said bluntly. Anything sounded better than Wynne, so Tamar and I both agreed.

There was a few seconds of silence. "Guess what I've been thinking?" Tamar said, stroking her chin like a scholar contemplating a new theory.

"Crystal, you know that business card that Sweets gave me in Searcy? Well… I've been thinking about taking him up on his offer. None of us are working, and I sure can use some money. I don't want to look like some cheap hoochie momma up in the clubs." She continued. "If I'm going to be a hoochie, then at least I want to be a high class one."

"I know that's real," I said giving her a high five. "I'm all game with that. I like to dance anyway. I might as well get paid for it." I added.

"What're you two talking about?" April interrupted staring at us in puzzlement. Tamar went on and filled her in concerning the strip-dancing offer Sweets had made us.

"He's the biggest drug dealer in Searcy!" I added proudly as if justifying what we were about to do.

"Girl, the brother is fine," Tamar said rolling her eyes upward as if in ecstasy. "The way he licks his lips turns me on."

"He has such a sexy smile," I added trying to convince her to join us in our plight. It worked.

"Count me in," April said shortly after.

"Wait a minute. Don't you have kids?" Tamar interrupted as if just remembering that fact.

"I only have one child, and finding a baby sitter won't be a problem," April said convincingly.

"Alright, then. It's settled," I said holding my glass of liquor in the air. "Let's make a toast." Tamar and April followed my lead. "This is to an exciting life, a new career, and lots of money." Each of them repeated after me. Afterwards, each of us took sips from our drinks.

That night and many nights thereafter, Tamar and I stayed over April's house and soon saw that it was just the sort of adventure we had been looking for.

The next morning after eating breakfast, Tamar said, "I'm going to call Sweets to see if he has some work for us."

She fumbled through her purse, found the business card Sweets had given her, and dialed his number. After answering, she explained to him that Tamar, April and I was serious about dancing for him. After making arrangements for us to meet him, she hung up.

"I can't wait to meet this guy you and Crystal keep talking about, especially if he's all about making us some money. I need some money!" April exclaimed. Her eyes twinkled as if envisioning dollar signs. Tamar and I both agreed by nodding our heads.

"Let's go tonight. If we are too tired to drive back, then we could stay over Tiger's house," Tamar suggested.

Late that evening, we all loaded into my Grand-Am and headed off towards Searcy. It was dark when we pulled into the yard of the address that Sweets had given us. As soon as I turned the motor off, Sweet's head emerged from the door.

"Hurry up, cut your lights off, and come on in! We don't want to announce to the whole neighborhood that you're all here, now do we?" I quickly cut off the lights and sat there thinking about what he had just said. I couldn't believe how far I was lowering my standards by subjecting myself to the orders of my soon-to-be pimp.

After building up our courage, we finally got out of the car and went into the house. There was no turning back now. We were quite aware of what we came to do—to make money—lot's of it.

"Come on in and have a seat, ladies," Sweets said, flashing his famous smile. "I want to see what each of you girls are working with, so I can give each of you your own special nicknames."

After smoking on a few blunts and sipping on a few beers, we were all in the mood to show him what we were working with. Sure enough, the weed and the slow music made me feel erotic, but I was still nervous. Jason had been the only guy to see me totally in the nude before and even then, all the lights were off. Although I was behaving very loosely, I still had some morals left, although they were rapidly diminishing. I knew that once I crossed this line, there were no limitations to what I would do.

One by one, we performed exotic dances for Sweets until the guys that we would be entertaining arrived. Just like dogs, he gave us our names, and with those names came ownership. We became his property. Disturbed as I am to say it, we were about to be sold to the highest bidder. Tamar's name became,

"Peaches;" my name became, "Exotic Chocolate;" and April's name became, "Cream." Over time, Tamar and I both got our names tattooed on our bodies.

As time progressed, Sweets set up "gigs" for us at local nightclubs and special VIP gatherings. He carried guns along with him to protect us while we performed. A few times, we even went on dope runs with him to create a diversion if the police were to stop us.

Tamar, April, and I became very popular throughout the towns we performed in. The quick fame along with the fast money gave me a false sense of power. These things masked some of my pain, but their false illusion didn't last long.

A New Found Love

When we had made it back to Forrest City early one morning after one of our strip-dancing escapades, my car died. I was thankful that I was going downhill and was able to park the car in front of April's apartment. I was too tired to figure out what had happened to it. I followed Tamar and April inside the apartment, and as soon as I hit the couch, I fell straight to sleep.

I didn't stir until about five o'clock the next afternoon. I awakened to the sound of talking outside. It suddenly dawned upon me that it was the Fourth of July. I jumped up and peeked out the window. People stood outside barbecuing and having a good time. Standing over by my car, I spotted my cousin Ray Jones and a tall, brown-skinned man. They seemed deeply engaged in conversation. Ray, perhaps in his late forties, only lived a few doors down from April.

"What are you wearing to the club tonight?" April asked, walking up behind me peering out the blinds.

"I don't know. I'll have to go to my trunk and find something to put on," I yawned.

"See if you can find something for me also," Tamar said

drowsily, throwing the covers back from her face. She stood up from the pallet she was lying on and stretched.

"Okay," I said, slipping on my house shoes.

"I'm still tired, but it's time to find something to do. I can't sleep the whole Fourth of July away," Tamar said. I opened the front door, adjusted my eyes to the sun's glare and stepped outside.

The smell of barbecue immediately awakened my senses. As I walked over to where my car was located, the guy that stood with Ray glanced up. There was nothing about him that just stood out, but he was handsome in an odd way.

"Come here Crystal. I want to introduce you to someone," Ray said after spotting me. I looked at the guy, and immediately our eyes locked. His mouth literally fell opened. He was far from my type—at least that's what I told myself. As if suddenly realizing he was gawking at me, a smile began to tear at the corners of his mouth. We shook hands as Ray introduced us. His name was De Angelo Winters. I could tell by the fire in his eyes that he was very interested in me—probably sexually, which was usually the case.

After our brief introduction, I turned to reenter April's house. As I walked away, I could hear him mumble under his breath. I turned around.

"What'd you say?" I asked.

"You don't know it yet, but you're going to be my wife," he announced with confidence. I smiled. Never before had a guy ever said anything remotely like that, and I was familiar with plenty of game. "Could I come by and visit you later on tonight?" he wanted to know.

Trying not to be rude since he was an acquaintance of my cousin, I told him, "Yes." Wanting to get Ray's input, I told him about my car breaking down. After he offered his assistance in checking it out the following week, I turned to leave.

While walking back towards the apartment, I thought about the look of desire that burned in De Angelo's eyes. After realizing that I was empty-handed, I came to a complete halt, turned around, and walked towards my car. The whole purpose of me going outside in the first place was to find something to wear for the club that night.

As I rummaged around in the trunk, I could feel De Angelo's eyes upon me sending shivers down my spine. It was as if his stare was burning through my clothes. Upon retrieving the items that I was looking for, I returned to April's place.

Once inside, I exploded in pure bliss, rambling on and on about the way the guy was staring at me. Tamar and April wanted to know every detail of our encounter.

"What is his name," April asked with a gigantic grin spread across her face.

"De Angelo Winters," I practically chirped. After mentioning his name, a weird expression came across her face.

"I know him. He's alright, I guess," she said. By the tone of her voice, I knew that she didn't think he was all that great. Since I was just looking for a good time and wasn't looking for a relationship, I decided that it would be quite harmless to entertain him that night.

For the remainder of the day, I cleaned up April's whole apartment, so it would be presentable when my company arrived. After April and Tamar left to go over to a neighbor's house to give me some privacy, I took a quick shower and put on a pair of white daisy dukes and a brown and white sleeveless shirt. I felt comfortable, yet sort of sexy. I glanced in the full-length mirror. The outfit accented my long, chocolate legs. I smiled, pleased with what I had pieced together.

After lighting a couple of candles, I glanced around to make sure everything looked fine. It did. Sultry lyrics by Jagged Edge played in the background as vanilla-scented incense burned, creating an atmosphere of seduction. There was a knock at the door. I stood up, ran my fingers through my hair, and quickly glanced in the mirror again to check for any flaws in my attire that I had overlooked. Everything was superb. When I opened the door, my heart sunk deep inside my chest with disappointment. I could hardly believe that this was the same guy I had planned on seducing.

There, in the dim light, DeAngelo appeared to have aged dramatically since I last saw him. He reeked with the smell of liquor. He didn't even bother to change his cloths from earlier. By the slur of his speech and his reddened eyes, it was inevitable that De Angelo was drunk—sloppy drunk. I put on one of my fake smiles as best as I could and politely stepped back, so he could enter in. He took a seat on the couch. After taking a deep breath and mumbling a few curse words under my breath, I did the same.

For minutes, he sat there speechless. I could tell that he was nervous, so I decided to break the silence that had started to envelop us. "How old are you?" I asked trying to sound remotely interested.

"Deuce, deuce," was his reply. *"He must be some kind of wannabe gangster,"* I thought. "So does that mean you're twenty-two?" I asked sarcastically.

"Yes, and I'm seven-four GD, Gangster Disciples, baby." I shrugged, showing him that I wasn't at all impressed with his tough gangster persona nor by his gift of Ebonics. I mean after all, I had been involved with some hardcore drug dealers.

I guess realizing he was losing my interest fast, De Angelo started speaking my language. "I have some weed, and it's some fire. Do you want to smoke some?" he asked. *I might as well get high,* I thought. *This conversation sure isn't going anywhere, and at least I would get something out of this whole ordeal.*

"Sure," I replied.

After De Angelo had finished rolling the blunt, I took a few puffs, and within minutes, I was high as a kite. I sat there listening to him brag about how he didn't take crap from anyone. Actually, when he finally stopped bragging on himself, he started looking somewhat cute to me. I don't know, maybe it was just the weed. Right then, it was definitely starting to stimulate me in places that it shouldn't have.

When De Angelo and I got totally "zooted" (so high that we could barely move), he somehow managed to bring the subject of sex up, and how good he was at it. *Yeah, right.* I rolled my eyes upward. *That's what they all say.* My body was starting to react to him, but my mind was definitely saying, *Yuck. Crystal, are you out of your mind?"*

To add a little fun to the evening, I decided to tease him. I fastened my eyes upon him, lowered my eyelashes, and slowly raised them back up. Whatever he was saying froze in his mouth. He was now watching me hungrily, enchanted by my every move. I didn't stop there.

I slowly stuck my tongue out and slid it across my lips until they were wet. I could tell by how his eyes darkened that my plan was working. De Angelo became trance-like as he leaned forward, wanting more. I slowly raised my index finger, placing it on his half-parted mouth. After stroking his lips with ease, my finger continued forming a trail down his neck and resting on his chest. Slowly, I raised my eyes to see if he wanted it just as much as I did. His heavy breathing answered the question for me. That's when I decided to stop. My mission had been accomplished. As soon as I leaned back onto the couch to show him that the fun was over, that's when he decided to pick up where I left off. His determination to seduce me excited me. So of course, you can imagine what happened next.

When our lasciviousness had ended, De Angelo passed out on the floor as tiny beads of sweat danced across his body. I lay back onto the couch, pleased with his performance.

When Tamar and April walked through the door minutes later, I was sitting on the couch grinning. When they saw me, April asked, "Goodness Crystal, what are you grinning about?" She followed my eyes to where De Angelo was sprawled out on the floor snoring rather loudly. Her eyes widened with surprise.

"Oh, that's why you're so happy. How was it?" she and Tamar whispered simultaneously.

"I must admit, it's the best I've ever had," I whispered back, still grinning from ear to ear.

"If it was that good, then let the boy sleep," April teased.

"I'm exhausted too," I said yawning. Then I rolled over on the couch, pulled the thin sheet above my head, and drifted off to sleep.

I awakened early in the morning to heavy breathing in my ear and massive hands exploring my body. I opened my eyes. It was De Angelo. We were at it again. We tried to keep the noise down, so we wouldn't disturb Tamar who was asleep on the opposite couch not far from us. After minutes of rough sex, he finally left. By then, the sun was high in the sky.

The next few nights, De Angelo showed up at the apartment. Just like the saying goes: "You feed a stray dog, he will keep showing back up at your house." He was both exciting and wild just the way I liked. I only looked at him as a sex partner. There was no way he was boyfriend material—at least I thought.

During the weekend, I was ready to go home. I needed time to recooperate from everything. I walked two doors down to where Ray, also known as Cat, lived. When he answered the door, I smiled.

"Thank you for introducing me to De Angelo," I said.

"You're very welcome cousin," he replied as if knowing the two of us would hit it off. "He's good people."

"By the way, will you watch over my car while I'm in Wynne for the weekend?" I asked. "I'm going home today."

"Sure. If you leave me your car keys, I'll see if I can fix it when I get off work tomorrow," he replied. I agreed.

That evening when Tamar's mother came to pick her up, I caught a ride back to Wynne with them over to my mother's house. That Saturday morning as Tamar and I were sitting in my mother's living room reminiscing over some wild moments we'd shared, I heard a noise outside. It sounded as if someone was pulling up in our driveway—the last thing I expected to see when I looked out the window was my car. Tamar could tell by the expression on my face that she needed to come and see what I was gawking at.

"That's your car isn't it?" she asked peering behind me in disbelief. We both ran outside to get a better view.

As soon as we made it to the front porch, I noticed my cousin sitting in the driver's side of my vehicle. I looked harder to make out the other silhouette. It was De Angelo. I didn't expect to see him so soon. I immediately looked down at my attire. I was raggedly. I didn't want him to see me looking so horrific, but it was too late. Ray opened his door and stepped out the car.

"He was the one that paid to get your car fixed," he said, pointing towards De Angelo as if trying to justify his reason for being there.

At that moment, De Angelo's tall and toned frame emerged from behind the passenger's side. He still looked as I had last seen him. Actually, I even think he had the same clothes on. I rapidly dismissed the horrific notion as he began speaking. "Will you go out on a date with me?" he asked giving me a gigantic smile, revealing a couple of missing teeth.

"You bet!" I answered, hastily remembering the ecstatic passion that the two of us had shared. *This will be the last time,* I told myself. *At least I could do this for him for fixing my car.*

"Oh, that's so sweet," Tamar said teasingly, acting as if she were wiping tears from her eyes.

"What are we waiting for? This calls for a celebration," I said excitedly. "I'll be right back. Let me grab some clothes to take with me." After doing so, all of us headed back to Forrest City in my car.

It was later that night at the Blue Flame that De Angelo told me that he was in love with me. I had been at that particular club many times before, but there was something mystical about this night. The setting seemed to be extra romantic. The music had a nice and soothing melody to it, and the lights were low. The whole scene enraptured me. Above us, hung a silver shimmering disco ball. I glanced across the table at De Angelo. The ball's light showered the surface of his face with raindrops of crystals dancing in every direction. I watched him fidget as if he was contemplating a serious issue. He hardly made eye contact with me. I brushed it off as a case of bad nerves.

Although I was sitting across from him, guys came up to our table and made comments like: "I think you are a very sexy woman," or "Do you care to dance?" They were totally disregarding the fact that I was with him. Each time, I would smile and shake my head to let them know that I wasn't interested—or at least not at the moment. By the crease in De Angelo's brow, I could tell that he was growing frustrated by their disrespect. I must admit, I was being a little flirtatious. I didn't want to give De Angelo all of my attention, just enough to let him know that I was grateful that he had fixed my car.

As I leaned back onto the red leather seats, he started to say something but then changed his mind. "Never mind," he said, his eyes watering.

"What?" I insisted, sensing the significance of what he wanted to say.

"You act as if I'm not even here. Can't you see that I love you?" His voice quivered. I could tell that it hurt him to say those last three words because afterwards he placed his hands over his face.

I never had a guy tell me he loved me before. Never. Actually, I never heard any man tell me that before, not even my own father. So, I was accustomed to equating love with hurt. For some weird reason, I burst out laughing. De Angelo got up angrily and stormed out the door. I continued to sit there, sipping on my Paul Mason and trying to digest everything that had just happened.

Within a few minutes, he returned and sat down facing me.

"I was not planning on saying that," he said. I studied his face closely. I could see the pain that was lying dormant just beyond the surface. "Not long ago," he began, "I moved back here from California..."

Briefly, he took it upon himself to explain how his baby's mama had treated him badly and had caused him to be attacked by her brothers. The two of them had been in a long relationship before he realized that it wasn't going to work. Since then, he had promised himself that he would never tell another woman that he loved her unless he was prepared to marry her. *That explains his rapid declaration of love for me,* I guessed. *This was "rebound" love. He just got out of a long relationship, and now he's vulnerable,* I summed up. That was perfectly understandable.

"I really meant what I said," De Angelo said, gazing into my eyes as if knowing that I doubted his feelings towards me. "For some reason, I want to be with you. I know it's really soon for me to be telling you this, but I know what I want—you," he said bluntly in a husky tone. "You're going to be my wife one day."

After a few more minutes of this conversation, I wanted to relieve some of the tension that was starting to develop. I knew that I wasn't ready to declare the same feelings of love to him. "Let's dance," I said grabbing his hands and leading him out onto the dance floor. I was definitely feeling the effect of the drinks I had been sipping on. For the remainder of the night, we danced until my feet ached. After the club had ended, I found myself wrapped tightly in De Angelo's arms at a hotel.

Because I enjoyed his company so much, we started going out every night. Shortly after, we became inseparable. I kept telling myself that the only reason I wanted to be around him was because we had great sex, but deep down, I knew that other reasons were starting to develop.

As months passed, I began to notice how frequent I mentioned his name to my relatives, and they noticed also. "Crystal, I think you're in love," Tamar said sarcastically one afternoon while sitting over April's house.

"Don't humor yourself," I said trying to convince her as well as myself that I wasn't. "I just like being around him because he's so funny." "Well," I said after pondering a few seconds, "and because he got some good loving."

"Whatever," she said rolling her eyes upwards. "I see how your face lights up every time you mention his name."

As if on cue, I started smiling. I couldn't possibly fathom how two opposite people could be in love. In fact, I tried to convince myself that it was impossible. We were definitely as different as night is from day.

The summer was soon growing to a close and for some reason; I was saddened by the fact that I wouldn't see De Angelo for a long time. I was going to miss him deeply. While away in Europe, I was frightened that he would move on without me. That really bothered me.

Before I was to leave, my cousin Felicia invited De Angelo and me to come and spend the night with her in Wynne. She and I were very close. She always seemed to enjoy my company, and since she had her own trailer, I accepted her offer on the Friday night before my departure. We all planned on celebrating at the local "hole in the wall."

That night, as De Angelo sat on the couch, I stepped inside one of Felicia's vacant bedrooms to get dressed. I wanted to surprise him by wearing something extremely sexy. I massaged my body down with scented body oil and then slipped into a long black velvet dress. It had spaghetti straps and a long slit that ran up the length of one thigh. The dress complimented my curves as it clung to every contour of my tall physique. I then put a silver ankle bracelet around my ankle and slipped into a pair of black open-toe heels. My hair was already pinned up nicely on the top of my head in a French Roll. Over the sound of the stereo that was playing, a repeated knock could be heard at the front door. Within minutes, muffled voices came from the living room. I grabbed my purse and was ready to make my entrance.

De Angelo's mouth dropped open when he saw me. He stood up as if in a trance and began to walk towards me, zombie-like. With one swift motion of his arms, he embraced me.

"I can eat you up right here and right now," he whispered in my ear sending a trail of kisses down my neck. He didn't seem to mind that some of my other relatives were in the room watching us. "I can't help it," he said out loud when he finally freed his mouth from my neck. "She does this to me. I mean look at her—she is so gorgeous."

I bathed in his praise of me. For a few moments, I was a princess suspended in a fairy tale book as I stood before my knight in shinning armor.

De Angelo and I never made it to the club that night. Everyone had to leave without us. "I figured that was going to happen!" Felicia mumbled agitatedly, walking towards the door with my other relatives trailing behind her. "You both act like a couple of dogs in heat."

After throwing nasty looks of disappointment in our direction, all of them walked out the door. I felt horrible for deserting them, but I wanted so badly to spend quality time with the guy I loved. I wanted to absorb his masculinity before it was time for me to leave. At that instance, I knew that I had fallen in love. I didn't know how I was going to say it, but I knew I would declare it that night.

As soon as we were alone, De Angelo hugged me tightly and kissed me over and over again. He told me how much he loved me and with each kiss gave reasons why. Then he backed me up to the bedroom where we made music until early that morning. *This is the perfect time to tell him,* I thought. As I lay in his arms, I looked up and called his name tenderly. His eyes came open.

"Yes?" he said breathing heavily.

"I love you." When I said it, I felt completely vulnerable as if I was internally naked before him. The words that I spoke came from so deep within that tears begin to flow down my face. He looked at me so passionately before kissing me again.

"I love you too, baby," he muttered. After that, we made love again and again until we both finally fell asleep in one another's arms.

The next morning, we both sat around watching television. We finally had to face the fact that we were going to be separated for a few months.

"All you have to do is tell me to stay," I said, gazing into his eyes breaking the silence. "I'll do it."

I wanted him to realize just how much I loved him. He hesitated for a few minutes then replied, "I really don't want you to go, but I know that this is a great opportunity for you. If I cause you to miss out on this, you'll never forgive me."

"Yes, I will," I said praying that he would only tell me to not go. I was willing to sacrifice this trip at a single word—stay.

"I will miss you so much," I said, whispering in his ear then tugging on it gently with my teeth.

The time arrived for us to say our good-byes. "I'll call you when I arrive in Italy. After I give you my address, you better write me or else," I said threatening him.

"Don't worry. I will," he promised.

After his friend, Derrick, arrived, De Angelo and I hugged one another again. Next, he and Derrick headed back to Forrest City. I felt so lost and alone. When my mother came to pick me up, I sat in the car in my own little world. All I could think about was how much I was going to miss him. Here I was on my way to Europe leaving my first true love behind. To soothe the ache that was in my heart, I found a pen and some paper in my purse and began to write:

> My feelings for you are like the budding of a rose after the dew of dawn has fallen across its surface—very soft and gentle. I can feel my feelings surmounting and reaching an apex of pure bliss that seems to leave me breathless and overwhelmed

in a zone of ecstatic sensations. Whenever I am in your presence, the melodies I hear are, oh, so sweet. The gentle vibrations of your voice are as silky strands of honey sending chills racing down my spine as they caress my features with gentle strokes of passion. By just standing close to you and not even physically touching you, I can still feel your touch. Your eyes give me a touch as gentle as the falling dew that covers the very façade of my heart. Your stare ignites a yearning within that burns with immense heat. Although we are apart, the memories of you and of the moments we've shared will continue to reach out their hungry fingers and stroke my heart. Time and distance is no obstacle that can constrain your gentle touches of passion for me. I'll wait until time and distance release us from our imprisonment. Good-bye, my love.

CHAPTER FOUR

It's a Setup!

> "But without faith it is impossible to please him: for he that cometh to God must believe that he is, and that he is a rewarder of them that diligently seek him."
>
> Hebrews 11:6

A Strange Land

Simultaneously, different emotions plagued me. Not wanting to pamper any particular one, I leaned back into the cushioned seat and stared into oblivion, awaiting the sound to come over the speakers that take-off was approaching. With my arms tightly nestled across my chest, I leaned forward to look at the wet pavement.

The fact that this was the first time I had ever stepped foot on an airplane was frightening in itself, but because I was traveling such as long a distance as Florence, Italy, the fear that gnawed at me superseded anxiety.

Within minutes, the flight attendant's voice resounded over the intercom in ripples of sultriness. "Please buckle your seat belts. We are now ready for take off." I sat there in silence, afraid to breathe as apprehension of what lay ahead surfaced. Clearing the cobweb of thoughts from my mind, I retilted my head back and tried to forget that I was on a plane.

Although I was traveling with other students from my university, I felt alone. *They don't understand me*, I concluded, enslaved by a victim's mentality. I longed for my peer's company; their consolation from the fear and grief that encapsulated me, ensnarling my soul. I wanted to voice my anguish, but pride constrained me.

Whenever I arrived to my new destination, I vowed to relinquish all of my bad habits and to live in complete submission to God. It was going to take a force greater than will power to keep me sane in a foreign land and to subdue the loneliness that had already evaded my spirit.

As the plane hurled us into the air, I clawed into the perspiration-soaked seat. After getting over the feeling that my stomach had dropped to my bladder, I soon drifted off into a world of dreams where I resided until it was time for dinner.

Finally, after enduring hours of the flight's turbulence, we arrived in Brussels, Belgium. Once inside the airport, each of us found our luggage, moved it to a luggage cart, and waited for further instructions. "We will meet our tour guide out front," said Mr. Stanley, one of our adult chaperones, as he motioned us onwards. As I departed the airport, the invigorating air awakened my curiosity. Miraculously, I wanted to live again.

A short, salt and peppered-haired man approached us. "Hello. My name is Mike Thrift," he said, extending his hand out. Each of us accepted it. "We're going to spend a few hours sightseeing here. Afterwards, we will all be driven to Florence, Italy. Now, everyone," he said, "follow me." We then followed him to the bus that awaited us nearby.

After a few hours of exploring the historic town, the bus

left for Italy. Around nine o'clock that night, we arrived at a little town called Scandicci which was located on the outskirts of Florence. As we came within city limits, the bus came to an abrupt halt. Since the street was too narrow and steep for the bus to ascend, everyone was instructed to walk the rest of the way to our new residence. After finding out we was expected to carry our luggage with us, I grew enraged. Realizing I didn't have much of a choice, I eventually surrendered.

When I stepped off the bus, the cold night air greeted my tired and aching body. Besides the bus' headlights, the celestial bodies that decorated the clear European sky were the only source of visibility for the dark path that loomed before us.

When I finally arrived at the villa, I was totally exhausted. The muscles ached in the back of my legs as if punishing me for not being physically fit. After everyone else had made it and had caught their breaths, each of us was greeted with hugs and Italian salutations from the family that would be hosting us for the upcoming semester. Next, they took us on a brief tour of the place then gave us a brief introduction of themselves.

Mr. Philip the director of the school was the son of the president of the International Program at Harding University in Searcy, Arkansas. He briefly introduced his family, telling how they came to live in Europe. His fervency caused me to perceive his deep passion for the Lord. His wife, Shelly, who stood alongside him, held a comical grin on her face (almost like the Joker from the Batman movie), adding comic relief to his seriousness. With each word, her chubby face depicted laughter.

Originally from the United States, our hosts had moved to Italy so churches could be established; and so Harding students could further their education through a wider spectrum of learning. Although their story was very fascinating, my exhausted body reminded me of the long day that we had just had. After meeting everyone, I quickly unpacked my bags, put its contents neatly away in its assigned place, and went to bed.

While lying underneath my warm blankets, I sensed the presence of God. I had a gut feeling that Europe was only a piece of the big puzzle that he was going to use to propel me into purpose. He awakened a quiet urgency that lay dormant in my spirit. Without a doubt, he had a plan for me, but what that plan was or the roads that I would have to travel to get there, I had the slightest idea.

After awakening early the next day, I threw back the covers, walked over to the window, and peered outside. Darkness still covered the sky like a thin blanket while hints of blue protruded through. In the distance, birds chirped cheerfully. The scenery befriended me, beckoning me to partake of its tranquility.

After hearing some of the young ladies rousing from their sleep, I snapped back to reality. I had to get dressed. Today would be a busy day. I rushed to the bathroom and stood outside its door with my clothes hanging loosely over my arm. I tapped gently. "Someone's in here! I'll only be a few more minutes," a voice shouted from within. I patiently stood there in the dark hallway, praying silently that God would allow me to handle sharing a room with eight girls and with only two bathrooms to use at our discretion.

The girl's head soon emerged from behind the bathroom's door. With a towel tucked tightly around her, she darted to the bedroom to finish dressing. I rushed in, quickly took a shower, clothed, and joined the rest of the group downstairs where devotion and orientation would be held.

When I arrived, Mr. Philip and his wife were introducing the rest of their family. This time, their two sons were with them. One of the boys was about sixteen and the other thirteen. Afterwards, Mr. Philip continued. "You will have two nice Italian women who will be living here with you all. They will handle all of the cooking, cleaning, and laundry. They can barely speak English, so this will be a good way for everyone to practice their Italian."

As if knowing their cue, two older Italian women appeared

out of the kitchen and greeted us with smiles. They were introduced as Renada and Martha. *Wow, I've only dreamed about having a maid. Now, I'll have two. This trip might not be so bad after all.* I concluded.

While trying to concentrate on what was being said, the sound of the wind seeping through the cracks of the old planks of the villa's floor disrupted my attention. I sat on the damp wooden chair with my hands tucked underneath me, quivering from the cold. Anticipation of what Florence had in store, mingled with the coldness, lured my mind away even farther.

The moment finally came when all of the introductions had been made. Next, Mr. Philip began to pass out maps of Florence along with local bus tickets. "Everyone has an assignment today. We'll all go downtown so that you can familiarize yourselves with the buses that run back to the villa. After exploring the town together, everyone will be responsible for getting themselves back here."

Confusion practically seeped from every pore of my skin. I glared at Mr. Philip as if he had suddenly and unexplainably lost his mind. *How is he going to do this to us?* I internally protested. *This man got some nerves making us find our way back by ourselves. We don't know anyone here. Anything can happen to us.*

He continued giving instructions, silencing the thoughts that were racing through my head. "I want everyone to divide into groups at least two people per group. Everyone in your group will work as a team to find themselves back here."

Only minutes after the orientation was over, everyone was busy packing their backpacks with bottles of water and with sack lunches that our new maids had prepared for us. Afterwards, everyone filed outdoors so Mr. Philip could accompany us to downtown Florence.

As I exited the large wooden doors, a rush of icy air stung my face sending loose tendrils of hair dancing wildly. Surrounding the villa, rows and rows of vineyards and olive patches could be seen. The pungent smell of fermented grapes lingered in the air leaving me woozy on the brink of intoxication. The darkened sky now had visible signs that daylight was approaching. Pink and blue ligaments were stretched out across its dark cloak. Far in the distance, hovered a mountain whose peak was covered in snow. Totally speechless, I stood in awe watching the day unravel before me.

Once everyone was outside, the journey began down the long treacherous hill that we had climbed the previous night. After making it to the bottom, we caught the bus that would take us into Florence. Within minutes, it began to fill with residents of the town. Fascinated, I sat on the cold seats staring out the windows and gazing at all the ancient-structured buildings that were so close to one another.

Somewhere in the back of the bus, a couple of elderly women greeted one another in Italian. I tried to quiet my thoughts, so I could tune in to their conversation. Not to my surprise, I only understood a couple of words that were spoken: "Pronto!" and "Buon giorno!" These two words meant hello and good morning. Other than English, the only language I knew well was Spanish and that sure wasn't going to do much good here in Italy.

The bus finally arrived in downtown Florence. Each of us poured out into the crowded streets. The bustle of people sent a wave of excitement washing over me. I darted my eyes trying to take in every detail of Florentine life.

Others in my group were busy admiring well known architecture that the tour guide was pointing out. "And that over there is the Ponte Vecchio," he said pointing towards what appeared to be nothing more than a bridge. By now, I was anxious about breaking up into smaller groups. This would give me a better chance to explore everything in more detail.

Suddenly, as if stepping into a gothic movie, one of the most amazing scenes towered overhead. Rising above every other building stood a massive golden dome. The sun's rays hit its golden surface at such an angle that fragments of light were illuminated on everything in its path. The light radiating through the glass of the surrounding buildings sent colorful prisms dancing wildly in every direction. I stood there gaping up in awe. For a second, I was unable to breathe. My eyes watered. *How could I not serve a God like this?* I questioned. *He loves us so much that he gives us such splendid beauty.*

By now, the sun's rays had chased away all traces of night. None of the buildings looked cold and dismal anymore. In order to find out everything about the dome, I moved in closer to the tour guide.

I noticed a few prejudiced stares from some of the Italians as they gripped their purses or wallets close to them as I walked by. I soon accepted the fact that I would never blend in with my upper and middle class peers. Eventually, I became so caught up in the explicitness of my surroundings that I began to disregard the stares along with my insecurities and began to focus on the mystic beauties that encircled me. They overruled the loneliness that ate at my heart.

Loneliness was one of the tools that God used to teach me many things about who I was in him. My flesh couldn't understand it then, but he was unraveling "religious" lies that were twisted inside my mind. It was needful for God to get people out of my ear so that he could speak to me. He used loneliness to strip me of the masquerade of being well-composed even when internally I was falling to pieces as a result of my hidden pain. He had to get down to the root of my "ice-princess" mentality, one that said tears showed a sign of weakness. It was needful for God to break these strongholds and mindsets in order for his true glory to be revealed. It was a process that wouldn't happen over night.

Black Crows

I half-listened to the tour guide who was discussing another well-known architecture. And once more I started focusing on the strange looks that I continued getting. I was nothing more than a country girl, raised straight out of the "dirty south" and was now surrounded by upper-class business people rushing off to climb another step up the corporate ladder. I probably was nothing more than a peasant in their eyes. *Wow, God must have a sense of humor,* I thought causing the corners of my mouth to twitch into a smile. I could almost picture Queen Esther as she was being pushed into exile, surrounded by people who once carried prestige. They perhaps overlooked her because she was nobody—a female, a Jew, and an orphan. At that moment, they all had something in common—captivity.

After turning a corner, I beheld markets that lined both sides of the street as far as my eyes could see. As I walked alongside the tables filled with merchandise, I noticed a few black men sitting on nearby cathedral steps. Like ravenous black crows, they gawked at everyone that passed by. Their skin color was that of dusty tar. It looked as if they hadn't bathed in a decade, mummified by the grime that was on their bodies. The texture of their hair was as matted wool that had been uncombed for some time.

Although my legs continued to propel me in the opposite direction, my eyes were fixed on them. Their whole demeanor captivated me. A big difference in their facial structures could be seen contrasted with that of black Americans. There was no doubt in my mind that these men were real Africans, maybe even straight from the Congo.

Eyes that were like black pebble's no longer suspended in a white sclera, but a yellow tainted one, rested on me. The coldness of their stare injected a creepy feeling within as if my thoughts were being read. Each of the crow-men sat upon the stairs as if time had frozen them. They were completely motionless except for their beady eyes. Disappointment overwhelmed me. I was happy to see black men, but I didn't expect them to look like this. I was hoping to at least get a few phone numbers on the trip. *If they all look like this, I will be one mad sister!* I cringed at the thought.

I kept glancing at them out of the corner of my eyes while slowly walking by. After a few minutes, I noticed that all of their eyes were fastened upon me as if suddenly aware that they were being observed. I quickened my pace. Soon the dusty statues started mumbling to one another while continuing to watch me. I hoped they weren't trying to put a spell on me. As I rounded the corner, I soon lost interest.

To my surprise, there were more markets. Surrounding me were so many different things to choose from at such reasonable prices. I was so accustomed to walking into a department store and purchasing items without speaking a word. Not here. All around me, bargaining for lower prices was heard from the mouths of consumers. It was completely amazing how people were talking down prices at unbelievable rates. I could just imagine being able to walk into Wal-Mart and saying: "I know that this shirt cost $25.00, but I'm willing to spend only $15.00 for it." How great it would be if the cashier would just reply, "Okay." as she stuffs the new shirt in a bag. Well, we all know that won't be happening here in America anytime soon.

Towards the end of the street, I noticed other black men. They looked better groomed than the previous ones. Their facial features held the same distinctness. As I began to pass by their booths, they eyed me as smiles of interest broke out across their faces.

"You mustn't be from this country," one of the guys said, leaving the group of men he was talking with to stand at my side. *Oh brother, he probably was sent over here to make sure I don't steal anything*, I thought.

"No," I said rather coldly glaring at him as if trying to turn him into a lump of ice.

"I can tell," he replied matter-of-factly while studying my face like it was a piece of exquisite art. "Your facial features are distinct."

I didn't know whether to take it as a compliment or not, so I just gave a slight smile.

"Where are you from?" he continued to pry.

At that time, another black guy approached us that had been listening nearby. "The United States," I said with dignity, quickly correcting my stance.

"Where in the United States?" they both pried.

"Arkansas," I said. Simultaneously, they both erupted with laughter. "Oh, the home of President Bill Clinton," one of the guys said, marveling in his knowledge about the ordeal with Monica Lewinsky. They started making hideous facial expressions.

"Yes," I beamed, tickled at their taunting.

The first guy that approached me then ran to grab a newspaper. "He made the front page of some of our newspapers." Some of my classmates that were standing close by heard the conversation and started laughing. All of us crowded around the newspaper to examine the pictures of President Bill Clinton and Monica Lewinsky.

After the hilarious episode, we resumed walking up and down the marketplace. While my classmates purchased items, I continued to look and admire the bustle of people. By this time, it had started to drizzle. Mr. Philip gathered everyone together in a huddle and made sure that we all had our maps with us.

"Me and my wife are getting ready to head back," he stated as his wife gave one of her comical mime expressions. "You are all on your own. I want each of you to pair up with at least one other person."

My eyes rested on a pale and skinny guy named Billy Young. He looked just like Shaggy from the Scooby Doo movie. The resemblance between the two was striking. I didn't know why, but for some reason, I always seemed to be drawn to loners and weirdoes. Maybe, it was because I had both characteristics myself. Billy's parents had accompanied him to Europe. His father, Mr. Young, was our new Bible class professor.

After Billy's acceptance to pair up with me, his mother immediately stood by his side. She looked at me over the brim of her glasses with disapproval. Finally, she announced that she and Mr. Young would be accompanying us also.

"This is going to be a long trip," I breathed heavily, not caring if they heard or not. I would have rather curled up with a good book locked away from the rest of the world than to be stuck with these people.

The New Groups

Everyone broke off into small groups. Afterwards Billy, Mr. and Mrs. Young, along with myself started on our own journey. Individually, each of us continued to speculate the many items that were on the market tables. To ease the tension that had started to circulate amongst us, I decided to add some comic relief.

"These things look like someone made them in their backyard," I said chuckling while holding up a pair of funny-looking earrings and a matching necklace. After giving a few more stiff jokes, they began loosening up. Soon, everyone was laughing and enjoying him or herself.

From that point on, Billy and I began to build a unique friendship in which I hold dear to my heart even to this day. He and I distanced ourselves a few paces ahead of his parents and made hysterical comments on everything we saw.

As both of us continued to walk, a guy approached me from the side. "Would you like to purchase an umbrella?" I looked in his direction. His eyes quickly raked over my body.

"No, thank you," I stated rather timidly due to his intense stare.

"I love your accent!" he shrieked, almost scaring me. Guys that were directly behind him began smiling. "Where're you from?" he breathed, yet eyeing me.

"Arkansas." I waited for the laughter that was bound to come. Simultaneously, he and the other guys that were listening in on our conversation began laughing, also showing knowledge of what was happening in the White House.

After the laughter subsided, the man extended his hand. "My name is Allah Bubba. "I'm a prince from Kenya, Africa. What's your name?"

"Crystal," I replied, accepting it. "Oh, he's a prince," I sneered in Billy's direction.

"Seriously, I am a prince," Allah Bubba repeated trying to convince me.

"If he's a prince," Billy whispered in my ear fighting to keep the laughter in, "then why is he selling umbrellas on the side of the road?" Unsuccessfully, we both erupted into a fit of laughter.

At this time, the rain began falling more rapidly. Soon people around us pulled out plastic bags and threw them on top of the items they were selling. Others were running around frantically placing items in boxes. "We better leave," Mr. Young stated walking over to where Billy and I were standing.

As I turned to leave, I felt a hand on my shoulder. "Pick out any umbrella. It is a gift from me to you. I hope to be seeing you soon," Allah Bubba said his voice slightly above a whisper. A warm look filled his eyes.

"Why thank you!" I exclaimed quite surprised. I grabbed a black one with white stripes as I raced to catch up with the Young's.

Like many others that had gotten caught in the downpour, we found shelter alongside a building to shield us until it subsided. Finally, after about twenty minutes, it only drizzled. Minutes later, the sun was starting to peep over dark clouds transmitting vibrant rainbows all across the sky.

We resumed a few more hours of sightseeing and finally decided it was time to head back to the villa. The Young's had no problem finding their way back. I was glad I had accompanied them after all.

Déja Vu

Since we were allowed to travel as we pleased after our morning classes, I signed out the next day and decided to explore the town by myself.

While walking, out of the corner of my eye, I noticed Allah Bubba across the street. He looked up from where he was selling paintings and started walking towards me. *Oh, Lord,* I thought. *What'd I do now?* Before I could answer my own question, it was too late.

"Hello, there young lady," he said approaching me from the side.

"Hi. How are you?" I replied nervously.

"What are your plans for today?" he wanted to know.

"I'm just exploring the city. So, tell me, what is there to do around here?" I tilted my head to the side, waiting for his reply.

"Well... how about I show you around?"

"Don't you have to look after your stand?" I added quickly, hoping he would remember.

"It can wait." He looked at my feet, inched slowly towards my hair, and finally rested on my eyes. I didn't know anything about him. For all I knew, his name wasn't even Allah Bubba. After internally debating, and finally concluding that it would be a good way to see the town, I finally answered, "Sure."

He ran quickly over to where his stand was located, and in a few minutes, had all of his belongings wrapped up and ready to go. While walking, I started singing softly, not aware that Allah Bubba was listening to the words of my song.

"Let's sit down over here." He pointed towards a bench.

After taking a seat, he turned to me and said, "Now, sing to me."

"You must be joking. Right?" I questioned, looking at the bustle of people around us.

"No," he breathed.

I searched his face for a hint of a smile but found none. I

gripped the back of the bench as if it was a boat, and the people around us were gigantic waves trying to sweep me away.

"I think you have a lovely voice, Crystal. I wanted to sit down, so I could enjoy it," he persisted.

"What type of song do you want to hear?" I asked, acting as if I knew a wide variety of songs other than gospel.

"Anything," he responded. "Sing what you were singing while we were walking."

"Well here goes." I inhaled then slowly exhaled. "I'll sing you a song about Jesus. It's called, 'No Greater Love.'"

Within seconds of singing, I became engrossed in its lyrics. I could feel the anointing of God descending upon me, and no longer did I care that I was in downtown Florence surrounded by a mass of people in the middle of rush hour. I continued to sing the song that told of how God sent his Son, Jesus, to die on the cross and how he came to die because of his love for us. I closed my eyes, lost focus of my surroundings, and focused on the message of the song. The song's lyrics stroked the depth of my soul as it reeled me into a whirl of holy passion.

By the end of the song, I realized that Allah Bubba hadn't spoken a word during the whole performance. I opened my eyes and looked at him. He sat there next to me with his head bowed in obeisance.

After a moment of complete silence between the two of us, he glanced up at me. To my astonishment, there were tears in his eyes. The salty substance flowed in a constant stream down his chocolate face. "What's wrong?" I asked.

"That was beautiful. You have the voice of an angel," he muttered barely above a whisper.

"Yeah, right," I chuckled, hitting him on the shoulder playfully. There wasn't a hint of a smile on his face.

"It's not everyday, that we hear the message of Jesus Christ in this country," he sniffled, fastening his eyes on mine. "I needed that."

There was a brief moment of quietness. "Tell me something good," Allah Bubba finally insisted.

"What do you mean?" I asked puzzled at his strange request.

"Tell me anything that's good." I assumed he knew a little Swahili since he was from Africa, so I decided to try some of my skills on him with "Munga Nakupenda." I tried to sound eloquent as the words flowed out of my mouth.

"What does that mean?" he wanted to know.

"It's Swahili, for God loves you," I answered. For a few quiet minutes, he seemed to be pondering everything I had both sung and spoken, trying to digest it all. The look on his face moved me deeply.

Instantly, it dawned on me how blessed I was. I, along with most people in the United States could hear the gospel whenever we wanted. Allah Bubba made me aware that there were people who were literally starving for the "good news." I felt an urgency to share the gospel by any means necessary. God had a greater plan for my being here thousands of miles away from home.

"Come on, let's go," Allah Bubba finally said. He then stood up. "Do you mind if we go by my house, so I can drop my things off?"

"Is it far?" I asked.

"No," he said pointing in the direction of a worn eight-story building across the street. "It's right over there. I just need to drop my paintings off."

"Okay, but I'll stay outside," I said, trying to make myself perfectly clear that I wasn't an "easy" woman.

"Sure, but you don't have to. I won't try anything," he assured me. I followed his lead as we headed towards the rusty-brown edifice alongside the street.

As he struggled to get the key in the door, he turned around and looked at me. "Are you sure you want to stay outside? I don't stay here alone. My uncle lives here also. I would like for you to sing to him." *Well ... it's for a good cause.* I justified. *There can't be too much wrong in this.* Suddenly, memories of being raped by

Jason began to plague my mind. Each incident that led to the rape came flooding back. With fear gripping at my heart, each of its *lub dubs* grew louder than the next. The anxiety caused beads of perspiration to become visible on the back of my palms. *This guy was different,* I told myself. After taking a few quick deep breaths, I finally agreed. "Sure. Let's not stay in long."

With a huge grin on his face, he opened the door and flipped the light on. I followed close behind. The fresh smell of bleach filled the air. The small living room contained a variety of photographs that covered each of its walls. It didn't take a genius to realize that only males occupied this apartment. There was nothing feminine about the place at all—no pretty flowers or silk curtains. Alongside one of the walls rested a stereo with a small television atop its well-polished frame. A dingy plaid couch and a wooden chair were the only other furniture that decorated the room.

"Would you like to watch television?" he asked, picking up the remote and pushing the "on" button.

"Sure," I lied. I took a seat on the couch. While sitting, I constantly tried to suppress the feelings of déj vu.

Allah Baba walked into the back room and came out with an older man. "Hello," the man said, welcoming me. He had long dread locks that fell at the center of his back. They reminded me of the huge tarantulas I had seen in Orlando, Florida. I shuttered at the thought.

"Hello," I responded. "Allah Baba tells me that you can sing really well." He then took a seat beside me. "I can hold a note if that's what you mean. I think he exaggerated a little," I replied modestly.

"Sing something for me," the man interrupted, cutting me off. I wanted to make the ordeal end quickly, so immediately I started to sing. This time I wasn't about to close my eyes and get caught up in the spirit. Upon completion, the elderly man peered at me with yellow-singed eyes.

"You sound really nice," he said.

"Thank you." I accepted his compliment with gratitude. Without another word, he walked back into his room and closed the door.

"Follow me," Allah Baba said, "I want to show you some pictures of my family." I stood up and followed after him into a small bedroom. He pulled out a small picture album from a drawer and began flipping through its pages. "Would you like a cigarette?" he asked, grabbing one from the top of the dresser.

The decision was a hard one for me, because I had just left the States smoking weed, cigarettes, and drinking beer. Now I was being reintroduced to those things. While wrestling with my fleshly desires, I was almost shocked to hear myself say, "No, thank you."

"Come on. I'm ready to go," I said heading towards the front door. "I'm getting ready to go back to the villa."

"Why? Are you okay?" he asked with questioning eyes.

"Oh, I'm fine," I yawned. "I'm just a little tired that's all."

"Well..." he lingered for a moment, still unsure of my honesty that everything was fine, "let me walk back to the bus with you." He insisted.

"You don't have to, but it's fine if that's what you want to do." Upon my saying that, he grabbed his house key and led me out the door.

Once outside, he walked me to the bus stop, took out a piece of paper from his shirt pocket, and began writing on it. "Here's my number. Call me sometime," he said handing me the wrinkled paper.

"I will." I promised.

"Can I have yours?" he asked.

"I don't have it memorized, but I'll give it to you when I call." I smiled politely as the bus came to a halt in front of us.

"I enjoyed the short time we've had today. You'll hear from me soon," I said.

"I'll be looking forward to it."

"Maybe, I can take you out to eat one day," he said with a smile forming on his thin ashy lips.

"Goodbye," I exhaled relieved I hadn't given in to any sinful urges.

I mounted the bus and found a seat close to the front. After minutes of riding, a strange sensation of being watched crept over me. I turned around. A middle-aged Italian man peered at me with a mixture of distaste and brutal desire in his eyes. I quickly turned back around. I dared not take my eyes off the buildings that passed by. I was too frightened of what I would find in the eyes of other passengers.

Emotionally, I was drained. A fusion of feelings stirred within me. Some were a result of culture shock. Others were due to rejection because of my race, and others were because of the dramatic sculpting of my inward man. I wanted to get back to the warm villa, so I could process the many different emotional peaks I was currently undergoing.

After about thirty minutes of riding, I finally arrived to the bottom of the treacherous hill. When exiting the bus, the sun's ferocious heat baked at my flesh causing me to throw my arms up across my forehead in protest of its torture. Trust me; I didn't want to get any darker than I already were. Although disturbingly hot, the day was beautiful. As I journeyed on, the scent of fermented grapes intensified. I tried to focus on the rows of grapevines that lined both sides of the road as a distraction from the heat.

After reaching the villa, I leaned against the building's cool wall. The muscles in my legs convulsed into climatic cramps due to the accumulation of lactic acid. Sweat poured from every pore of my body. I took quick gulps of air, so that when entering the front door, I wouldn't appear too overworked. Often, I joked about losing weight; now, it seemed I didn't have much of a choice.

I finally mustered up enough energy to open the tall wooden doors. The cool air greeted me. I looked around, and when I didn't see anybody, I found the nearest table and lied on top of it. Its coolness soothed my parched skin. The starchy aroma of freshly cooked pasta teased my aching stomach, causing it to growl. *I can get used to the idea of someone cooking a good home cooked meal for me everyday,* I thought glancing at my watch. It was only three o'clock. I had approximately an hour and a half until dinner. That left me with plenty of time to lie down and contemplate. I got up from the table and stretched.

While slowly ascending the stairs, I suddenly became aware of the peace that trailed me. The creak of each time-weathered stair filled the silence. Once in my room, I threw my backpack underneath the bed, kicked off my shoes, and climbed underneath the sheets with my clothes still on. Immediately, my thoughts gravitated towards De Angelo. Tingles rippled over the surface of my skin as my heart skipped a beat. *Why didn't he stop me from leaving?* I questioned as tears sprang to my eyes. *Does that mean he never really loved me?* Hard as I tried, I couldn't erase the last night we shared together. I envisioned lying in his arms as he repeatedly kissed me softly on the forehead. "I love you so much, baby," he had whispered over and over in my ear. "I love you too," I whispered back looking up into his stormy eyes. The connection we shared at that moment moved me. I couldn't refuse the tears any longer. That night had been the first time I had expressed my love for him or for any guy for that matter.

I threw back the covers, walked over to the phone, and dialed DeAngelo's number. Just as I was about to hang up, he answered. Not long after, he told me he didn't love me anymore and to stop calling. I was shocked. Mixed emotions of hurt and rejection wrestled their way to the center of my throat. It was hard to fathom that my first love would abandon me when I needed him the most. It seemed that every active man in my life ended up abandoning or hurting me. His remarks only carved a bigger wound in my already damaged heart.

Being overtaken with grief, I sat on the corner of my bed and cried. To find solace, I sought for a pen and some paper. The feeling to write was urgent. The sorrow I was experiencing was too immense. I felt alone. I felt neglected. I felt unloved. There was no greater way to pour out my anguish than releasing it through my writing. It was my prayer, my supplication to God. I allowed my emotions to write for me. As tears fell, nearly blinding me, I wrote passionately:

> Of a surety, tears have become one of my consolations. I cry constantly. It's as if the only substance within me is the salty elements that form tears. Two fiery demons stand smirking behind my desolate eyes, causing tears to flow down my pain-ridden face. I try to constrain the enraged beasts but to no prevail. I don't know if there is much hope left for me. I don't know how close my time is to return to that final exposition within the earth; the conclusion called death. Neither do I know what my destiny holds. Oftentimes, I feel like a foe of the Almighty instead of a friend. I can't perceive the amount of pain that will be inflicted on me, but of a fact, I die daily. Like philosophical Socrates, "The only thing I know is that I know nothing." Why do the Holy Scriptures teach that it is not good for men to be alone when I am the loneliest of God's creatures? Living a life of loneliness is making my existence bitter. Hard as I try to smile at couples who snuggle up against one another, I can't ignore the great battle between the demons lurking behind my eyes. The constant struggle between the two grips me to the core of my existence—whatever that may be. I knew love once in a prior life, but now, I stumble upon a question: Was it really love or mere infatuation? It is as if I were not born of a woman at all but of despair. Every part of my being is encompassed with hopelessness including my eyes and smile (which isn't a smile at all but a hypocritical lie that tries to cover the truth of my reality; pain.) If I never again hear the melodic tunes of the ocean washing its great crest upon massive stones, please do not be sad. My life was miserable here. I am ready to ascend into that mount called Sky. Let the memory of me fade quickly because my life was worthless and filled with vanity and vexation of spirit. "For me to live is Christ, and for me to die is gain" (Philippians 1:20–21).

After writing, my frustrations slowly began disintegrating. I stuck my writings in the side of my backpack and lay back onto the cool bed. My face was ashen from the tears that had dried. My eyes throbbed in their sockets.

After hearing footsteps coming up the stairs, I rapidly threw the covers over my head as if asleep. The light came on followed by voices. Two of the young women started discussing some of their purchases they had bought at the market. Upon noticing me lying in the bed, one of the girls whispered softly, "Be quiet. Crystal's sleeping." Immediately, the light was cut off, and the sound of footsteps descended the stairs.

I peeked from under the covers to see if they were really gone. After seeing that they were, I threw the covers back and jotted to the bathroom where I splashed cold water on my face. If anyone noticed that my eyes were a little red, hopefully, they would suspect it were due to a bad case of allergies.

I glanced at my watch. I had fifteen minutes before dinner. I tiptoed back to the bedroom and lay once again upon the bed. I took a piece of paper that was lying on the floor and began to fan myself with it, trying to subdue the stinging from my reddened eyes.

Fifteen minutes went by rapidly. I could hear the faint sound of the dinner bell ringing downstairs, beckoning everyone to come and eat. I got up, returned to the bathroom, and glanced at my reflection in the mirror once more to make sure I was presentable. My eyes, no longer red, now contained a brownish tint to them. I figured no one would pay much attention anyway. I quickly turned and walked down the stairs.

Everyone was already sitting down to eat. I scanned the area quickly to find a seat by someone that didn't talk much. I spotted one by Billy and took it. "Good evening," he said as I sat down. "Good evening," I returned glancing down the table to observe what was being served for dinner. It looked delicious. There were two types of pastas, garlic bread, fish, and a variety of mouth-watering fruits. I gathered a little of each item and as usual waited for grace to be spoken over the food.

"I want to say something," said Mr. Philip as he stood up to gain everyone's attention. "Tomorrow morning, I'll be giving everyone schedules for their classes. Each of you will meet in the classroom at 6:30 a.m. sharp. Are there any questions?" He asked, glancing around the room. After giving everyone a chance to speak, he sat back down.

After hastily eating my food, I took my plate and utensils over to the window, so the maids could clean them. Once upstairs, I decided to prepare for bed before the rest of the crew came up. After showering and putting on my pajamas, I jumped in the bed and pulled the covers over my head. It wasn't long before exhaustion overpowered me and lured me to sleep.

Instructions

Early the following morning, the sound of faint chattering awakened me. I opened my eyes. Some of the girls were already taking turns going to the bathroom and getting dressed for the day's activities. I yawned a few times before realizing how well rested I felt. My body was equipped for conquest. Already having prepared myself the night before, I lingered a while longer in bed, toying with a lock of my braids. My mind drifted to Allah Baba's startling reaction to my singing the previous day.

At six o'clock, I got up, quickly fixed my bed, and threw my clothes on. Next, I went to the bathroom to finish getting groomed. Mr. Philip was walking through the front door just as I was coming down the stairs. I ran and grabbed the nearest empty seat.

"Is everyone here?" he asked, causing heads to turn to see if anyone was missing. There wasn't. He proceeded.

"I'm assuming everyone's here." After pausing a few minutes to do a last check, he said, "I'm going to call each of your names. When I do, I want you to come up and get your class schedules." He called each name one by one, and when my turn came, I arose to retrieve mines.

"Now the schedules are very similar," he continued. "The only difference is that half of you have volleyball for recreation, and the other half will have racquetball. After a few weeks, everyone that's taking volleyball will rotate over to racquetball and vice versa."

I examined my schedule. I had volleyball for the first rotation. *Good,* I thought. *This'll be fun.* I skimmed over the rest of my classes. I was scheduled to take Elementary Italian, Acts of the Apostles, International Politics, art, and volleyball. Mr. Philip continued to talk.

"We will not be having a lot of classes here at the villa due to the fact that we'll be doing a lot of traveling. Now, I'm going to give each of you a ticket known as a Eurail Pass. With this," he held the object high over his head so we could all see, "you can travel anywhere by train or boat in Europe." My ears immediately perked open. He continued. "It expires only a few days before the end of your stay here. Do not lose them. Keep them with your passports."

He then began to pass each of us a Eurail Pass with our names on them. I was so excited. *God is just awesome,* I thought. *Who would've ever imagined I would one day travel all over Europe.* I smiled at the thought of being able to see places I've only heard of in my history and art classes.

"The next thing I'm passing out is your syllabus. Your homework assignments for all of your classes are in it. Even when you are on your free travel, you will be responsible for turning each assignment in on time." After saying this, he began passing out a syllabus along with a calendar that contained scheduled activities we would be doing throughout the semester.

He continued. "Next week, we are going to travel to Rome as a group. While there, we'll be looking at the Coliseum and other well-known, archeological sites. I want each of you to keep a journal of everything while you are here in Europe. At the end of your stay in Italy, they'll be retrieved and graded." Mr. Philip paused and looked around as if making sure everyone was paying attention. Satisfied that we were, he resumed.

"Now, three days before we are to go to Rome, a mission trip will be available to those who would like to go. If anyone is interested in going to Geneva, Switzerland, to help some of our fellow laborers of the gospel pass out flyers about the new Church of Christ they're building there, raise your hands."

Without hesitating, my hand shot up along with some of the others. "Now let me explain the conditions there. Once you commit to partaking in this great experience, whether it rains or not, you will be passing out flyers from six o'clock a.m. until six o'clock p.m. I will not promise any of you a comfortable sleeping arrangement nor a lavish meal. Keep in mind this is a work for the Lord." He paused before going on as if allowing the information to sink in. "Anyone that is still interested in going on this mission trip, please sign your names on this paper."

He then sent a piece of paper around. When the paper reached me, I quickly signed it, seizing the wonderful opportunity of working for the kingdom of God.

When he had finished going over everything that he thought was important, he cleared his throat and said, "Clear off your desks. We're going to start your first class for the day—Italian. I'm going to pass out the books that you'll be using for this class. I expect you all to take good care of them because I'll be recovering them at the end of the semester." Soon we were all enraptured in trying to learn Italian.

A Fire Kindled

The trip to Switzerland had finally arrived. The night before leaving, excitement caused me to be restless. Despite the fact that I didn't always do the right things, the desire to do mission work never left me. I wanted to introduce God into people's lives. I wanted to generate a fire in them that would burn away any pain, any false illusions of what they thought salvation was all about and to acquaint them with my God of grace and mercy.

When we finally arrived to Switzerland, something began to stir within me. Whatever "it" was it moved like a snake leaving a trail of fire behind. As soon as I stepped off the train, a friendly young couple that would take us to our lodging for the night greeted us. Somehow, I knew this trip would be an experience that would forever be held close to my heart. I couldn't explain it, but deep down, I just knew.

After arriving at the couple's house where my companions and I would be staying, they formally introduced themselves and told of how they began their missionary work. Their passion for Christ left me totally amazed and in reverence of them. My ears were alert. I leaned in closer, so I could take in every word.

When their dynamic introduction had concluded, they gave each of us a stack of flyers that we were to pass out the following day. "You'll all split up into groups of two or three so that as much ground as possible is covered," the husband stated. Maps were also given to us so that we could find our way around the town.

"In the morning, everyone will be fed breakfast. Afterwards, each of you will be given a sack lunch to take with you."

For a brief moment, I zoned off. I couldn't quite figure out why I was so excited about passing out flyers for the newly established Church of Christ in the area. Suddenly, it dawned upon me. I knew what "it" was that moved in me earlier. It was the anointing of God. I felt it again, but this time it was more powerful, consuming me. Every cell in my body seemed to tingle. It was a spiritual fire that engulfed me in flames. At that moment, I knew that whatever my purpose of being created was, sharing the gospel was a part of it. I reached for a nearby pen and began to enscribe these words on the back of a flyer:

> The flame flickers within my heart. It ignites a burning within me that travels through the abyss of my soul. The flame of God lightens every dark substance within me. It liquefies all of

my hardness and makes me fragile under its heat. Surely, "the anointing destroys the yoke"(Isaiah 10:27). I can feel my nature transforming as my heart conducts the massive heat into a passion that is so great that it must burst forth and transmit its energy to all of its surroundings. When the flame is at its maximum radiance, it overflows and is seen through my speech, my actions, and my life. The flame is in the center of my existence, fueled by the Spirit, the very essence of my God.

When I refocused back on the married couple, the solidity of their ministry almost made me sick with envy. Instead of the woman's husband using his leadership to subdue her in her "rightful place," they were working together for God and having dominion over things instead of each other. This is exactly what I wanted. After seeing this, I knew that I would never be happy in settling for anything less than this.

De Angelo's face flashed across my mind. I wanted him so much to be saved. I loved him. He was the guy that my heart longed for. But in order to have a relationship that was based on ministry and not just sex, I had to face the truth that De Angelo currently didn't fit that description. The Scriptures say, "How can two join together accept they agree," (1 Corinthians 1:10) and "Be not unequally yoked with unbelievers," (2 Corinthians 6:14). I could no longer deny the fact that the only way I would have a relationship like the one I was witnessing was if I allowed God to put me and the man that he had ordained for me together. God didn't need my help. My job wasn't to go and find a husband, but to prepare myself to be a wife. When God saw that I was equipped to be a helpmate, an asset instead of a liability, then he would send a man who was whole and complete in him that would love me like Christ loves the church.

After informing us of our task for the next day, the woman and her husband gathered in the kitchen and started preparing dinner for us. As the smell of food began to taunt me, I realized just how famished I was. "Make yourselves comfortable," the man said from the doorway of the kitchen. The long train ride left me feeling weak. I trembled with exhaustion. I had been too excited about the mission trip to fall asleep on the train; but now, I just wanted to crawl on the couch and fall asleep. The hunger that taunted my stomach prevented me from doing so.

When the food was finished cooking, we all gathered around the table to say grace. After everyone was fed, we all took time showering, first us ladies and then the men. When I saw the couple drag out sleeping bags and a battered mattress on the floor, I tried to hide the disappointment on my face. I said a short prayer of forgiveness and quickly dismissed the ungrateful spirit that was trying to erupt. I should have been happy to sleep on the floor. I thought about the time when my family, and I lived in our van in Orlando, Florida. Back then, there weren't any option about where I slept. I had some nerves to have quickly forgotten where I had come from.

I took one of the sleeping bags and went to the farthest corner of the room. While lying there, the drowsiness began to kick in overdrive. The last things I could remember before sleep finally confiscated my conscience were my prayer to God that he would forgive me for being ungrateful, that he would change my heart, and that he would use me in ministering to his people.

In the wee hours of the morning, I awakened to the sound of down pouring rain. One by one, everyone around me begin to stir. After getting dressed, all of us gathered around the living room for a brief devotion. Afterwards, we put our sleeping materials away and proceeded with packing up all of the items that we'd need to take for the day.

The remainder of the day, with joy and the feeling of accomplishment, I passed out flyers door to door. Many of the French speaking inhabitants were extremely pleasant as they humbly took them and offered refreshments in exchange. While dripping with rain, I habitually smiled, acted like I knew what they were saying, and walked off.

At the close of the day, everyone met at the designated

pickup location to be taken back to our guest's residence. After giving our reports of how much ground we covered and our experiences with the townspeople, we packed our things and were taken to the train station where we met up with Mr. Philip and the other students. We were now on our way to Rome.

Help! I've Been Robbed!

From the moment I stepped foot on European ground, I contemplated on what I would bring back to the States for my family, friends, and of course, De Angelo. On this particular trip, I decided to take five hundred US dollars, which had been exchanged for Italian Liras to do some early Christmas shopping.

When we arrived to Rome, everyone took their belongings and exited the train. After a few minutes of walking, Mr. Philip led us downstairs to a worn and overcrowded subway station. The sub was standing room only. It was so jammed that people were literally crammed against one another—butt cheek to butt cheek. I was already raging with PMS, so the last thing that I wanted was someone all up in my face.

Questioning eyes glared at me as I found a snug place against my professor's thigh and directly in front of a gypsy lady who held a baby in a pouch that was nestled against her bosom. Although Mr. Philip had warned us of frequent thefts that had occurred on Italian trains, I didn't believe it could happen to me. So with my proud, American self, I held my purse in front of me.

Just as it dawned on me that maybe I needed to be a little wiser, I looked down at my purse and noticed that its flap was unlatched. Before I stuck my hands in it to examine my belongings, I knew that I had been robbed. My heart felt like it had been pushed to the back of my chest, daring me to take another breath, so it could shatter into a thousand fragments. Upon my discovery, I tried to gain control over the situation by forcing my will power to restrain me from grabbing anyone by his or her throat and demanding my money back. I was like a ravenous bull ready to charge the first person that smiled knowingly in my direction.

I took a deep breath and looked inside my purse. As I had suspected, all $500 was gone. Suddenly, a commotion erupted from my side. "There's a hand in your purse!" An English speaking voice yelled out. Immediately, I glanced in the direction the voice came from. Gracie, one of my classmates, swung at Mrs. Young's purse.

"There's a hand trying to get in your purse!" She yelled again, reddened with anger. I looked towards her purse and noticed a hand disappearing into the crowd.

"My money has been stolen," I whispered towards Mr. Philip, but others close by overheard.

With quivering lips, I fought back the tears. "Everyone, get closer to one another," he declared. "Crystal's money has just been stolen."

When he said those words, I swatted at a tear that had slipped from the corner of my eye. I became aware of how severe my situation was. I was now broke. In only a few minutes, the remainder of my money was gone.

Our stopping point had finally come. I was reluctant to get off the train because I knew that my money was still on there. How was I supposed to survive now? Before the train left for its next destination, I finally decided to get off.

When we gathered in a group to discuss what had just happened, Mr. Philip discovered that his Italian Bible, which he had snugly tucked away in his sock, was gone. My guess was that someone thought it was his wallet. I didn't want to feel like a charity case, so I refused any money from anyone that offered, including Mr. Philip. I gave a Christian-like response. "God will provide. Maybe whoever stole it needed it more than I did?" Everyone looked at me in amazement at how well I was taking my dilemma. It was all a lie. I wanted to seek revenge. I was hurting. I wanted to scream from the top of my lungs. Better yet, I wanted to cuss, fight, and have a fit. Instead, I continued to refrain myself from doing anything stupid. Deep down, I knew that God was going to supply all of my needs.

We ventured on to the well-known Coliseum. While there, some of my classmates purchased post cards and other items that were being sold nearby. Some of them resumed asking me if I wanted to borrow some of their money. And because I was used to being independent and taking care of myself, I declined their acts of love once more. Pride refused to allow me to be looked down upon. My misconceptions of their thoughts towards me caused me to sink into a deep depression.

After hours of feeling envious towards everyone around me and feeling angry at myself for taking all of my money with me, I finally surrendered to the fact that maybe God was trying to teach me a valuable lesson. Perhaps, he was allowing me to be reduced to nothing so that I could learn how to depend on him instead of on people and money.

The robbery would lead me on an expedition of faith in which I trusted God daily for my needs. For the duration of the trip in Europe, I was led to travel without taking anything with me—no food, water, or clothing—only my Bible and my reliance on Jesus. And through this act of faith, God totally blew my legalistic mind. He showed me that, through faith, he could do anything according to the power that operated and flowed through me. He becomes limited only when we limit him through our faith.

Walking by Faith

After leaving Rome, our group took a two-day boat cruise to Athens, Greece. It reminded me of the Titanic. When I stepped onto the ship, royalty surrounded me. As I ascended the carpeted steps onto the first floor, I felt like a princess. Huge chandeliers accented the ceilings and gave the room a crystallized splendor. I could just imagine how Esther felt as she stood in the palace of King Ahasuerus. I could picture her eyes darting about her taking in all of the finery that she could only dream about. I didn't do anything to deserve all of these blessings from God. I knew that his grace had brought me this far. I trusted that it would be his grace that would take me even further.

Even as a child, underneath my dirty rags, and my worn shoes, I felt like a queen. During my early childhood years when I started having dreams and visions of where God would one day take me, I saw myself through the eyes of God. I was whole. I no longer felt broken, rejected, and ugly, but in these visions, my head was held high because I knew I was the righteousness of God. Royal blood pumped in my veins. I was a "chosen generation, a royal priesthood" (1 Peter 2:9).

For the remainder of the luxurious boat ride, I basked in the few hours of splendor, dismissing the fact that it had to end. Sooner or later, I had to face reality. I was broke.

As soon as I stepped off of the boat when arriving to Greece, a manager from a pizza parlor walked up to me and said, "Are you hungry?" Of course I looked at him puzzled but eventually managed to utter, "Yes." His next words puzzled me even more than the first.

"Come on. You can eat free." Members of my group could hardly believe their ears. They looked at Mr. Philip as if he had planned it, but he shrugged unexplainably.

As everyone followed behind the man into the restaurant, he suddenly spun around. "Everyone can't eat free, just her," he said pointing at me.

"Well, if they can't eat, then neither shall I," I retorted as I backed out the door.

Before I could fully digest what I had just witnessed, someone in my group spotted Anthony Hopkins. He was so handsome. To be honest, at the time, I didn't even know who he was, but because someone said he was famous, I jumped in the photograph just as my classmates posed to snap a picture with him. Since that day, he has become one of my most favorite actors.

Strangely, during my travel in Greece, people literally walked up to me on the street and handed me free merchandise such as genuine leather boots, slippers, belts, and other things. I knew then, that a person's money didn't determine whether or not they were blessed, God did. I didn't have a dime in my pockets, but I had the favor of God on my life; and he was blessing me abundantly.

Our next trip was to Amsterdam. As soon as my classmates and I stepped from the train we were greeted by sexual images displayed on billboards for all eyes to see. I was baffled. The entire atmosphere reeked of sexual lewdness. I entered a nearby store to purchase post cards. Once inside, graphic sexual pictures surrounded us. After my peers made their purchases, a young and cheerful cashier handed each of us a single colorful condom. "Enjoy yourselves," she said with a smile, hinting at the sexual exploitation she assumed we would partake in.

Once outside, to our surprise even the billboards alongside the streets had nudity displayed on them. *Do they even care if children see this?* I wondered. *It seems like this whole country represents sex. Its motto should be: "Have sex; it does the body good."* As I shuttered at how much Amsterdam reminded me of the biblical Sodom and Gomorrah, I took a deep breath and ventured on to the Ann Frank Museum with everyone else.

After arriving, since I didn't have any money to enter, I stayed outside and waited until the others had finished touring the museum. At this point, it didn't matter much. I was about sick of going to museums anyway. I had seen almost every well-known sculpture, architecture, and museum all across Europe anyway.

After leaving the Ann Frank Museum everyone decided on going to yet another museum. Because it had started drizzling and because I didn't want to wait outside like a wet puppy, I decided to meet them back at the train station. It wasn't long after I started walking that I realized I was lost.

For hours, I tried hard to retrace my steps back to the train station, but as hard as I tried, I couldn't remember the route. Nightfall seemed to have come quickly, and to my dismay, I ended up at the infamous Red Light District. Rumors of open-prostitution were proven to be true. Nude women were standing in windows and were being rented by sex-starved customers. Nearby, guys that could have easily been gang members were huddled over a fire as they puffed on cigars. I turned my jacket upwards, so they couldn't tell if I was a female and walked by them quickly. The air was pungent with the smell of marijuana.

Nightfall encircled me like a cave. I wanted to cry but was too frightened of my surroundings. Nearby, a bus expelled passengers. They rushed off the bus and into the night. *Please God, I wish there were someone around here that speaks English well enough to direct me back to the train station,* I prayed. Suddenly, a woman that had just gotten off the bus walked past me. Something stirred inside me. Slowly, I turned around in the woman's direction. She turned around as well and looked at me. As if in a trance, we walked towards one another looking directly into each other's eyes.

"Are you lost?" she asked.

"Yes," I sighed, breathing a breath of relief that she spoke English. *Thank you, God.* I groaned inwardly.

"Where are you trying to go?" She questioned.

"To the train station," I replied. I rapidly explained to her my situation of how I had gotten lost.

"For some reason, when I passed by you, I knew I had to stop," she explained. "I've had this desire to know God more, and I felt like you could help me."

"I'll tell you everything you want to know," I said. "I have almost four hours left before it's time to go back to the train station."

"Good," she interrupted. "You can come back to my place, get a hot meal, and freshen up. Afterwards, you can tell me about God. When my boyfriend gets off of work, we will then drive you to the train station. Follow me."

I dispensed all fear as I followed behind her into the subway. As cold, hungry, and lost as I was, I had little choice but to trust her. During the ride to her house, she notified me that she was a schoolteacher who, in addition to learning more about God, desired to learn how to sing. I sat quietly, marveling in the fact that God was continuously setting me up in the right place at the right time to tell people about salvation and in return, he blessed me also.

After arriving at her apartment, I freshened up in the bathroom then ate a delicious, hot meal that she had prepared. Her generosity had me on the verge of tears. A few times, I swiped at the salty substance that fought to break free, trying not to let her see. In the meantime, I spoke to her of how God loved us and gave us Jesus to take away our sins through the death and resurrection of his body. I explained the importance of reading and learning the bible. She sat listening attentively to every word. Before leaving, she tried to sing for me. Afterwards, I realized immediately that she really could use singing lessons. I spent a few minutes giving her some pointers such as singing from her diaphragm.

When her boyfriend made it home from work, she introduced us to one another and explained to him why I needed a ride to the train station. The three of us then loaded into his Bronco and rode into the night.

Once I made it to the train station, within seconds, I spotted my group. I waved goodbye to the nice couple, told them I would never forget them, and walked towards my peers who greeted me with sighs of relief that I was okay.

Another lesson on faith came when I traveled to Germany. It was a cold night in November. Sooty snow littered the streets in Berlin. I trampled over its white mass towards the tattered Berlin Wall. Members of my group along with myself took turns writing our names on the wall. Next, we tore its deteriorating fragments and placed them in zip lock bags as a memorial. Some of my classmates decided to explore some of the town.

But since only three hours remained before we were to travel back to our villa in Italy, I told them I would stick around at the train station.

I found a seat close to the main entrance and began observing everyone as they came in. Three days had passed since I had last eaten anything. The hunger mixed with the cold left me feeling weak. Although physically my strength was growing weary, my spirit was growing like an overstuffed giant. As minutes turned into hours, my eyelids began to get heavy. Surrounded by strangers, I didn't trust myself to fall asleep. I wrestled to wait on the train ride back to the villa before resting. To stay awake, I decided to explore the train station. It was huge. I stepped onto the escalator and descended down to the bottom floor. Out the corner of my eyes, I could see guys throwing admiring looks in my direction.

Once downstairs, the smell of sweet pastries teased me to a stupor. I sat down again, long enough to regain my composure, and then window shopped in many of the little shopping stores. I glanced at the clock. Two hours had already gone by. As I turned to ascend back to the top floor to wait for Mr. Philip and the others, an old man reached out his hand and touched my arm.

"Hello, there," he said. His eyes beamed. I could tell that he wanted to engage me in conversation.

"Hi," I replied as I continued to walk on. *He might as well forget trying to hit on me with his old self. He looks like a homeless bum*, I thought. He was clothed in layers of dirty and worn clothing. The only part of his body that I could make out was his face—which was nothing much to look at. Suddenly, these words dropped into my spirit, "I have no respect of persons."

Immediately, as if another force had taken over, I did a U-turn, and walked over to where the old man stood still gazing at me.

"Where are you from," he wanted to know.

"The United States," I replied.

And before he could question me about how I ended up in Europe, I gave him a brief run-down of the story.

"How about we take us a seat over there," the man said with discerning eyes as he pointed to a nearby pastry shop. "Let me buy you something to eat, and then we can talk."

"Thanks for the offer, but in my country, people don't just take things from someone they don't know," I said pridefully.

"Well, you're not in your country," he stated sarcastically.

I decided to take him up on his offer. I realized that God had placed this man in my path so that he could be a blessing to me. *Maybe, he's an angel,* I thought. *The Scriptures do say, "Be careful to entertain strangers for you entertain angels by unawares."* He and I walked over to the pastry shop where I ordered a mouth-watering cinnamon roll with raspberry filling in the middle and a refreshing soda to wash it down with.

"May God bless you," I told the man, staring at him with compassion-filled eyes.

"I'm Muslim," he chuckled. "But I know what you mean."

"Thank you anyway. I pray that my God will bless you," I said.

Within minutes, we began discussing the difference between Christianity and the Islamic religion. I was astonished when he enlightened me on the fact that Muslims believed in giving a tenth of everything they own—not just money, like most Christians do.

"It is a part of our culture to give of ourselves. For that, we are blessed," he said quite humbly.

"I'm so grateful that you've shared some of your blessings with me," I said, chuckling. "I should be leaving now. Those whom accompanied me from the States will be looking for me. In a few minutes, we'll be catching a train back to Italy. I don't want to delay them."

"Wait one minute," he said standing up abruptly. "Stay right here. I have to run to my apartment to get something. It is right around the corner, so it won't take long." I didn't understand what he was talking about, but I shook my head as if agreeing to wait on him.

As soon as he turned the corner, I gulped down the remainder of my drink, licked the raspberry cream that had gotten on my fingers, and adjusted my clothing to leave. When I made it to the first floor, I spotted a few members from my group standing outside of McDonalds. Although I had eaten the pastry, my stomach still growled for more food.

When I approached the McDonald's, Mr. Philip walked up to me and placed a hand on my shoulder.

"Crystal, we've missed you," he said.

"Yeah, well, I've been exploring the train station. I should be a pro at that by now," I said.

I didn't feel like trying to explain to him that pride was the reason I wouldn't borrow money to go with him or the others, so I just smiled and acted like I didn't pick up on his sarcastic implication.

After hearing the announcement that our train had arrived, everyone gathered their belongings together. I waited patiently by until we were instructed to form a line. A hand tapped me on the shoulders, startling me. I turned around. It was the old man.

"Here you are," he said. "I thought I'd lost you."

Shocked to see him, I thought of something to say. "I'm sorry for leaving, but I didn't want to miss my train," I quickly explained.

"That's okay. Are you still hungry?" Without waiting for my reply, he walked over to the McDonald's counter and purchased a triple cheeseburger value meal and handed it to me.

"You're so sweet." I gleamed. "God will pour his blessings upon you for being so nice to me."

As I turned to follow my group towards the train, he thrust a handful of money into my hands. Without even looking at how much it was I thrust it back into his.

"I can't accept this. You have already done so much for me."

"But I want to give you this," he said placing it into my coat pocket. "Never forget me." He then handed me two pictures of himself.

"Thanks. I'll never forget you as long as I live." I didn't even try to conceal the tears that now flowed from my eyes. I ran to the train as my last classmate was boarding.

Having been notified by Mr. Philip a few weeks earlier that we would need $94.00 to purchase a plane ticket from Paris, France to Heathrow, England in order to catch our flight back to the United States, I had been sickened with worry. I didn't know what to do, but I trusted that God would provide. I reached inside my pocket, pulled out the money that the man had given me, and counted it. God was just too good. I had enough money now to purchase a ticket as well as buy food for a few more trips. I leaned back into the chair and meditated on God's goodness until I drifted off into a sweet sleep.

Throughout the remainder of my travel in Europe, God revealed many things to me. He taught me valuable lessons concerning faith and trust in him at all times. When I didn't see a way, he provided a way "in the wilderness." When I didn't have any money, his favor followed me and provided me with the best. He was indeed Jehovah Jireh, the God that provides!

The time for my departure was rapidly dissipating. I had to endure two more days of uncertainty before flying back to the United States. And by now, I was missing the U.S. terribly! Our semester had ended at the villa, and everyone was free to travel. A few of us decided to go on to Paris, France before going home.

After arriving in Paris, once again, the others wanted to visit important museums and other costly places, so as usual, I decided to stay at the train station until we met up again later that evening. This time, they never came back, or if they did, I missed them. Hours went by. I got something to eat and continued waiting. Before I knew it, dusk was starting to fall. I had no place to go, and I was freezing. It was so cold that my butt felt like it was freezing to the seat. I had a few dollars left, so I walked over to the customer's service desk to ask about securing my luggage. It took every penny I had left to rent a twenty-four-hour locker.

Night was finally upon me, and people continued to walk by as if I didn't exist. Around midnight, the train station was starting to shut down and by now, customer service had left, so there was no one around to interpret for me. I walked up to an on-duty patrolman and begged him to let me stay in the station for the night. After minutes of using my hands to create gestures to make him understand me, he finally got the gist of what I was saying and granted my request.

A heavyset man and his family, a couple of security personnel, and I were the only ones left in the building. It was so quiet in the train station that I could hear the heavyset man breathing heavily across the room. I tucked my feet underneath me and tried to get comfortable. Nothing worked. I was too cold to sleep. All night, I tossed, turned, and prayed that I would soon arrive back home to the comfort of my bed.

Before the sun rose, I could hear the train station coming to life again. I stood up to stretch my legs. After minutes of doing this, I decided to walk around, so my blood would thaw. Seemingly from out of nowhere, a young and handsome Frenchman walked over to where I stood. I could tell by the bulge of his front pants what was on his mind.

"Hi there, can I teach you how to French kiss?" he said in a rich French accent which, sent the smell of mints up my nostrils.

I burst out laughing. This had to be some sort of joke. But by the expression on the young man's face, I knew that it wasn't. He stepped closer to me. No one seemed to notice. Before I knew it, the man was rubbing himself up against my thigh and trying to stick his tongue down my throat. I was enraged. Without trying to put up a fight, I walked away, leaving the man lingering behind to entertain himself.

For the remainder of the day, I explored the enormous station. It was more like a mall. Of course, I ended up getting lost.

It was huge. Just as discouragement was starting to set in at being lost, I glanced up, and to my surprise, I spotted Bishop T.D. Jakes, Kirk Franklin, and his wife—all giants of the faith. They looked in my direction. I waved, and they waved back. I could hardly believe my eyes. I wanted to run over to where they stood so badly, but I looked down at my attire and noticed how scummy I appeared. I decided against it. I wanted to follow after them and demand a prophetic word from the Lord. Was I going to be okay? What was the end result of all the trials and tests that I was encountering? I wanted to hear anything that God had to say even if it was words of rebuke. But of course, I stood in the same spot—warring with the decision to move and sinking deeper into despair as they moved farther away from my vision.

In the distance, an elderly man observed my sadness. He walked over to where I stood and began talking to me in French. I had no clue what he was saying. "I don't understand you," I said. He realized that I spoke English, so he quickly switched to the little English he knew. He wanted to know if I would have coffee with him in a little coffee shop next door. The incident in Germany taught me how to dismiss my pride and to trust God. I accepted.

Once there, the guy and I communicated with one another by switching from Italian to English and then to the little French I did know. I would have tried Spanish, but he didn't know any. Whenever we didn't know a word in one language, we would translate it in another language. It actually worked. Whenever we got totally lost with comprehending one another, we drew pictures on a napkin. It was hilarious. I found out that he was from Africa. Again, when I didn't see a way, God provided a "ram in the bush." This man ended up feeding me, buying me things, and treating me with the utmost respect. By that evening, I was teaching him, along with some of his friends, how to read English from the Bible.

That night, I made it back to the train station to get my luggage out of the locker, so I could catch a shuttle to the airport. To my dismay, I had lost my retrieval ticket. The people behind the desk refused to let me get into the locker without one. I had approximately two hours before my plane was to leave for Heathrow, England. I hung my head down and found a seat. I had to think. I couldn't catch the shuttle without my luggage; it contained my plane ticket back to the States. I felt cursed. Every time God had blessed me, it seemed an attack of the enemy followed.

As I sat there for over an hour, a handsome soldier walked over to me and sat down. "You are too attractive to be looking so sad. Try smiling," he said turning to look at me. He had the smooth rich color of a golden brown paper bag.

"I don't have much to smile about," I stammered dismissing the desire to be flirtatious. "I can't get my luggage out of storage because I lost my ticket and my plane is getting ready to leave in less than an hour," I whined.

"Find out how much it'll cost to get it out, and I'll pay," he said startling me. A huge smile suddenly crept on my face.

"You'd do that for me," I exclaimed.

"Why not? You're a beautiful young lady."

After saying that, we both went to retrieve my luggage. I turned around and gave the man a gigantic hug.

"I come to the United States a lot," he said, pushing back from me.

"I would love to see you again. Maybe, we could make some arrangements to do so?"

"I'd like that very much," I said putting on my "royal" smile. He took a piece of paper out of his bag and wrote a phone number on it.

"Call me," he said extending it to me. I took the paper, got my luggage, headed towards the shuttle, and boarded. Through the window, I waved at him until he disappeared from view.

As soon as I made it to the airport, I could hear the last boarding call for my plane. I ran as fast as I could to the gate where my plane was to leave. When I arrived, I was disappointed when a stewardess revealed to me that the plane had already taken off. I could hardly believe it. I wanted to scream from the top of my lungs, *Okay. God, I get the point. I understand that you want to break me down, so that I can learn to trust you. Honestly, I do, but now this is a little too much!* I whirled around, walked up to the ticket desk, and asked the agent when the next flight to Heathrow would be leaving. By now, I was getting used to disappointing news, so it wasn't a huge surprise when she said, "Tomorrow morning." Without uttering another word, I turned around, found myself a seat and prepared myself to spend the night.

I awakened the next morning from having spent the night at the airport. I was cold, hungry, and frustrated. Every muscle in my body ached from having remained in the same position during the majority of the night. Outside, darkness continued to array the sky as tiny diamond-like stars decorated its mass. I glanced down at my watch. It was now five forty-five a.m. I had almost three hours before my plane was due. To soothe my aching muscles, I stood up and stretched.

While stretching, the tension in my body began to diminish. An old lady slept a few seats away. The way she carried on all throughout the night, I didn't blame her for yet being tired. Throughout the night, she had screamed and said things to people as they walked past her. They all walked by, shook their heads, and mumbled underneath their foreign breaths. I didn't understand anything she said, but my assumption was that she was drunk or something.

I took my suitcase to the bathroom to freshen up. I glanced in the mirror. I was horrified at what I saw. I looked horrible. Reaching into the side pocket of my suitcase, I pulled out my toothpaste and toothbrush. I quickly brushed my teeth and replaced them back into their compartments. The rest of my clothes were dirty, so I knew that I had to make out with what I had on until I got back home to the States. I ran my fingers through my braids to untangle them and then applied gel to the edges of my hair to rid some of its kinkiness. After washing my face, and applying some make-up, one could never tell that I had just slept in the airport. *I look pretty, good as a bum*, I thought as I smiled at my quick "extreme makeover."

When I arrived at the gate where my plane was to arrive, a few people were already waiting in line. I stood behind the last person and sat my luggage down beside me. While waiting for the attendant to take our tickets, I occupied myself by studying everyone around me. Since being robbed, people's clothing, their dialect, and their behaviors became my only means of entertainment.

When the plane finally arrived, I handed the agent my ticket. Once on board, I found a seat next to a window and sat down. I exhaled. The flight would only last an hour and forty-five minutes before arriving in Heathrow. Acknowledging my salvation helped relax me, I knew that I was saved. God had brought me this far for a reason. His presence was accompanying me on the trip. I was at peace with myself, and in that peace, I begin to drift into a deep sleep.

I awakened to a loud booming voice over the intercom: "We are preparing for landing. Please buckle your seatbelts. Make sure your luggage is secured under your seats or in the overhead compartments. Nothing should be blocking the aisle."

I jolted upright. I had slept the whole trip. *One more plane ride and I'll be back in America!* The soul part of me screamed. I felt like jumping up and down. It wasn't that I didn't like Europe—because I loved it—I was just emotionally drained. God had taught me so much on the trip. I needed time to digest everything. I was ready to get back to familiar territory where people spoke the same language as I did.

When the plane stopped, I looked at my watch. I had two hours before my next plane was to leave. I rushed inside the airport to check my luggage in. To my surprise, some of my classmates were there. We spotted each other approximately at the same time. I was so happy to see them that I wanted to give each of them a hug and a kiss. The expression on their faces made me realize that the thought was not such a good idea.

"We were so worried about you Crystal," one of the girls stated with a hint of disapproval in her voice. "We didn't know what to do about your leaving the group to travel by yourself, so we called the instructor back at the villa."

"I told everyone that I was going to meet them back at the train station." I interrupted as my happiness in seeing them began to fade.

"I think Mr. Philip called your mother." she retorted back at me.

With hearing that news, adrenaline began to surge through my body. Fear and dread overtook me at once. My mom was expecting me to make it back to the states at a certain time. I knew how she could get whenever she panicked. If she got the phone call from my instructor, she would worry about me until she found out where I was.

"I got to go," I told them abruptly. "I have to catch my plane."

"Are you all leaving now?" I asked as my heart continued to pound in my chest.

"No," one of the guys stated, "our plane doesn't leave until later on this evening. We're trying to meet up with some of the others from our group, so we can tour London together. Good luck. We hope you make it back home safely," a few of them said simultaneously as I hugged each one goodbye.

To my alarm, when I arrived at the front desk to check in my luggage, the lady at the counter shook her head. "I'm sorry, but you're at the wrong airport. The airport that your ticket has is located about an hour and a half away from here." I could hardly believe what she was saying. I refused to hear what she was saying. I thrust the ticket in her direction once more as she repeated the previous statement, only slower this time.

Suddenly the words the instructor had mentioned earlier at the villa came back to me: "Once in Heathrow, you'll have to catch a bus to the London airport. It runs about every twenty minutes." I had completely forgotten about that. I didn't even bother to ask her how much it would cost to catch the bus. I was broke again. I didn't even have enough money to buy anything to eat. Deep down, I knew that God would make a way. He hadn't failed me yet. All of my classmates had already left. I didn't know what to do, so I decided to walk outside, hoping that my angel would appear to rescue me.

When exiting the building, I noticed an Arabic man eyeing me. Soon he headed towards my direction.

After approaching, he looked down at my luggage and asked, "Do you need a ride?" His voice was diluted with a strong British accent.

"Yes, I do!" I exclaimed. He grabbed my luggage.

"Follow me. I have a taxi over here," He pointed in the direction of a nice turquoise minivan with a taxi sign displayed on top and started walking towards it.

"I don't have any money," I said continuing to stand still. "Please, you have to understand…" I rushed to catch up with him so I could explain my situation.

He persisted in pulling my luggage across the street leading me to his vehicle. "I have to get to the London airport, or I'll miss my plane. I don't know what to do," I continued near tears.

"Come on," the man said as he lifted my luggage into the vehicle. I was amazed at how understanding he was. *God is so good*, I thought as I leaned back into the thick cushioned chair and closed my eyes to intake a deep gulf of air.

As the man began to pull out into the flow of traffic, he spoke. "That will be twenty pounds." My eyes flew open. I bolted upright. "Excuse me?" I questioned calmly with an edge to my voice hoping I misunderstood his words. He repeated himself once more. "I told you I don't have any money." I whined realizing he had misunderstood my plea earlier.

By now, we were on the main highway and in the flow of traffic. The man glared at me with disgust in his eyes. He stopped on brakes rapidly and did a U-turn in the middle of the street. "This cannot be happening to me," I uttered. I became filled with rage. I wanted to hold the man hostage and take off in his van. It's amazing how a difficult situation can bring out the worst in a person.

I was starting to guess I had a mission here in Europe that God wanted me to fulfill. That was the only rational explanation I could come up with for all the turmoil I was experiencing. At that moment, I was willing to give up everything for God. I had already lost De Angelo. A sharp pang went through my heart upon realizing I possibly would never see him again.

As the taxi cab driver pulled over on the side of the road, I grabbed my bags out of the back, threw them on the ground, and I got out without saying a word as his tires screeched away. Here I was, in heels, carrying a huge raggedly suitcase in my hands and a dirty backpack on my back stranded on the interstate. While walking, I increased my pace trying to make it back to the airport as soon as possible, hoping I didn't freeze to death first.

My feet ached when I finally made it. No matter how hard I tried to hold back the tears, they propelled on. I looked down at my watch. There was no way I would make it in time to catch my plane. I was miserable. I wiped my hands across my face and walked over to a chair to sit down. As I sat there, I bowed my head and prayed. *Lord, it's hard to say this, but despite what I'm feeling, let your will be done.* I couldn't say too much more. Discouragement gnawed at me. Defeat wasn't far behind. I wasn't just broken, but I felt as if God was crushing me.

In the midst of my tears, I began reflecting on God's provision for me while in Germany, Paris, and Amsterdam when I didn't see a way. Although I felt like my back was up against the wall in many different circumstances, God always had at least one person that he used to provide me with the things I needed. This time wouldn't be any different. Without realizing it, I had just ascended up another notch on the ladder of faith.

Suddenly a hand was placed on my shoulders. This caused me to turn around abruptly. I looked up, staring through the tears that now burned at my eyes. There stood a caramel-skinned lady. Her facial features were strong and delicate. "Are you okay?" she asked looking at me with concern in her eyes. "No," I explained as I poured out my story to her in between sobs. Without any hesitation, she said, "Let me go to the ATM machine, and I'll give you some money." I didn't want to get too excited because if I were let down one more time, I probably would've fell out in the floor and ranted like a spoiled child. There was no doubt in my mind that security would have had to escort me out.

Praise the Lord, the woman returned. "The bus is out there now," she said. "I pray that you'll have a safe trip back to the States."

"Thank you so much. God shall bless you," I said looking directly into her eyes and then hugging her. Next, she handed me some money, and I boarded the bus.

"I knew you would do it, Lord," I exhaled once comfortably positioned in my seat.

On the journey back to the United States, I flew from Paris to London, from London to New York, from New York to Atlanta, and from Atlanta to Memphis. By the time I reached Memphis, I didn't want to step foot on another plane.

CHAPTER FIVE

The Crossroads

> "Thus saith the Lord, Stand ye in the ways, and see, and ask for the old paths, where is the good way, and walk therin, and ye shall find rest for your souls. But they said, We will not walk therein."
>
> Jeremiah 6:16

Reunited

When the plane finally landed, I let out a breath of thankfulness. I had finally arrived on American soil. As soon as I descended the escalators in the Memphis Airport, I immediately spotted my mother. Years of worry and disappointment outlined every crease of her face. Upon seeing me her disposition transformed into one of glee, chasing away all visibility of a lifetime of hardships.

As she neared me, she started talking at once. "I didn't know what to think when you didn't arrive on your designated flight.

I called your instructor back in Italy, and he told me that some of your classmates called to notify him that you had left your group and decided to go your own separate way."

"Now, does that make sense?" I asked, stopping her parade of railings. "I was in a strange country. I didn't know anybody, and I didn't have any money. Now, why in the world would I want to travel by myself?" My mother chuckled as the revelation of truth suddenly struck her.

I walked over to the checkout area, retrieved my other belongings, and followed my mother into the freezing night. "Everyone knew I had been robbed and didn't have any money," I continued trying to prove my innocence. I watched the fog twirl before me for a few seconds before continuing.

"So I wouldn't have to stand outside in the cold when they went to museums, I simply told them I would meet them back at the train station. Somehow we missed each other, and I ended up by myself." My mother already knew how stubborn I was, so it really didn't surprise her how I had reacted.

Finally arriving at her white minivan, I stood silently as she unlocked the doors. After loading everything, I got inside and strapped on my seatbelt. It felt good being back in the United States. I had learned so much while living overseas. I could not comprehend exactly what had happened to me, but I knew that God had done some major internal reconstructive surgery. Although a sense of newness surfaced, just knowing that I was back on familiar territory, strangely disturbed me. Once more, I would be faced with the same demons of lust and riotous living. Satan would try to use the same baits to lure me again.

I leaned back in the cushioned seat and rested my head against the cool window. Mother was still talking, but my mind had drifted to sweet thoughts of De Angelo. I envisioned him before me with his six feet two, toned frame wrapped in smooth caramel skin. I peered out the corner of my eyes hoping my mother didn't notice the smile that had crept on my face. Thankfully, she was to busy concentrating on the road. Sinking deeper into my seat, love nestled me in her wings and flew me to a land of exotic thoughts of De Angelo. I completely suppressed the fact that he had dumped me and left me wounded and bitter.

It was past midnight when we finally drove into our driveway. Cold and exhausted, I grabbed my luggage out of the back and followed my mother up the creaky, termite-eaten steps that led into the house. Everything looked just as I had recalled, only cleaner. The scent of laundry detergent filled the air giving the room an aroma of freshness.

I walked into my bedroom and fell backward onto the bed. The tidiness and freshness of the room enveloped me with peace. Deciding against unpacking, I quickly changed into my pajamas and climbed into bed. Not long after, sleep came.

The next morning a light tapping outside my bedroom door awakened me. I peered through crust-filled eyes as it opened. My mother's head suddenly materialized. "Tamar's on the phone," she said. Slightly hesitating, I pulled the pink and white, coral-knitted cover back and stretched. After yawning several times, I finally made my way to the phone.

Since I hadn't spoken to her while in Europe, Tamar didn't know that I was confessing to be saved again. I wondered if my speech would give me away.

"Hey, girl!" I said with exaggerated excitement.

"Hey!" Tamar responded. "I see you finally made it back home."

"Girl, I was ready to come back. My chocolate self was almost stranded over there." After chuckling, she resumed. "Girl, I can't wait until you give me the full story." I yawned again. "Yeah, well, I'm too tired to go into it right now. I need a lot of energy, so you can get the full effect."

There was a brief pause on both ends. Tamar's voice penetrated the silence. "So, what are your plans for your birthday tomorrow?"

Surprised she hadn't forgotten my birthday; I answered. "I don't know."

"How about we hook up with Sweets and make us some money?" she asked.

Before I could catch myself, I blurted out, "Sure." I could hardly believe what I had I just said.

"So that's the plan," she said rather quickly. After we had talked a few more minutes, we finally hung up.

I walked back to my bedroom as if in slow motion. I couldn't understand where all the teachings that God had just taught me overseas went. I didn't understand why I replied to Tamar as if I didn't just have a special encounter with God.

I retreated back into my bedroom and started unpacking my luggage. I pulled out a Kill Army CD I had purchased for De Angelo. It gave me a good excuse to go by his house. To show off my well-defined muscles I had acquired, I chose a short black miniskirt, a silver low-cut spaghetti-strap top, and a pair of black and silver pumps. All of the long hours of walking across Europe had paid off.

After getting dressed, I walked to the back door of our house and opened it. I found mother outside raking leaves into piles. I was pretty sure the December air would send more leaves dancing wildly back into our yard. I stood there and watched her for a few seconds. Her back was hunched over as if the year's hardships had finally beaten her down. I was convinced she was the strongest woman I knew. How could she possibly have endured raising seven hardheaded children practically by herself, dealing with a drunk and abusive husband, enduring the insults and the drunken slurs that he threw at her, cooking, cleaning, and still remaining sane? I knew it was no one but God that was preserving her, waiting for the moment when he would manifest King David's words, "Many are the afflictions of the righteous, but the Lord delivers him out of them all" (Psalms 34:19). No matter what she had to encounter, she never lost her ability to smile although the sparkle in her eyes were dying daily.

I decided to speak. "I'll be back if anyone is looking for me," I said startling her.

"Okay," she said turning to smile at me.

"Did you find something in there to eat?" she asked being the overly concerned mother that she was.

"I'm not hungry," I said. "I'll get something later on." She turned and resumed raking.

I found my car keys hanging on a nail in the dinning room where I usually kept it and walked out the front door. I was so excited. It felt good to be home. It felt good to be in my car again; and most of all, I felt good because I was going to see De Angelo again. As I cranked up the car, immediately the engine light came on and I noticed the gas hand was on E.

I jumped out of the car and ran back around the house to where my mother was. "Mom, Marsha left my car on empty and didn't put any oil in it!" I said brewing with indignation. Mom paused from raking the leaves to look at me.

"Well, I can give you five dollars, but that's all I have to spare (those were the days when five dollars could put an average vehicle at a half tank of gas)."

I never liked taking money from her. She always gave long speeches about how she needed it back due to the fact she didn't know when she would get anymore. Her speeches always left me feeling miserable that I couldn't help her more. I took the money that she extended. I was grateful she refrained from giving me a long speech this time. Once settled in the car, I drove straight to the gas station then drove straight over De Angelo's.

When I made it over to his house, fear immediately seized me. As I got out of the car, I clutched the Kill Army CD tightly next to my side. I knocked on the door. After deciding that no one was there, the doorknob turned. My heart pulsated rapidly as I watched De Angelo emerge from behind the closed door. His face immediately lit up when he saw me standing there. That was definitely a good sign. "Hey, baby!" he exclaimed as he gave me a massive hug. At that precise moment I wanted so badly to give him a piece of my mind for having the audacity to tell me he didn't love me anymore but decided to wait a while longer.

After we embraced, I handed him the CD. "This is for you. I bought it in Italy."

"Thanks. You are so sweet," he said, smiling down at me ravenously. He stepped to the side. "Come in." I had never been inside his parent's house before. Not because he hadn't invited me, but because my shyness restrained me. I wasn't sure if I was ready to meet his parents. Reluctantly, I followed close behind him into the house.

His mother was in the kitchen cooking but came out as she heard De Angelo and me conversing. As soon as she saw me, her face glistened with joy.

"Oh, so, you must be Crystal," she said knowingly while extending her hand. I nodded. "My name is Mrs. Pearl. My son has said so many good things about you." I continued to smile. "He tells me that you went to Europe?"

"Yes ma'am. I just got in last night," I stated trying to sound proper.

"What in the world were you doing in Europe?" She interrogated pleasantly, taking a seat so not to miss any of the details.

At that moment, De Angelo's sister walked through the front door. I figured it was her because De Angelo had previously mentioned her in a few conversations. She was only two years younger than me. After noticing me, she mumbled and then walked right by us into the back room. Within minutes, she returned and sat down across from me.

"Hello," she said looking at me blankly, "my name's Nikki." Her elongated body formed a perfect sculpture of a figure eight. Her golden brown, blemish-free skin seemed to radiate, heightening the effects of her dark-brown hair streaked with honey highlights, which barely touched her shoulders. She was absolutely beautiful. The striking resemblance between her and De Angelo amazed me.

"Hello, I'm Crystal," I said extending my hand. She accepted it.

"She's a pretty chocolate girl," De Angelo's mother stated to no one in particular having not taken her eyes off me the entire time. "I want to hear all about your trip to Europe."

"Well..." I said pausing briefly not really sure where to begin. I finally decided to tell the story from the beginning of how I got the international scholarship. I concluded by telling her some of my adventures while overseas and how I almost got stranded over there. They were totally absorbed into what I was saying. Soon, I was starting to feel right at home, and all of my nervousness dissipated.

I ended up staying over De Angelo's house for a few hours talking with his mother and sister. As the evening progressed, he and I decided to take a ride. I hopped in the passenger seat as he stepped into the driver's seat of my car.

"You know my birthday is tomorrow don't you?" I asked, not the least bit surprised when he shook his head that he had forgotten.

"What do you want to do?" he questioned as he began to caress my nearest thigh and with his other hand continued to grip the steering wheel.

"I don't know yet," I lied, hoping he had some better plans that would persuade me to stay with him instead of going to Searcy.

"I'll figure something out. I'll make sure you have a good time if you decide to spend your birthday with me," he said as he reached over and kissed me on the cheek.

I glanced over at him. I didn't know why I wanted to be with him so badly. For some reason though, his rough exterior intrigued me. I wanted to let him go, but his bad-boy ways captivated me. The nurturing part of my creative being challenged me to change him for the better. I thought that with good sex, and by being submissive to him, it was enough to make De

Angelo want to change. I was in for a rude awakening. My love wasn't going to be enough to get the job done.

The Birthday to Remember

The morning of my birthday, after Tamar and I drove to Forrest City to pick up April, we headed for Searcy. We didn't even make it out of Wynne, when my car started to decelerate on its own. The farther I pushed my foot on the accelerator, the slower the car became. Everyone was silent. Finally, the car came to a complete halt. I managed to maneuver it to the side of the road. "What happened?" Tamar asked. "I don't know, but I think the car just died." I turned the ignition. Nothing happened. I turned it again. The gargling sound of the carburetor trying to turn over could be heard. The look of doom became visible on each of our face.

As soon as we all unloaded the car, an old man and his wife pulled in front of us in a beat-up station wagon. Paper and clothes littered the floor and seats of the tattered vehicle.

"Do you gals need some help?" asked the old man getting out of the car.

"Yes, sir. My car just died. I don't understand what happened to it." I ranted.

"Are you sure it didn't run out of gas?" he asked as he walked over to my Grand Am and stuck his head inside to research the situation for himself. After seeing that the car had a full tank, he turned the ignition.

"This sounds like a problem with your motor. Can I give y'all a lift somewhere?" Upon accepting the fact we weren't going to Searcy, I accepted his offer. Tamar, April, and I loaded into the rusty vehicle. There were huge cracks in the floor that revealed the pavement underneath. Chuckling softly, I mouthed the word "Flintstones" in Tamar's direction. We fought to keep from laughing out loud.

After dropping us off over to my mother's house, we thanked

the elderly couple and went inside. "I can't stay home all night. I have to find something to do," I whined.

"I know, girl," Tamar said, agreeing with me.

"All of us are broke. Maybe, I can call De Angelo to come and get us. We can at least get high," I said glad to have a good reason to spend my birthday with him.

After calling him and confirming that he would pick us up later, April, Tamar, and I sat around talking.

"I can't believe this," April said with the sound of frustration audible in her voice. "I had my mind set on hooking up with Sweets and making some money.

"I'm sorry your birthday sucks." Tamar agreed. I wanted to tell them that spending my birthday with De Angelo would be the best birthday present I could ever have, but I refrained from doing so.

Instead I simply said, "That's alright. Maybe next year will be better."

Later that evening, De Angelo and his sister arrived to pick us up. When we made it to Forrest City, we dropped April off at her apartment. Afterwards, De Angelo shouted, "Now it's time to go celebrate my baby's birthday!" Tamar and I looked at one another with widened eyes not knowing what he was up to. Suddenly, Nikki pulled in front of Ray's Place, a nightclub in which I was very familiar with.

"Get out," De Angelo said. "It's time to party!"

To my astonishment when I walked into the club, there was a small surprise party for me (about four of his old drinking buddies). Different drinks were lined up on a table. His friends waved at me motioning for me to come over.

"Happy birthday, baby," De Angelo whispered as he kissed me softly on the neck. "This will be a night you'll never forget."

I was stunned. I didn't expect him to do anything for my birthday especially with such a short notice. Tamar and I pulled a seat up and partied until the club was ready to shut down. For the whole night, De Angelo treated me like a princess. The love that I had for him began to grow even stronger. It seemed like the two of us would be a couple again after all.

After the club, De Angelo decided we would walk over to one of his friend's house, I was glad. I needed to walk off some of the alcohol that ran through my system. While walking, my stomach churned. But to play like I was a professional drinker, I started talking to psych myself from getting sick and embarrassing myself.

"I don't get drunk. I can always handle my liquor." I lied.

"Girl, please, you're through," Tamar laughed.

"No I'm not," I slurred. I staggered and uttered deranged words until we arrived at our destination.

Once there, I remained outside while De Angelo went inside. I started feeling dizzy, so I sat on the porch with my head between my knees. Tamar sat next to me. I felt as if I was floating in the middle of a turbulent ocean, being tossed to and fro.

A few minutes later, De Angelo reemerged with a sandwich in his hand. "Crystal, you need to eat this so your high can subside." I refused. Tamar agreed that I needed something on my stomach. I ceased from struggling and allowed him to stick a piece of the sandwich in my mouth. It seemed to work for a few minutes, but by the time his sister arrived to pick us up, I could feel it coming up.

"I'm going to puke," I said squinting at him as if he had millions of blinking lights radiating from his body. Everything around me seemed to sway back and forth.

"Just wait until we get home," he said laughing.

Tamar stood on one side of me, and De Angelo on the other as they both helped me into the car.

"Where are y'all going?" Nikki asked looking frustrated at having to play the roll of "taxi cab" at about three o'clock in the morning.

"I'm going over April's house up on Grandma Circle," Tamar answered. Before I could open my mouth, De Angelo had already spoken for me.

"Crystal is coming with me over to mamma's house."

I didn't have any strength to protest. I wanted to go with Tamar, but De Angelo's decision seemed final. I tried to raise my head to speak, and that's when I felt all of my stomach's contents come up.

As I vomited, De Angelo's hands caught the smelly gush just in time before splattering on the floor. I could hardly believe he allowed me to throw up in his hands. Although it was a disgusting act, he had just won major points with me. Nikki immediately jerked on the brakes. I was so embarrassed. She turned around, and saw all of the puke dripping down the sides of her brother's hands.

"Ugh! You're nasty De Angelo!" she blurted out. "There isn't that much love in the world that'll make me catch anybody's throw-up! I'm going to hurry up and get y'all out of my car."

She turned back around and sped over to her mother's house. Meanwhile, De Angelo found a paper bag nearby and handed it to me to stick up to my mouth. After we arrived over their mother's house, as soon as I hit De Angelo's bed, I passed out.

The next morning, De Angelo and I laughed about the previous night's events. The queasiness I yet felt quickly subsided as I began to eat the delicious breakfast that he served me in bed. Throughout the rest of the day, we watched movies and, of course, had sex.

For the remainder of the summer, we were inseparable. We did almost everything together. Many late nights, we often found ourselves playing in the park like a couple of giddy school kids. As he'd push me on the swings, I'd lean my head back and imagine I was flying higher and higher into the sky. Other times, we would go for rides in the country and talk about our childhood days. No matter what we did, as long as we were together, I was happy. During those times, the whole concept of love seemed so beautiful.

The summer ended rapidly, and soon, it was almost time for

me to go back to Harding University. I hated the fact that I had to leave De Angelo again.

"I promise I'll come up there and see you," he said. "I'm sorry for not writing while you were in Europe. It was hard for me. You were just too far away. I couldn't stand for us to be separated from one another that long. I was lonely, so that's why I told you I didn't love you anymore. It tore me up when I told you that, but it was untrue. I did and always will love you, Crystal." I dismissed the brewing resentment I had against him and kissed him on his half-parted lips. Somehow I believed him.

The moment finally came when it was time for me to leave. We said our good-byes, and then I was off to school. Since my Grand-Am never got fixed after it broke down, my mother had to drive me to Searcy.

The Face of Death

When I arrived on campus, the atmosphere was very dismal. A feeling of gloom hung in the air like moss darkness. Trying to ignore the ominous dread, I went to register for my classes. After registering and getting the key to my dorm room, I went to search for Rachel.

When I didn't find her, I found my new room and decided to unpack. That semester, I hardly brought any belongings only some covers, one suitcase of clothes, and a backpack filled with personal care items. The trip to Europe had taught me how to pack efficiently with only the things I needed.

After getting everything unpacked and put away, there was a knock on the door. It was my new roommate. She came bouncing into the room as her short golden locks swayed with her every move. *Oh, my goodness*, I thought. *This girl is just way to cheerful for me. I hope she isn't a snitch.*

Not long after we had introduced ourselves to one another, there came a knock from the inside of our bathroom's door. To my bewilderment, my roommate and I found out that we were sharing our bathroom with two other girls who stayed in the consecutive room next to ours. They both turned out to be just as bubbly as my roommate. *"Just great,"* I thought. *"I'm stuck with the Beverly Hillbillies."*

When I introduced myself to the both of them, they appeared to be extremely friendly. *Maybe, they'll be helpful in getting me back on the right track.* I hoped. I liked competition, so I could use them to help me become studious again. After minutes of chattering away, they left our room.

"Did you hear about what happened on campus yesterday?" My roommate asked after the others had left.

"No. What?" I asked.

"They found a guy lying in his dorm room dead."

"For real?" I asked, turning to look at her. "How did he die?"

"Some believe it was because of an insulin overdose. They found an IV needle stuck in his arms, and his diabetic medicine lying next to him."

"That's sad," I said shaking my head. I guess that explained the feeling of dread I had felt earlier.

Later that evening, I ran into Rachel. It was she who told me that Justin had died in his dorm room. I was in shock. Our friendship was one that was rare. Although he had been interested in dating me, he seemed more like a big brother. I could talk to him about anything without fearing it would be repeated to others. He helped me get through some tough times. A wave of sadness overtook me. I was pained to know that I would never see him again.

Only a few weeks before I came back to the States, Justin had been on my mind heavily. Early one morning, I felt a strong urge to pray for him. I didn't understand why, but I obeyed. I prayed that God would save him and help him to come into the knowledge of Jesus Christ and his love for him. I even sent him a letter about how God loved him and wanted to save him. I truly believe to this day that he had gotten the letter because my other friends had received theirs. They were all mailed at the same time to the college. I was glad I had obeyed the unction of the Spirit. Whether I felt worthy to witness or not, God had just used me to send someone a message.

To escape the feeling of self-pity for not remaining the witness that I once professed to be, I craved for something to subdue my thoughts of unworthiness. So once again, I resumed the everyday lifestyle of running from my pain instead of facing it. By walking off of campus and finding my cousin Tiger, I found that escape. I stayed over to his place getting high until a few minutes before curfew. Not long after, I fell into such a depression that school didn't interest me anymore. Competition no longer excited me. The only things that did were beer, and marijuana, and of course, De Angelo. He was my favorite drug of choice.

So Long, Fair Love

At first, De Angelo started coming to Searcy on weekends to visit me. Soon, he started coming on weekdays as well. When he did, I would stay off campus as much as possible. As long as I was wrapped in his arms I was happy. During his visits, he oftentimes complained about me not spending enough time with him. The more frequent his comments came, the more serious I took them.

I was overtaken by the fact that I felt more love from him than I had ever felt from anyone before. Since he had become the remedy to my loneliness, I wanted to do whatever necessary to make him happy.

Somewhere in the middle of my third semester, I decided to drop out of college. I didn't want to lose De Angelo. Many of my professors questioned my decision. Because I was so into sin, it didn't bother me when I lied to most of them and told them that I was ill. Each of them expressed genuine sympathy, and one instructor even prayed with me. *How could I have possibly sunken so low? I know better than this. Lord, please forgive me.*

I bowed my head in repentance at the sincerity of her petition of healing.

As soon as I finished taking my final exams, I packed all of my things and was ready to leave. When I told De Angelo that I had dropped out of school, disappointment was the only thing I received from him. I thought dropping out would prove the depth of my love. I was willing to push my dreams aside by devoting my time to him. I thought he would be thrilled that now we would have more time with each other. He wasn't. To him, I was starting to become too needy and clingy. I was. The more he pushed away, the harder I clung on.

Our happy little fairytale relationship had come to an end fast. Eventually, whenever I'd call him, he was never at home. He often made excuses when I wanted him to come and see me. Whenever he did see me, it was only to have sex; then he would leave again. Constantly out of the blue, he started accusing me of cheating on him. I became suspicious of his accusations, assuming he was the guilty party.

One afternoon, De Angelo called me. "Crystal, I have something to tell you." He and I had been together a little over two years at this point, so by the tone of his voice, I knew that something was wrong. "I love you and don't want to hurt you." He hesitated briefly before continuing. "Promise me that you won't get mad?" he said anticipating a response. My heart began to beat frantically. "First, I have to know what it is," I said as fear began to grasp its fingers around my lungs. I didn't expect to hear what came out of his mouth next. "I had a one night stand with a girl a while back." On impulse, my grasp tightened around the phone. He continued. "She just had a baby a few days ago, and she's saying that it's mine. I don't think it is because I only slept with her once," he tried to explain in one breath.

I could hardly believe what I was hearing. I felt sick like I would pass out at any moment. I've heard of that kind of thing happening to other people. Never did I anticipate that it would happen to me. This was some Jerry Springer type of mess. A parade of railings rushed through my mind like a tidal wave. *Why would he do this to me? I know how to treat a man, don't I? I'm pretty submissive. I'm respectable. I give him great sex whenever and however he wants it, and I do mean some pretty kinky stuff! I fulfill my womanly duties of grooming myself nicely. Why could he possibly want to cheat on me?*

"Well, if it's yours, you definitely need to take care of it," I snapped. "I knew you were holding something back from me!" I temporarily lost my suave composure. "I should have listened to my womanly intuition!"

In order to keep him from basking in my hurt, I played tough and subdued my anger. De Angelo resumed. "I wasn't going to tell you, but I knew that you would eventually find out. In fact, my mother told me that if I didn't tell you, she would."

After taking a deep breath, I spoke. "We've been through so much, De Angelo. This will be difficult for me to get over, but I know that we can get through this together."

I could hardly believe what I had just said. What I really wanted to say was, "Negro, please. I guarantee I can find another man. You can get to stepping. Holler at you!" Better yet, I wanted to get real ghetto by rolling my neck and screaming deranged Ebonics like, "*Aight. Me and my dogs are on our way. So you want to play me for a fool? Since I'm obviously your trick, I'm going to bring you a treat! I'm about to open up a can of whoop—*"

Instead, all I said was, "I love you. We can make this work." I stifled the madness that I felt at my own self for being a so stupid. I continued. "I have something to tell you also. I've been thinking about moving to Texas with my brother and his family. But now, you have just finalized that decision for me. I'm going to accept my brother's offer. I need to get away for a while. After finding a good job and saving up some money, I'll try to get us a place. There are too many bad memories here for the both of us. I refuse to stay in Forrest City if we are going to try and make this relationship work," I hoped he'd agree with my decision.

"Crystal, don't go," he whispered. The plea of desperation was audible.

"I have no other choice." With that, I hung up the phone and wept bitterly. My heart was broken. Once again, I was left abandoned and betrayed. .

The very next week, I was on my way to Fort Worth, Texas to live with my brother. Other than working at a Labor Ready once, no jobs came through for me while there. So I could have some money in my pockets, I babysat for my brother and his wife. With the money that I made, I bought calling cards, so I could call De Angelo. He was rarely at home. And when he was there, he always rushed me off the phone by saying he had other business to handle.

Naturally, I turned to God again. He was my remedy for my broken heart. I didn't turn to him because I just wanted to be saved although I did but because I needed an escape route from hurting so bad. My action was good, but my motive was bad. Therefore, I became the parable Jesus spoke of in Matthew 13:20–21 concerning the sower. "The seeds that fell on rocky ground stand for those who receive the message gladly as soon as they hear it. But it does not sink deep into them, and they don't last long. So when trouble or persecution comes, because of the message, they give up at once" (TEV). I was a hearer of the word and not a doer. That's why there was no stability in my life.

After living in Texas for almost two months without employment, I was ready to go back to Forrest City. My brother drove me to the greyhound station to catch the bus. Blinded by tears, I watched him disappear as the overcrowded bus pulled away from the terminal.

When the bus finally arrived to Forrest City, I caught a ride over April's place. By this time, she had relocated to a trailer.

When I showed up, she greeted me with open arms and allowed me to stay there with her.

One morning, I awakened early. Nothing stirred. Only the sound of heavy breathing could be heard. I didn't get much sleep the night before since many things boggled my mind and since the sound of April's boyfriend loud snores kept me awake. In order to clear my head a little, I decided to take an early morning stroll. I threw the covers back and quietly as I could, slipped on my shoes, tip-toed to the door, and then opened it.

After about fifteen minutes of walking, to my dismay when I had returned over April's, I discovered that the door had been locked. I sat down on the trailer's cold and damp steps and rested my head in the palms of my hands. *Why is my life full of so much trouble? No matter what I seem to do, I keep meeting some type of resistance along the way,* I moaned. *I must be cursed or something. Why can't anything go easy for me for once?*

I wanted to go over De Angelo's house, but somehow, I knew that we were no longer a couple. Valentine's Day had just passed, and I didn't hear a word from him. Nothing. So without knowing where to go, I got up and started walking. I prayed for God to lead and direct my feet. About twenty minutes later, I ended up at a Super Stop gas station. I sat down in front of the store, hoping I would run into someone I knew.

A crack fiend, which I was accustomed to seeing loitering outside the gas station, approached me. She looked like the living dead. Her clothes were tattered, and her eyes seemed to have sunken in the back of her head. "Do you have fifty cents?" she asked. Nothing seemed to have changed about this woman, only her weight. She was thinner than I remembered, but was still the same half-dressed woman that I was used to seeing performing tricks and begging for money.

After telling her that I didn't have any, she looked at me with serpentine eyes and said, "I hear you and De Angelo aren't together anymore."

Startled at her comment I asked, "Where'd you hear that from?"

"It's all over town," she boasted. "I saw his new baby, and he's a pretty little thing. It's too bad that y'all aren't together. Y'all would have made a pretty baby too." As she talked, I could feel anger brewing to the surface at her venomous words.

Trying not to let her see the effect of her poisonous words on me, I continued to compose myself.

"I just got back from Texas, and to be honest, I don't know what's going on. I haven't heard from him," I said.

After giving her enough gossip to spread to someone else, I headed towards Grandma Circle over to Tina and Steve Hancock's apartment (a couple that De Angelo had introduced me to during the initial stages of our relationship). He and I had spent many nights over at their house talking, drinking, and of course, making love.

Tina was hilarious. She was short and chubby with hardly any hair on her head—barely enough to make a pony tail. Many times, she would look at me cuddled up next to De Angelo with her crossed-eyes and start laughing outrageously revealing tobacco-stained teeth. "What's so funny?" I would ask puzzled. Her reply was often the same, "Nothing." Then she would spit a squirt of snuff in a jar. Without warning, she would repeat bouts of uncontrollable laughter.

After minutes of trying to coax the answer out of her, she'd finally answer, "Girl, you are in love. That boy got your nose wide open."

I would just look at her and shake my head because she found that to be so hilarious. "You're crazy," I'd say, often joining her in fits of laughter. Her husband Steve, a big monster of a man, weighed about four hundred pounds. He would look at the both of us and boom out, "The both of you are absolutely nuts."

When I made it over to their apartment, I could hear singing coming from inside. With my hands poised ready to knock, the door opened. Out came Tina clapping her hands and stomping her feet as if the Spirit had just touched her. After noticing me standing there, she encircled me with a smothering hug.

"Crystal! You look good!" She stepped back to examine me. "How are you?"

"I'm fine," I replied with the same amount of overemphasis.

"Who is that singing?" I asked curiously. "That's my sister, David, and Steve. All of us just started going to this new church down the hill. Since they didn't have a choir, we decided to start one. We're in revival this week. You ought to come."

As she spoke, I began to realize that maybe it was God's will for me to get locked out of April's house. I had a purpose to fulfill. I was at the right place, at the right time, getting ready to attain a piece of the puzzle that would formulate my divine destiny.

All that week, I attended church with Tina and some of the other's that lived on Grandma Circle. There were only a handful of us there, but from those, a choir was formed. With a strong desire to stay busy for the Lord and increase the church attendance, I started going door-to-door, inviting people out to the anointed services that were being held.

One night while at church, the preacher stood up. "Someone go look outside. I feel it in my spirit that someone has been standing out there for a while but is afraid to come in." Yet submerged under the powerful grasp of the anointing, I didn't give his words much thought.

Within minutes, one of the deacons came and tapped me on the shoulder, untangling me from my trance-like state. "Crystal, someone outside wants to see you." I looked at the person in bewilderment.

"Who is it?" I asked. No answers came. Questioning eyes followed me as I approached the front door of the church and exited.

Standing there propped up against the tainted siding of the church was De Angelo. I could hardly believe my eyes. "The devil is a liar," I mumbled. *This is nothing but the devil trying to tempt me.*

"Hey. I miss you," he breathed smiling up at me. The cool November air gathered at his mouth emitting fog with each word.

"How'd you know I was here?" I asked looking at him in obvious frustration but secret glee.

"I can always track you down." He toyed. "I wanted to come in, but I had drunk a beer earlier. I wouldn't have felt comfortable in church knowing I had been drinking."

He paused slightly, licked his lips, and then continued. "I saw you through the window. I've been standing out here for nearly an hour contemplating on whether or not to go inside." I was speechless. "Will you come and go with me?" After seeing the look of distaste on my face, he changed the question quickly. "Can I meet you over Tina and Steve's house when church is out?" he asked practically begging with his eyes.

"That's where I've been staying anyway. I'm going back over there when church is over, but right now, I'm going to get my praise on."

At that moment, people started exiting the church. It had concluded earlier than I'd anticipated. Tina walked over to where we stood and hit De Angelo on the arm.

"Hi, De Angelo!" "What's been happening with you man? Why don't you come back over to the house with us?" She chimed.

"Is there enough room in the car for me to ride?"

"No," I snapped. "The car is packed."

"Well, I'll walk over there then." He turned to gaze into my eyes almost hypnotizing me. "Crystal, will you walk with me?" With shoulders squared, I looked him in the eye without giving in to his wishes.

"No. I'll meet you over there. I have a ride."

During the ride to the apartment, I gloated on how good it felt to have put my foot down. I was so used to letting De Angelo have his way. If he wanted to see me bad enough, he would have to make an effort.

Ten minutes had barely passed when there was a knock at the door. I rushed to open it. "You got here fast," I said laughing as De Angelo walked through the door. Tiny beads of perspiration had formed at his temples. Before the door closed completely he grabbed me by the waist and nestled me in his arms.

"You've lost some weight," he breathed only inches away from my mouth. Loosening from his vice-like grip, I said,

"While in Texas, I exercised almost every day." I marveled that he had noticed.

"Well, you look delicious," he said looking me up and down voraciously.

I could tell that he expected us to resume where we'd left off before I moved away, but it wasn't going to be that easy.

"I heard you were back in town," he said after realizing I wasn't going to give in to his seductive stare.

"Why did it take you so long to come and visit me then?" I asked sarcastically.

"I've been busy," he snapped, sensing that I was upset. "Carol, don't even start with me," he added in his usual easily agitated way.

I guess he thought I was dense or something because the last time I checked my birth certificate it said Crystal and not Carol. He quickly corrected the name mistake as if it were an honest one. I glared at him without saying anything. *So, that's the girl's name,* I cried inwardly. There was an awkward moment of silence. De Angelo quickly filled it with nonsense babble so that his "honest" mistake wouldn't seem too obvious.

Everything was making sense now. De Angelo was wearing jewelry that I had never noticed before—a huge yellow-gold Herringbone and two gold-nugget rings; each with the letter C engraved on it. "What does the letter C stand for," I asked placing my hand on his necklace stroking it. I was accustomed to his lying, so it didn't surprise me when he said,

"It stands for Crystal." *Yeah right, you toothless snake. I'm sure it means Carol!* I ached to yell.

Since I was trying to do right by God, I decided against arguing with him and making a scene. I resisted the urge to go ghetto on him. Even if I did, I knew that De Angelo would've made me seem like I was the one in the wrong. Blame was his usual tactic.

I couldn't understand why he wanted to lead me on. I could've dealt with the fact that he didn't want to be with me anymore, but it was hard to accept the fact that he kept popping in and out my life whenever he chose. He didn't want me to be with another guy, but yet he didn't fully want to be with me either. He had me so confused.

I wrestled to swallow down the all-too-familiar agony. I couldn't even try to imagine him being with another woman, but it had happened before; and I knew it was happening again.

I looked him straight in the eyes, took a deep breath, and calmly stated, "De Angelo, you don't have to lie to me. Just tell me the truth. What does the letter C really stands for?" Despite my brewing rage, right there in that dimly-lit apartment I wanted to grab him and plant sultry kisses all over his peanut butter-colored body. I shuttered at the hideous thought and silently prayed to be released from his voodoo-like spell.

"I am telling you the truth!" De Angelo bellowed.

The pitch in his voice began to grow higher with each word, causing his nose to flare. I quickly dismissed the anger-birthed sexual tension that had started to surface. After seeing that I wasn't going to react to his anger, De Angelo softened. "I love you," he said as if it would convince me that he did. Regardless if it was love or not, he had just called me by another women's name; I was determined to find out who she was. I didn't play that.

Shortly after his declaration of love, the true reason why he stood before me came out. He looked at me tenderly with passion-filled eyes. "I want some loving, baby. I need you badly. You know how to satisfy my needs." Caught off guard, I chuckled nervously trying to ignore his comment. When I realized that he was serious, it was almost too late.

As he started kissing me on the neck, I spoke up. "I love you so much, but I will not sleep with you. I'm saved. We have to wait until we're married." It took everything in me to resist him. My body was ablaze with passion.

"I'm glad you're saved," he said surprised at my reaction. His dark and cloudy eyes were hungrily gazing into mine. "You don't realize how much you're helping me when I see you trying to do what's right."

He resumed kissing me on the neck. "Baby, I got to have some of you. I need it. I need you. Your loving is just too good to me. Can't no women even try to compare to you, Crystal." At the mention of another woman during the topic of sex made me want to puke right there all over him. It brought to mind all of the betrayal again.

When he saw that I wasn't going to give in, he stood up and began to throw accusations at me from the top of his lungs. "You must be sleeping with someone else, while you're sitting here trying to play that good-girl role. That's probably why you won't give me any loving!" After saying all of that, he stormed out the door. Once again, I was left alone and abandoned.

I didn't know whether to cry or rejoice. I was happy that I didn't yield to temptation, but yet I was saddened because I had let him down. I had practically just pushed him into the arms of another woman.

After hearing the door slam shut, Tina came into the living room and saw me sitting alone. "Where's De Angelo?" she wanted to know.

"He left. He got mad because I wouldn't have sex with him," I said bluntly.

"Girl, that boy loves you. He'll be back," she said trying to cheer me up. It didn't work. As soon as she went to bed, I cried myself to sleep.

The next few nights, I continued to go to revival at the new church that I was attending. It was extended due to the fact that a lot of people were giving their lives to the Lord. Of course the more I worked in ministry, the harder the enemy fought me. De Angelo reappeared. Through eyes of enlightenment and hope, I saw him as my soon-to-be husband.

He showed back up over Tina's apartment late at night. He was very drunk. To give the two of us privacy, she and Steve left to go over to a neighbor's house.

After sitting down beside me, he kissed me innocently on the cheek. When he saw I allowed him to do that without slapping the mess out of him, he tried to kiss me on my half-parted lips. At first I retreated, but not wanting to discourage my "soon-to-be-husband," I compromised. Soon, he was all over me—kissing, touching, and rubbing at those secret places. Within minutes, we were breathing heavily in one another's ear begging for more.

After having sex, I felt disgusted with myself. I had just given my pearls to the swine again. I gave up something that was so precious to me—my relationship with God for a dream, an illusion of what I thought De Angelo would be one day. Stupidly, I figured since I had sex with him, he would love me enough to leave the other woman alone. Of course, I was wrong.

The next morning, before the sun had risen, De Angelo woke up. Thinking that I was yet asleep, he left without any explanations or excuses. I stared at the closed door in disbelief. *"Maybe, he just went out for some fresh air,"* I tried to make myself believe. After an hour had passed, I knew better.

I could almost hear the devil laughing at me for being so foolish. I had chosen a few minutes of pleasure instead of peace with God. In the end, I had lost both—De Angelo and my relationship with God.

For some reason, I kept falling back into the same dismal cycle of choosing him over what God had planned for my life. I wanted to break free of our "soul ties," but no matter how hard I tried, I kept going back.

The prophetess' words came to mind. "If you sin against God, repent and get back up." I sat on the couch sobbing for hours while rocking myself back and forward contemplating on her words. The immense grief I felt left me feeling naked and ashamed. It seemed easy to just repent, but even after I did it, I didn't feel worthy enough to be forgiven. I hated myself. Basking in condemnation was my only comfort.

The next day, feeling like there was no hope for me, I slipped back into the same old behavior of pampering an "I don't care" attitude. This proved to me that one sin usually lead to an overflow of others. Because I wanted so badly to be an example of holiness to everyone I came into contact with that when confronted by Tina about the previous night with De Angelo, I denied having sex with him. I wanted to prove to them that one could live a sin-free life. I had failed and was too embarrassed to admit it.

A few hours later, while lying on the couch playing Nintendo, a knock came at the door. Thinking that it was De Angelo, I jumped up and opened the door. My heart sunk; it wasn't. It was a short guy named Little Pete, a beastly looking man who stayed a few doors down. He constantly voiced to me how he'd love for me to be his lady. He smiled. I was in no mood for his stuff today. I left him standing at the door to resume playing the game. "What's wrong with you?" he asked walking in. "Nothing. I just need a vacation," I hissed not taking my eyes off the television screen. A few minutes later, Tina entered the room.

"What's up Tina? I'm trying to see if y'all have any plans right now," Pete said. I already knew what was coming next. "I got a blunt if anybody's up for smoking it."

Tina hesitated as if seeking my approval, then finally said "No. I better not. I'm trying to stop." I abruptly cut through their conversation and walked to the door.

"I'll be outside," I said.

My conscience gnawed at me because I was letting so many

people down. I was so in love with De Angelo that my spiritual life was constantly being compromised. There was no doubt in my mind that he had become my idol. He was my god. I worshipped the very ground he walked on. I couldn't imagine living without him. He was my addiction. Although he wasn't treating me the way I desired, I lived off hope that he would eventually transform. This agonizing hope became my own private hell.

By the time Pete walked outside a few minutes later, I was drowning in despair. Once again, instead of dealing with my emotions, I sought a way to escape them. As he walked off, I ran to catch up with him.

"Can I hit the blunt?" I asked.

He smiled. "Sure. Follow me."

While smoking marijuana with him, an eerie feeling overpowered me. Death was nearby. I could feel him waiting for the go-ahead from God to snatch my loathsome breath away. I knew that if I didn't get my life together soon, death was inevitable.

After getting high, Pete and I departed our separate ways. I went back over to Tina's house and fell asleep to escape the eerie feeling that hovered over me.

That night, I told Tina that I was going over April's house. Truthfully, I planned on going to the nightclub first. I hoped to run into De Angelo, so he could see that I was the old me again—wild and fun.

When arriving at Ray's Place, I sat at the bar watching everyone that came through the door. Dismissing dance proposals and flirtatious comments, I continued to examine every face that entered the hot and over-crowded nightclub. De Angelo never came. By the time the club had ended for the night, I was drunk. I had downed almost four forty ounces of Colt 45.

While walking from the club, I gripped my coat tightly around me as the roaring wind nudged me on causing me to lose my balance. As I fought to regain my composure, somewhere in the distance, the faint sound of a female's voice could be heard. As I drew closer to the sound, it became magnified. The voice was recognizable. It was Nikki, De Angelo's sister.

As I crossed the street from the club, I could barely make out her petite frame located in the dark dugout to my right. To my astonishment, she was dangling across a man's shoulder in midair, fighting to be freed from his grip. I could hardly make out any faces because it was too dark.

After adjusting my eyes, I recognized Anthony, Nikki's boyfriend. He was standing directly in front of a short, small-framed girl, preventing her from getting to Nikki. I didn't know what was going on, but from the look of things, this appeared to be some type of relationship drama. Out of a sense of obligation to De Angelo, my only concern at the moment was making sure that Nikki was all right. And from what I could see, she wasn't.

Maybe it was because of the alcohol's illusion of bravery or because I wanted to gain the respect of my hopefully one day sister-in-law. Whichever it was, I found myself screaming from the top of my lungs, "Leave my sister alone!" Everyone froze at the sound of my roar. All eyes were on me. The alcohol provided fuel to my new surge of adrenaline. As if in slow motion, the tail of my coat seemingly flapped in the wind as I ran over there and demanded the guy to put Nikki down. He did.

After throwing degrading comments back and forth between one another, Nikki finally left the girl standing there and got in the car. "Come with me," she demanded me. Gladly, I followed her orders. My drunken self needed to sit down badly. Once in the privacy of the car, she pleaded. "Will you spend the night over my house tonight? I'm scared to stay there by myself." I agreed.

Once there, we spent half the night talking about guys and the other half we spent crying over pain from past wounds that had left our hearts tattered. Night after night, she insisted that I stayed with her. Before long, I found myself moving in.

I eventually went over to Tina's apartment, got my clothes, and took them over to Nikki's. One day while staying over to

Nikki's, I decided to take an early morning walk. Not far from her apartment, I saw De Angelo and another guy approaching from the opposite side of the street. For the moment, I didn't care if he only wanted me for his sexual gratifications as long as he wanted me. I ran my fingers through my hair making sure that none of my split ends were sticking up.

As he drew nearer I inhaled, waiting for him to say something. He and the guy passed by as if I didn't exist. I wanted to throw a tantrum, but with my head held high, I continued to walk as if I wasn't bothered. Without a doubt in my mind, we were finally through.

Shortly after, I found out through his sister that he was living with the women he had admitted to having had a one-night stand with before I moved to Texas. And of course, it turned out that her name was Carol. I was truly heartbroken. That explained why he was never at home when I called or why he always disappeared for days at a time.

Because of all the emotional anguish, I made up my mind that I would move back home to Wynne. I needed time to find myself. I had lost my identity by trying to conform to what I thought De Angelo wanted me to be. I valued myself by how much interest he had in me. And because he didn't appear to have any, I felt worthless. So, I called Tamar and pleaded for her to come and pick me up.

When she arrived, I explained to Nikki that it was time for me to go home and recuperate, but I promised to stay in contact.

One afternoon, having been in Wynne for almost three weeks, I stared at the television as if only seconds from having a nervous breakdown. The fuzzy screen seemed to suck me in as I lost myself deep in thought. I needed something good to happen. I was tired of living from place to place. I was ready to get something that I could call my own. As if by will power, the telephone rang. I groggily picked up the retriever and answered. "Hello."

"May I speak to Crystal McDaniel," a female's reply came. I

paused thinking that maybe it was a bill collector trying to collect some money that I owed.

"This is she," I stammered.

She continued. "We have a job opening at Mullay Plastics in Forrest City. I was calling to see if you still needed a job."

"Yes, I do," I said quickly, jerking upright in my seat.

"Come into the Interim Office as soon as you can and fill out an application. You can start this evening." Suddenly, I remembered signing my name up for a job at the temporary service office a few days ago.

"I have a friend that needs a job also," I quickly added remembering Nikki. "Can she come with me?"

"Well..." the lady said hesitating briefly, "she can come in and fill out an application. She will then be placed on a waiting list, but I can't promise you anything." That was enough for me. I had at least tried.

When our conversation had concluded, I quickly called Nikki. "Do you want a job?" I excitedly asked her. "If you do, then you'd better come on down here. I just got a call from Interim, and a lady said we could start tonight. She will put you on the waiting list, but hopefully, someone won't show up."

"Yeah!" she screamed. "I'll be right there!" I believed that by faith, both of us would get the job.

About thirty minutes later, Nikki was outside my house, tooting her horn. We sped to the Interim, and within minutes, we were both hired for the job. That night from six o'clock in the evening to six o'clock the next morning, the both of us worked at Mullay Plastics.

After getting my second paycheck, I moved to Forrest City into my very first apartment. The news somehow got to De Angelo, and one evening, he showed up at my front door. Because of the fact that I was still deeply in love with him, I let him in. He apologized for all of his wrongdoings and promised to make everything up to me. For about three days, he did just that.

Since I was off for the weekend, we cuddled and made love

without leaving the house for anything. He whispered all of the right things, making me think that he was serious about working harder to keep me.

That night as I lay in his arms, I had a dream that he and I were walking somewhere. Out of nowhere, a girl approached me with a knife. She was trying to stab me over De Angelo. I woke up with sweat pouring off my body. I never told him about it.

The following Monday morning, after telling me he was leaving to do some work with his father, De Angelo left. I didn't see him any more that week.

Once again the cycle of him jumping in and out of my life resumed. I couldn't blame him; it was my fault for letting him do it. I was getting to the point where I was sick of my own self. I realized that the cycle would continue until I got tired enough to do something about it.

The following weekend, after picking up my paycheck, De Angelo reappeared at my apartment. I found it strange how he always seemed to show up when I had money. The only explanation he gave me for staying gone so long was that he had been busy.

I wanted so badly for things to work out between the two of us, but I was getting fed up with his games and his lame excuses. It was hard accepting the fact that our relationship now consisted only of sex. His love for me was gone. His actions dictated that to me. We were no longer best friends but strangers to one another.

One evening when De Angelo suggested we go over to one of his friend's house to drink a few beers with them, I accepted his offer. I yearned to feel like a couple again. It had been a long time since we had been outside of four walls together, so I didn't mind the fact that he expected me to pay for the beer and the weed as long as we were together.

To show him that I was still sexy, I slipped on a black miniskirt that had two slits up the side and put on a white silk shirt. I decided to wear my black spaghetti-strap sandal-heels to add the finishing touch. His mouth fell open when he saw me. *That's the De Angelo I'm used to,* I thought. Immediately, he began pulling my miniskirt up around my waist, and with a quick shift of his hand, began fondling me. His hunger for my body made me burn with lust. With my back arched and my head held back, I screamed for him to devour every inch of me. With sweat dripping down the side of his face, I watched him climb to sweet ecstasy as a shadow of pure serenity crept across his face.

He was my addiction. It wasn't just the sex or drugs that had me feening, but it was my love for him. I sought after his approval. He gratified my cravings of wanting attention and affection. Since I had never been validated before, I identified my worth through his eyes. I wanted to please him at any cost. Without a doubt, he was my idol.

On our way over to De Angelo friend's house, we decided to walk along the railroad track. While walking, I heard a sound at my rear as if someone was running on the tracks. De Angelo turned his head before I did. Out of the corner of my eye, I could see him stiffen. When I turned around, I saw why. With wild, matted hair, a barefooted woman ran towards us with the look of anger on her face. "What are you doing with her!" she screamed at De Angelo pointing at me.

Because a few observers were standing nearby, I remained calm. *So this must be Carol,* I guessed. *I finally get to meet her.* I noticed a black car pulled over to the side of the road with its door ajar. Apparently, while driving, she had spotted us. Enraged with jealousy, she had leaped out to vindicate herself.

I continued to stand there without saying anything. De Angelo was going to have to settle this for himself because apparently he had been lying to us both. The girl was hysterical. Tears streamed down her face as she continued to yell at him. I threw a sharp look in his direction. I wanted to smack him right there, but due to the fact that a small crowd was gathering, I refrained myself. I knew that by the end of the day, everyone that knew De Angelo and I would have heard about what had happened.

De Angelo walked over to where the girl was standing and whispered something to her. She immediately began calming down. Shortly after, she turned and walked away. I didn't know what he said, but I gloated in glee when he left the scene with me.

In silence, De Angelo and I resumed walking. *Why am I with this big liar?* I questioned myself. *There is no way he could possibly ever love me the way that I deserve. I am so stupid for letting him use me.* In utter distaste, I had unconsciously stopped in my tracks.

"What's wrong with you?" De Angelo asked, looking at me suspiciously.

It had just dawned on me that I had already been forewarned in a dream that I was going to be confronted by a woman over De Angelo.

"Nothing," I snapped, resuming walking.

When we arrived over to the Hill's, we stayed there until late that evening, drinking and getting high. Afterwards, De Angelo walked back with me to the house and left. He didn't make any lame excuses about leaving or any explanation for that matter—nothing.

When I looked in my secret stash to sort out my bills for the month, I found out that some of my money was missing. I could hardly believe that De Angelo would steal from me. For three days he didn't show up. My patience with his trifling ways were growing thin.

One night later that week, his sister came over to my house, wanting to know if I would go out to the club with her. I agreed. I didn't care about paying the rent that month. Since my money was stolen, I didn't have enough anyway. Instead, I bought a short leather outfit to wear. I longed to feel sexy because inside I was dying.

While at the club, many guys were trying to hit on me, but I decided against letting anything transpire to more than just a friendly conversation. I just didn't feel comfortable. After being there for a while, De Angelo walked through the door. My heart began beating frantically. My emotions were so mixed up. Part of me was happy about seeing him, and the other part was filled with disgust.

There was no doubt in my mind that he was both, drunk and high. I could smell him when he came to sit by me. "Come on let's go," he said, eyeing me with reddened eyes. I looked at him as if he had lost his mind. *How dare he have the audacity to tell me what to do? He was the one that walked out and had stolen from me. He got some nerve.*

"I came here with Nikki," I said sternly glaring at him. "I'm not leaving her here by herself. You know she has enemies after her."

"She'll be alright. Now, let's go," he demanded.

Nikki had already made me promise before we left my apartment that I would not desert her. Although frightened, I did not bulge. Out the corner of my eyes, I could see De Angelo's nose flare. Hoping he would get fed up with my rebellion and leave, I excused myself and walked to the bathroom. To my dismay, when I returned, he was still sitting at the table where I had left him. Both disgusted with how the night was turning out, Nikki and I both agreed to leave. Neither of us felt like hearing De Angelo's griping all night.

When we got up, he followed us into the humid night. I continued to ignore him. Irritated by my nonchalant attitude, he reared back and punched me in the face. I was shocked and humiliated. I never thought he would ever put his hands on me. For the last past year, he had turned into a stranger.

With one swift motion of his hand, the shimmer from the designer's knife I had given him as a gift was pulled out and pointed in my direction. I saw absolute rage in his eyes. Someone I loved so much wanted to kill me. That was a hard pill to swallow.

"Come on, De Angelo," I cried hysterically. "Let's go home."

Meanwhile, I backed away slowly to show him that I was

surrendering to his will. When he realized that he had me where he wanted me, he began to follow closely behind my footsteps. My heart pounded in my chest as he cursed me all the way home.

"I'm tired of you disrespecting me! You probably don't even have any underwear on underneath that dress!" he snarled. Just as I started to climb up the stairs to my apartment, he grabbed the end of my dress and pulled it up.

"I do," I said weeping bitterly, too afraid to move his hands.

Violent shakes of fear rippled through my body. It became almost impossible to get my keys to fit into the door. When I finally made it into the house, I flung myself on the bed and wept. I never believed that a guy would hurt me so much. I've watched my mother get disrespected and slapped around by my father. Now one of my worse nightmares had come true. I was following her footsteps.

"Stop all of that whining!" he retorted. I quickly stifled my cries but continued to shake uncontrollably.

"You were going to kill me," I said looking at him blinded by tears.

"I wasn't going to kill you. I just wanted to teach you not to disrespect me!" he shouted. After saying that, he walked out of the room. Within minutes, I could hear the shower running.

After finishing, he stood before me with beads of water dripping from his body. As if nothing had just happened between us, he threw sexual jargon at me in hopes of getting me aroused. Pretending that he had not just tried to kill me was impossible. Biting my lips to keep from crying, I fulfilled his desires. I prayed that it was the last time.

The next morning, when he left to go to work with his father, I packed all of my things and left his stuff in the apartment. I had his sister to drive me back to Wynne. I sat in silence all the way home. I was so tired of moving back and forth. I was tired of being restless. I realized that it was not going to be easy for me as long as I neglected the call that God had on my life.

At Death's Door

After living in Wynne for about a month and quitting my other job, Nikki called me one Friday evening. "Mrs. Rose at the Blue Flame needs some extra workers this weekend. I'm going to see if I could work there. Do you want to work with me?" I hesitated, afraid that I would run into De Angelo and that he would kill me for leaving without telling him anything. But since I was broke, I finally agreed.

"I'll be by to pick you up after while. You have to wear black and white," she added before hanging up.

Later on that evening, Nikki picked me up. We stopped by her mother's house first before going to work. When I saw De Angelo sitting in the front yard with one of his friends, I ducked in the seat. Nikki started laughing. "Girl, that boy won't do anything to you. My mom is at home, and besides, she doesn't play that."

As Nikki stepped out the car, I locked myself inside but quickly decided against it after recalling the type of strength De Angelo had. I opened the door, jumped out, and bolted up the stairs into their house.

De Angelo's eyes widened when he saw me. He leaped out of his chair and rushed up the steps behind me. "I got a good mind to crack your skull," he threatened glaring at me angrily. "Get this girl out of my house right now!"

"Leave her alone," Mrs. Pearl practically hissed. "There will not be any of that in my house. I pay the bills in here and not you. I'll let whoever I want to come into this house."

I slowly started backing towards the door. "Gone with that stuff, boy," Nikki said laughing.

"We both just got hired at the Blue Flame. We're getting ready to go to work."

"She better leave now!" De Angelo ranted as tears of anger welled up in his eyes. After his threatening remark, Nikki and I dashed out the front door.

Once inside the car, I took a deep breath. Thank God I was still alive. I was glad I had already gotten our confrontation out of the way, so I wouldn't have to constantly look over my shoulders trying to avoid from running into him. Finally, without a doubt, our relationship was over.

That night, Mrs. Rose only needed one worker. I was in no mood to be working anyway, so I quickly said that Nikki could do the honors. "Mr. Ray could use a worker at Ray's Place down the street," she said looking over the brim of her glasses at me. I guessed that was my cue, so I told Nikki that I would meet her back there when I got off of work.

I walked the short distance to Ray's Place. There wasn't many people there. I extended my hand and introduced myself to Mr. Stanford Ray, the owner. "Mrs. Rose told me that she was sending me a worker over here," he said with a pleasant tone to his voice. "I'm glad you could make it."

Throughout the night, he walked me through how to work the cash register and how to be an effective waitress. At the end of the night, I found myself pleased when he stated with a smile, "I'll see you back tomorrow night". That whole weekend, I showed up at the restaurant. The owner was so pleased with my progress that one night he asked to speak with me after work.

"How would you feel about running this place one day?" he questioned watching me with discerning eyes.

"That would be awesome!" I said believing he was talking about the distant future. "As long as you teach me what I need to know!"

"I want you to be my new manager," he said as a matter of fact. His words froze the smile on my face. "I believe you would do an excellent job."

"Are you serious?" I questioned. There wasn't a hint of a smile on his face.

"Yes, I sure am. You have excellent skills, Crystal. I've been watching how customers open up to you. Most importantly, I've noticed that you are very honest. You can start tomorrow in your new position."

"On weekdays, I want you to open up at 11:00 a.m. every morning, and close at 11:30p.m. On weekends, I want you to open at 12:00 p.m. and close at 2:00a.m." He instructed. "I know it is long hours, but I think you can manage it." After going over formalities, he shook my hands and handed me the keys to the place.

Working long hours didn't intimidate me because I didn't have anywhere to go anyway. I was single with no children. Therefore, I didn't have any obligations.

During my first few nights of employment, whenever money came up short, I always took it out of my own pocket to make up the difference. I didn't realize he had noticed. Although I was a sinner, I was an honest one. Nevertheless honest or not, I was still on my way to hell because I was not saved.

For the first few months of managing Ray's Club, business picked up as never before. I worked the cash register, cooked, served food, cleaned the place, waited tables, and did the inventory. I was responsible for paying the D.J, hiring and firing employees as well as paying them. I loved the job. It required a lot of time and energy, and I had both.

Sometimes when the business was slow, the days seemed to be never ending. To make the time pass, I'd sit at the counter and watch people get drunk and act a complete mess. Soon, the nightclub atmosphere toughened me. I grew used to being cussed out, throwing people out of the club, and calling the cops. I became even more popular throughout the town, but this time instead of as an exotic dancer, it was for being sort of like a young entrepreneur. I became a spectacle. Many new faces started showing up at the nightclub to see the new girl everyone was talking so much about. Most of the guys knew that I was single; therefore, I had many admirers.

During this time in my life, a jewel in the night developed while dealing with those that came inside Ray's Place. My genuine love for people grew especially for those that were deemed as social rejects. I found myself spending countless hours getting to know drunks, prostitutes, and crack addicts along with their drug dealers. They often found themselves pouring out their souls to me. I listened to them, what they had to say interested me. I was eager to learn all that I could about their way of life. Somehow all of this would be a piece that would fit into the plan that God had for my life. Although the enemy was trying to destroy me, God was going to use my pain for his glory. I felt as if he was teaching me a valuable lesson for a special project that he was orchestrating in my life.

One morning, while on my way to work, I noticed a guy gawking at me with a sly smile. By now, I was used to guys looking at me in this way, so I smiled back and continued walking.

"Hey, what's your name?" he called after me.

"Crystal," I threw back over my shoulder not stopping to entertain him.

"What's your name?" I said yet trying to be polite.

"Drake Gardner," he returned proudly.

I had never seen him come into Ray's Place before; but after our brief introduction, I was starting to see him on a regular basis. Oftentimes, he would sit in the back by himself and sip on a few beers. I couldn't mistake the fact that he was constantly watching me. There were glass mirrors alongside all the walls, and I would look up and find his eyes resting on me through one of them. I would smile and resume working.

Since I was a bit flirtatious, whenever I was extremely bored, I would put some money in the jukebox, pick out a good position on the small dance floor in front of a mirror, and dance exotically for the few customers. Drake always ended up so mesmerized that he would move closer to get a better view.

It didn't take long for me to realize that he wasn't like most guys that came in. He was sort of shy—so it appeared. He didn't throw himself all over me like I was accustomed to but watched me in admiration from a distant. I must admit that his mysteriousness turned me on in a strange way. I desired to win his affection. Trying to do so became a challenge for me. Little did I know that playing with fire was about to get me seriously injured.

One evening after my little dancing serenade had ended, I walked up to Drake to see if he wanted to place an order. He did. He wanted another drink. Upon my return with his purchase, I looked at him seductively, biting the bottom part of my lip playfully.

"How are you today?" I asked.

"Fine, what about yourself?" he replied. He then took a small sip of his remaining Bud Ice.

"Great," I answered. "I see that you're sitting back here by yourself. I figured you would like some company."

"I'm alright," he said confusing me with his coldness. Then he smiled, revealing some of the prettiest teeth I had ever seen. Getting him to open up was going to be harder than I thought.

After a few more minutes of conversation, I was getting bored. Drake wasn't revealing anything about himself. I was so used to guys bragging on what they got or how good they could do something, but he was definitely different.

The following morning, I came to work upset, and it showed. One of my brothers and I had argued very badly the previous evening as a result of a confrontation between his girlfriend and myself, which left me pretty much homeless. Now, I was stuck in a dilemma. I had to find somewhere else to live. Due to the fact that I didn't pay rent at my previous apartment and had moved out without notifying anyone, it was going to be hard for me to get a good recommendation to obtain another apartment in Forrest City.

Although in a sullen mood, I yet managed to smile at customers. But when I guessed no one was looking, I frequently caught myself staring off into space. A few of those times I caught Drake watching me from the mirrors again. I quickly diverted my gaze and pasted a fake smile. He wasn't deceived.

He slowly got up and walked towards me. *Oh, brother*, I thought. *He finally decides to speak when I don't feel like talking.*

"Where's that pretty smile I've grown used to?" he asked, tracing the curves of my lips with his eyes and then bringing them to rest on my saddened eyes.

"I am smiling," I said. "I just have a lot on my mind."

"Do you want to talk about it," he asked taking a seat at the counter next to me. I usually don't open myself up to strangers, but for some reason, I poured out my heart to him about not having a place to stay. "I have a three bedroom house," he interjected without letting me finish. "Anytime, you want to get away, you can stay with me."

"That's a nice proposition," I said, "but no thanks."

"In case you're wandering, I stay by myself," he added. "I just recently ended a relationship, and I'm not looking for another one." He almost convinced me that he wasn't interested in me.

"Well, I might take you up on that offer if things get any worse," I said. I found myself smiling again, and soon I was back to my happy self. "Here. Have a beer on the house," I said handing Drake his favorite beer.

That night, I ended up staying inside the club by myself. The place was eerie. Falling asleep was almost impossible. Being surrounded by mirrors gave me the illusion of a haunted house. The sleepier I became, the more shadows I saw. It wasn't until morning that sleep finally came.

I awakened to the sound of a tapping noise on the solid-glass front door. It was Drake. I looked down at my watch. It was 10:35 a.m. I usually didn't open the doors until 11:00 a.m., but I unlocked them anyway.

"Hey there," I said rubbing my eyes. "I figured you slept here last night. Would you like some breakfast?" he asked. I stuck my head out the glass door. Drake's immaculate and perfect symmetrical teeth glistened as he smiled at me.

"No thanks. I'll cook something on the grill in the kitchen. First, I need to go freshen up." I yawned.

"I'm getting ready to go to work. I just wanted to stop by and check on you," he said, turning to leave. "I'll be back when I get off work."

I watched him for a few minutes through the glass door as he walked away. He was short and semithin in physique but was well toned. I quickly locked the door behind him and then turned to go freshen up. I needed to hurry and get dressed before customers started pouring in for lunch.

Throughout that morning, and days to follow, I found myself thinking about Drake quite often. His dark brown eyes seemed to make me vulnerable whenever they were cast in my direction. They left me feeling naked. Because of his quietness and calm demeanor, I assumed he was a nice guy. His discretion spoke volumes.

After about a week of Drake coming into the place and throwing his gorgeous smile in my direction, I started thinking, *Maybe this is my chance to actually hook up with Mr. Right. Maybe he's that special one."* Many lonely nights, I had longed for someone distinguished to come into my life, revealing a fairytale type of romance. A virtuous woman was buried somewhere deep inside me as a result of years of pain and mistrust. She was tired of "casting her pearls amongst the swine." She was aching to be set free—to throw away the filthy rags of compromise and to put on her rightful garments of royalty.

Here is my prince, I thought as I saw Drake walk through the doors of Ray's Place many nights later. Our eyes met. He walked over to the counter where I stood and whispered in my ear. Do you want to come and stay over my house tonight? I won't bite. His pearly whites glistened as usual. I became nauseous with hope, believing that my rib was the missing link that was designed to fit his body. He was the one God had ordained for me before the foundation of the world. "I'll think about it," I whispered back. I'll let you know before I close the store."

The remainder of that night, I observed him closely. I cringed in disbelief as he took crisp one and five-dollar bills and toyed with them in his fingers before setting them on fire. His bizarreness captivated me. I glanced at the clock. An hour remained before closing time. I had made my decision. It was final. I stood up, took a deep breath, and walked in his direction.

"I've made up my mind," I said taking a seat next to him. I felt very uneasy about my bluntness but yet continued. "I would like to stay with you tonight."

"That's fine," he returned. "In case you're wondering, I'm not expecting sex in return, and to be honest, I don't even want it."

"That's cool," I said a little offended. I wrestled with the reasoning of his bluntness. "I just don't like the idea that you're staying in this place by yourself," he added sensing my uneasiness, "it's just not safe."

"I guess I'll meet you later then," I said, leaving his side to attend to a customer.

After work, Drake waited outside while I finished cleaning and locking up. I grabbed a few beers to take with me and wrapped them in a brown paper bag. Just as I was turning the lights off, nervousness seized me. Although De Angelo and I had not been together for a few months, I felt as if I was cheating on him. I quickly dismissed the notion after remembering that he was now living with another woman. After all, it was his fault we were no longer together. I rechecked everything once more and then walked outside to greet Drake.

When we made it to his house, he entered through the back door to let me in through the front. Once the lights were turned on, I noticed that the place was fairly decent. There was a queen-sized bed in the living room right in front of a fourteen inch television. Although there were no signs of anything feminine, the room appeared rather cozy. When Drake disappeared to another room, I sat on the edge of the bed and waited for his return.

After a few minutes, he stuck his head inside the living-room door. "Do you want some ice for your beer?" he asked.

"Yes, please," I replied. He returned shortly with two ice-filled glasses.

After sitting them down on the nightstand besides the bed, he turned towards me. "Is it stuffy in here to you?" he asked taking a seat next to me and pulling off his shirt. "I'm burning up."

"Yes. It's pretty hot in here," I replied. He then got up and plugged in the fan that was already snuggly fitted inside the window. Immediately, a wave of cool air began to circulate into the room.

I poured some of the beer into my cup and then kicked off my shoes. "We'll have to watch a tape since my cable isn't on," he said while rumbling through his tape collection. After finding one, he put it in the VCR. He continued. "I've been thinking about moving in a few weeks. I'm going to sale this house and find me a smaller apartment to live in." To tired to actively listen, I finished drinking my beer and stretched back onto the bed to relax from having been on my feet the majority of the day. The beer began to take affect on me leaving me feeling warm and tingly. The tenseness of the day began to subside, and I found myself drifting into a deep sleep.

I awakened around 9:00 a.m. with Drake lying next to me. He looked so peaceful. I glanced down the length of his body and saw that he was aroused. Being the seductress that I was, I started to caress his body with the tips of my fingers. His eyes immediately flew open.

"No," he said sternly, gently removing my hands, but his eyes begged for me to continue. I wasn't used to begging for sex, so I refrained from touching him. Seconds later as if not wanting the moment to pass, he picked up where I had left off. To my astonishment, like a ravished animal, he was all over me, kissing and enjoying himself in my garden of love.

After about a week of spending each night together, Drake started confessing his love for me. As weeks turned into months, the happiness I felt with him seemed to supercede the disappointment that De Angelo had caused me. It appeared I had finally found true love.

One day before work, Mrs. Rose, the owner of the Blue Flame approached me about how I had turned out to be an asset to Mr. Stanford's club. After expressing her gratitude, she continued. "I have a small apartment you can stay at until you are able to get on your feet. You don't have to worry about paying me any rent. The place is not much to look at, but at least you can save up some money to get something better."

I could hardly believe my ears. Everything in my life finally seemed to be lining up. I had a man who was protective of me, and who gave me almost anything I asked for. I was a store manager working for a nice and understanding boss. And now I was getting a free apartment. For once, it felt like I was living on top of the world.

That night after getting off of work, Drake and I went to find the apartment. It was located right in Mrs. Rose's back yard. The edifice was more like a shed than an apartment. Nevertheless, I was happy that I had a place to go to that I could call home. Inside contained one medium-sized room with a bed, a small table, and a bathroom. After fixing the place up with the help of Drake, it became livable.

By our three-month mark together, I started noticing a glimpse of Drake's jealousy. If any of the male customers spoke to me longer than Drake thought necessary, he often spat out threatening remarks at them. At first, I was flattered, but his paranoia soon became irritating. My provocative fashion drew male customers to the nightclub, and I loved the attention that came with it. In return for spending their money, I provided them with good service, a friendly conversation, and nothing more. Drake somehow figured that every guy that came into Ray's Place wanted me sexually. Maybe that was true, but business was business.

One particular day, Drake came into Ray's Place intoxicated. This was normal for him. He looked around. When he noticed that there was only one customer in the building and that it was a male, he became furious. He figured that we had something going on. I tried to explain to him that the guy was only shooting pool and was waiting for some of his work friends to meet him there for lunch. He wouldn't listen.

Drake walked up to the guy, and started throwing accusations at him, causing him to flee outdoors in anger. Afterwards, Drake started walking in my direction. Within minutes, his countenance had changed. It was like staring into the face of one that was demon-possessed. Without any warning, he picked up my spiral notebook pad that was lying on the counter and slapped me with it. I was totally devastated. It was hard to digest what had just happened. Instead of a prince, he was nothing more than a frog, after all.

After screaming degrading things at me, he continued his abuse. Like a track athlete, he jumped behind the counter where I sat crying uncontrollably, grabbed the club's baseball bat and began threatening me with it.

"You're quitting this job, slut! I know you like them men all in your face, but that's going to end right now!" He yelled causing spit to fly in my face. "You're coming with me!"

Anger sprung out from behind his eyes like a Venus flytrap latching onto its prey. Without any hesitation, I followed his command. After locking the doors, I walked behind him while eyeing the baseball bat he held tightly onto. "I will quit if you want me to," I cowered, hoping to calm him down at least until he sobered up.

When we made it back to the apartment, Drake consistently cursed me. His drunkenness, his anger, and his jealousy sickened me combined with the fact that I had left work without making it known to anyone. I had to figure out a way to get back as soon as possible before the boss found out.

I sat on the bed and looked at him with utter disgust. I wasn't going to put up with a lot of unnecessary hell from him like I did with De Angelo. The cold truth stood before me like a mirage in a desert. I was lonely and on the rebound; that was the reason I had hooked up with him. Getting involved with Drake was nothing more than a scheme to fill a void that had developed in my life. And now that he had completely changed from being the nice guy I thought he was, I was ready to dispose of him. I wasn't about to subdue to his abuse. I could tell by the look in his eyes that if I didn't get away from him soon, he would end up killing me.

When he walked into the bathroom, I knew my moment had come. I had to escape. I gathered up the courage to stand, then tip-toed to the door. I flung it open, and with all of my might, ran as fast as I could. Thankfully, I saw Mrs. Rose's car parked in her driveway. I beat on her door as rapidly as I could, willing her to open it. She finally did. After seeing the horror on my face, she let me in without asking any questions. As soon as I made it indoors, Drake had made it to her front porch and began banging frantically on the door.

Almost out of breath, I explained to Mrs. Rose everything that had just happened. Without saying a word, she walked past me and went into another room. She returned shortly with a pistol in her hand. "Drake, get away from my door. I'm warning you," she said, opening the wooden door. The storm door was still locked. Looking at his face through the bars of the glass caused me to hyperventilate.

"Let me speak to Crystal," he demanded.

"You see the girl don't want to talk to you right now. Now get away from the door right now! I know what'll solve this nonsense. I'm going to call the police on your sorry behind." At the mention of the word police, Drake retreated off the porch and around the corner.

"After you calm down, go back to work," Mrs. Rose said looking at me over the brim of her glasses.

"I'm afraid to go back," I stammered. "He'll come and get me."

"We'll fix that. Put a restraining order on his butt." She then picked up the phone and did just that.

About thirty minutes later, she dropped me off in front of Ray's Place. Hard as I tried, I couldn't shake the ominous feeling that surrounded me. Safely inside, I hurriedly locked the doors behind me. After about an hour of building up my nerves, I opened the nightclub back up. Within hours, a steady flow of customers started coming in.

Just as I was starting to relax, I looked up and saw Drake through the glass doors. I glanced at the phone and then back at the door. I couldn't decide whether to call the cops or to lock the door. It was too late to do either. He had already entered the nightclub. After spotting me, he headed in my direction while calling me everything but a child of God. He then grabbed me by the arm. "You're coming with me." I was too afraid to put up a fight because I suspected he had a gun. My instincts told me to do whatever he said.

I walked up to the DJ and handed him the key. "I'm leaving," I said, silently praying he would discern the trouble I was in and call the police. With no other words, I left. I knew the boss would be in later that night, so I was comforted that he would get the keys from the DJ. He always arrived on Thursday nights because they were the busiest. I held my head down in pure embarrassment and anticipation of what would happen to me next. "We're going over to my momma's house to spend the night," he growled, "just in case someone tries to call the cops."

After arriving at his mother's, we stood outdoors for a while. He continued his harassment with threats and drunken slurs that were aimed to terrorize me. It worked. Every chance I got, I tried to run. He always caught me. My attempts to escape made him madder and madder. He finally grabbed a mop that was propped up against the back wall of the apartment and held it against my neck. "If you try that one more time, I'll kill you," he breathed only inches from my face. The veins that distended from his temples made me believe he was angry enough to carry out his threat.

Later that night, as I lay ensnared underneath his arms grasped around my throat, I listened to the sound of his breathing. I cried silently trying to time his snores, so I could make my escape. Fear restrained me from action. All that night, I fantasized about leaving. I didn't want to be in his presence any longer. Thoughts of being with him disgusted me.

Early the next morning, after he had wakened, I couldn't hold back my true feelings any longer. "I can't be with you anymore," I said. "This relationship won't work for me."

After rubbing his hair back, he looked at me and stammered, "I love you Crystal, but I don't want you with me if you're not happy. I can't make you love me."

Tears began to stream down his face. I knew better than to feel sorry for him. His tears were nothing more than a manipulation tactic. He had used it before. This was my opportunity to escape, and I was going to use it.

Without waiting for another word from him, I put on my shoes and sprinted out the door. It had started to rain, but I didn't care. I ran as fast as I could back to my apartment to pack. I knew that as soon as he got a hold of some liquor, he would come looking for me again. And this time, maybe, even kill me.

After packing, I walked to the nearest gas station to use the pay phone to call someone from Wynne to pick me up. Since I didn't have any money, I could only make collect calls. Most of my relative's phones didn't accept collect calls, and the ones that did, refused to accept mines. I was stranded. Death stalked me. I could feel him nearby, waiting for the moment to snatch life out of me.

I went inside the gas station and persuaded someone to buy me a 40oz of Colt 45. I unscrewed the top and gulped half of its contents down. Next, I walked over to the Hill's house that was almost directly across the street from the gas station. Mr. and Mrs. Hill were surprised to see me without Drake.

As I began speaking, fear was easily detected in my voice. "What's wrong," Mrs. Hill questioned searching my face for any clues. I began telling her and her husband about how violent Drake had become and how I had just left him.

"You should've stayed with De Angelo. That boy really does love you," they both said in unison, adding to my despair.

"Yeah, if he really loved me, then he wouldn't have left me for another woman," I snapped sarcastically. Both De Angelo and Drake had contributed their fair share of chaos in my life. Whether physical or emotional, all abuse was the same to me.

An old cream-colored Caddy pulled into the Hill's driveway. As soon as I noticed the driver, I rushed towards his car and practically begged for a ride to Wynne. I only knew him vaguely, but yet, he agreed to take me after first taking care of a few errands. "I'll show you where I stay, so you'll know where to pick me up," I said opening the passenger door and getting in.

After the driver dropped me off, he promised to come back and pick me up after handling his business. I went in the apartment and looked around making sure Drake wasn't inside. After seeing that everything was untouched, I changed into a brand new outfit hoping it would make me feel better. As the warmth of the sun from the opened window grazed across my face, I lied upon the bed to await the guy's arrival to take me to Wynne. After an hour of waiting, the beer from earlier began to tire me. Soon, I fell asleep.

When I awakened, the sun had nearly gone down. I could hardly believe it. The guy had stood me up. Drake was probably near drunk by now. Sooner or later, after realizing he shouldn't have let me go that easily, I knew that he was going to come looking for me. Since the apartment would be the first place he'd look, I decided to walk over to Tina and Steve's apartment in Grandma Circle.

When I finally made it over their place, they were in the process of rolling up a blunt. They were no longer churchgoers but had completely reverted back to their old lifestyle of partying.

"Crystal!" Tina yelled in surprise as she opened the door for me to come in. The room reeked of freshly-smoked weed. "Where's Drake?" she probed glancing behind me. By now, most of the town knew that I wasn't with De Angelo anymore.

"I left Drake. He's crazy. I should've never hooked up with him in the first place." Afterwards I begin telling her how he forced me off the job with a baseball bat and other incidents of violence he displayed. When she extended the lit blunt in my direction, I accepted. I wanted to suppress the feeling of dread that was now spreading like a malignant cancer.

As I sat in front of their living-room window, puffing on the blunt, I heard voices outside. I automatically recognized Drake's. I turned and immediately spotted him. A tall, dark-skinned guy escorted him. They both appeared to be under the influence of something. Within seconds, Drake banged on Tina and Steve's front door. "Open up this door!" he cursed.

I leaped up and ran into the bedroom. Due to the fact that the apartment building was located on top of a gigantic hill, I couldn't jump out the window. It would have been the equivalent of jumping out of a three-story building. I didn't see any other option. I tried to pry the window open, but it was too late. Drake had already made it into the house.

When he spotted me, he picked up an iron chair and ran towards my direction. I dived across the king mattress barely escaping the swing of the chair as he hurled it at my head. I ran towards the door with him close on my heels. In the process, I grabbed a nearby chair, stopped abruptly, and plunged it into his chest trying to block him from getting out the door. The plot was effortless. When I saw his eyes widen with surprise of the fact that I had tried to fight back, I panicked. This was the first time I had ever tried to defend myself. His look frightened me so badly that I dropped the chair and took off running outdoors. Within a short distance, one of my heels broke causing me to tumble to the ground.

Drake caught up with me and started stomping me in the head, kicking me everywhere he could. Everything after that was a blur. A crowd began to develop, watching me get beat to a pulp. No one dared to help. While trying to stand, a hard object came crashing against my skull knocking me back down. On impact, the sound of my skull cracking penetrated my ears as a warm substance poured down my face and into my mouth. I looked down at my shirt and saw blood—lots of blood. I was on the verge of going into shock. The voices of the crowd became faint as Drake began to pull me up from the ground by my hair. There was no doubt in my mind that I was going to die.

By now, I couldn't see much of anything since the side where I had been hit had swollen, causing my eye to close. "Come on, I'm going to teach you about playing with my emotions. When we get to the bottom of the hill, I'm going to kill you." I trembled at his words. They were ferocious. I knew he had the strength and the rage to carry out his threat. Blinded by the night and by pain, I walked before him like a sheep to the slaughter. All the way down the hill, Drake pulled my hair, kicked me, and cursed at me. The tall dark guy I had seen earlier through the fan, walked at a distance, following our trail.

When we made it to the bottom, we were completely surrounded by gross darkness. I was ankle deep in mud. A thicket of trees and bulrushes welcomed Drake's devious plans of murdering me. The wild thickets prevented any attempts to escape.

A massive stone with the words engraved, "This is Hollow Ground," hovered above me. I knew this because I used this path as a short cut many times before to go to the community store located at the bottom of the hill. According to rumors, the area where I stood was an old Indian burial site. I shuttered at the thought of myself lying amongst those nameless bodies. I imagined my cadaverous face with the look of horror imprinted on its features, frozen in time.

"Give me my gun!" Drake yelled at the tall, dark guy that was now standing at his side. "Man, she's not worth it. Can't you see you've already done enough damage to the girl?" the guy asked apprehensively. I could sense that Drake was pondering on his words because he got quiet for a few seconds.

"Keep talking to him," I pleaded slightly above a whisper. "Shut up!" Drake screamed in my face. "Don't talk until I speak to you!" Once again, he turned and demanded the young man to give him the gun.

As fate stared me in the face, I wanted to pray but didn't feel worthy enough to do so. I deserved to die, and I knew it. I bowed my head in submission to what was inevitable—death. My life began to flash before me. I had been raised to know God. He had shown me his goodness numerous amounts of time. I knew his grace, but yet now I stood only minutes or even seconds away from going to hell. I was without excuse.

It was at this moment of truth when the strangest thing happened. The sound of prayers on my behalf surrounded my head like a swarm of bees. Then a vision appeared. I stood transfixed as I watched unrecognizable faces kneeling to petition God for protection on my behalf. Their supplications were fervent, heartfelt. The vision didn't last long, but I knew that someone was interceding on my behalf. And like the scripture says, "The effectual fervent prayer of a righteous man availeth much" (James 5:16).

In the distance, sirens were going off. This startled both men. Drake decided to send the tall dark guy away with the gun in the opposite direction while he and I took the railroad tracks to his mother's house.

As we walked the long dark tracks, I became very lightheaded from losing to much blood. This caused me to stagger.

"I dare you to fall," Drake said as he picked up a big stick. "I'm going to teach you about playing games with me." Hatred filled his voice. I had to think quickly.

"I love you, Drake. I really want this relationship to work.

You just have to be patient with me." I lied, telling him what he wanted to hear hoping it would soften his hardness towards me. Thankfully, my plea of desperation caused him to temporarily calm down.

It was hard for me to dismiss the fact that approximately four weeks before this incident Drake had gotten stabbed in the back by a guy at the night club. The fight started with one of Drake's jealous rage. After getting a pool stick and hitting the guy across the head with it, the man pulled out a knife to defend himself. The stab had punctured Drakes' lungs. I was there for him through the whole ordeal. It was I that had washed his wound every night and took his stitches out when his wound had healed. Here I was, now being wounded by him. Sometimes life could be so ironic.

On the way to his mother's, we stopped by my place first. After going in, he wiped vigorously at my face. He didn't want me going over to his mother's looking like I had been slaughtered. After realizing I was too afraid to look at my reflection in the mirror, he started laughing deviously in my face. Hatred filled me as tears began to flow down my cheeks.

After arriving over to his mother's, Drake paused before entering, glancing back at me. "If my mother asks you what happened to your face, tell her a woman hit you with a brick and took off running." Without lifting my eyes to look at him, I shook my head to agree with his plans.

As soon as I entered the house, his mother looked at me with widened eyes. "What in the world happened to you?" she asked studying my face. After feeding his mother lies, Drake finally went outdoors and left me alone in the room with her.

She looked at me and calmly asked, "He did this to you, didn't he?" I couldn't hold the masquerade any longer. The tears gushed down my face.

"Yes ma'am, he did," I said as I sat on the crimson colored couch crying uncontrollably. "I kept telling that boy that his anger was going to get him in trouble one day."

At that moment, Drake walked back into the house and ushered me into a back bedroom. I quickly wiped at the tears with the bottom of my shirt. His mother didn't say anything else. She only shook her head at him in disapproval.

Once behind the bedroom's door, Drake's threats resumed. When the pain in my face had reached an excruciating level, I begged him to take me to the hospital. He refused. He left and walked out the room. When he returned, he held a huge butcher knife in his hand. He swiftly walked towards me and grabbed me by the throat, putting the cold blade against it. "Stop crying or I'll slice your throat," he demanded. I immediately stifled my tears and began to shake. I couldn't get enough breath to my lungs. I was hyperventilating.

For three days, he held me there against my will. And during those three days, I slipped in and out of consciousness:

> The darkness engulfs me all about. It reaches its stagnated finger's out to grip at my weary soul. It darkens my path so that I am unable to see. I fall and sink to oblivion. All around me is darkness, and all I can smell is death. Together they both compass me about, becoming a reality to my burning eyes. I cannot see for there is no light within me. The gross darkness is so thick that it nearly suffocates me. The immense evil that's held in this thickness holds chains of bondage onto my legs for entrapment. All around me are voices that I cannot discern. They intertwine with one another to become unified. Each voice cries out their own sad stories, but their words are unrecognizable due to utter anguish. Because of the lack of light, I can barely make out faces of desperation. A struggle erupts nearby, but the exact location, I know not because my paths are dark. Someone reaches for my hand. I try to pull free of the cold and clammy grip, but we both fall together into a bigger pit of stagnation.
>
> In the bottom of this pit, linger the souls of those that had hit rock bottom. In this cold, secluded place lies the final exposition of being. As I began to fall among the corpses, silence

echoed all around me. No longer did I hear the moaning of antagonizing souls, only the sound of my breathing. I slowly looked around. No longer was I running from death, for I no longer had anywhere to run but was staring him in the face. I could see his face quite clearly. I could depict him from the darkest of dark. He stood there piercing into my eyes as if daring me to scream. I was spellbound. I stood cold and shivering, looking into his gaze. I hardly believed it. I heard so much about him but was caught by surprise to meet him so soon. Everything started to spin as I became overcome with dizziness. "The wages of sin is death," his voice shrieked. My heart felt faint, but I was too afraid to surrender to its vulnerability. Death reached out his arms to grab my mesmerized soul. Just as he touched my face, I heard a voice somewhere in the distant. It was quite demanding, but simultaneously gentle and soothing. "Not so!" the voice exclaimed. All of a sudden death was no longer staring at me. Yet I stood in outer darkness, all alone, but yet not alone.

I walked back and forth throughout the dark pit. I stumbled over and over again. Just as I was about to give up hope, I looked up. At that moment, I noticed that the darkness above me was a little brighter than the darkness that I was in. I began to climb on top of all the dead bodies. I could feel people pulling at my legs, but I was determined that I would break free of this horrible hell.

Once out of the horrible pit of decomposition, I glanced around me. Nothing had changed since I had fallen beneath. Everything still reeked of death, and I still couldn't see my path well enough to prevent myself from falling.

"There's no hope," I cried. I wanted out so badly, but there was nowhere I could turn; for all around me lurked darkness. As I fumbled consistently through the thickness, I got a small inclination that touched the root of my spirit. I must look up. I looked up, and there was a small hole about the size of a quarter that contained a small glimpse of light. I could see a hint of its brightness coming in through the portal. I had hope. Without trying to comprehend how I would climb this massive cave and reach its orifice, I started on my journey. I stood up and began to shake the mud from my clothing and my face. "Lay aside every weight and the sin that do so easily beset you..." rang in my spirit. I noticed that I felt lighter than before. I clung to the sides of the cave with all my strength.

After climbing for some while, I began to get tired and weak. A voice that resounded all around me spoke in a demanding yet gentle tone. "Be still, and know that I am God." Suddenly, I stopped trying to climb. I rested my fragile body against the cold damp walls of the cave, so I could see where the voice was coming from. "Where are you?" My soul cried out to the voice. Immediately, the scenery began to transform around me. The darkness conformed into light, and instead of the smell of stagnation, I smelled the aroma of scented oils. My senses awakened as from a deep sleep. Everything became filled with color. As I stood in my new array of light, looking at the world in its new vibrancy of color, my heart began beating with anticipation. At this moment I realized how much "life" I was missing. It was I that had chosen to live in a world of darkness.

While allowing my eyes to adjust to the scenery and their explicit details, I began to vow within to watch my steps more closely, so I wouldn't fall back into that horrible pit from whence I had come. The air was so fresh and cool. The sun's rays rested gently upon my face warming my skin while sending blood racing to its surface. Peace began to descend upon me. Much closer than the previous times, the convicting voice spoke. "Here I am." Immediately our spirits connected with one another, and my feet began to become anchored to the ground. I wanted to run, but the voice spoke once more. "Peace, be still." I obeyed as I allowed him to do whatever he pleased in my life. "Pain is a part of the process, and discouragement is a part of destiny. This is the journey of transformation," the voice echoed to the depth of my being, down to the "created in his image" part of me. It was then that I knew that all I had to do was trust him, and all would be well with my soul.

During those brief unconscious episodes, I began to realize that a world without God is like a dark cave. No one can help each other because everyone is fumbling in their own pit of stagnation. Just going to church wasn't good enough. The darkness was a little brighter there, but yet, it was still dark. Until I was able to look up to God and give my entire life to him, I would remain in darkness.

On the third day of my disappearance, someone pounded outside Drake mother's apartment door. When he leaped up to go answer, I was too weak to look out the window to see who it was. After returning, he had a weird expression on his face. "Do you know who that was?" Drake asked, taking a seat on the bed beside me.

"Who?" I asked not understanding what he was getting at.

"That was your mother." As I digested what he had just said, Drake watched my reaction carefully.

From somewhere within me, I conjured up strength. Thinking I was finally free of him, I leaped up in excitement. He continued quietly. "I told her you weren't here." Those words were more painful than any physical damage he could've done to me. Because of those words, my mother was probably somewhere sick with worry. Someone at Ray's Place must have told her how I was forced off the job. I guessed that was how she found Drake mother's apartment. She had driven all the way from Texas to come and check on me.

Without saying a word, I dropped to my knees and wept bitterly. I couldn't believe it. I ached for him to finish me off. I concluded that death was better than staying with him another minute. I was miserable being held against my will. I made peace within that either he was going to kill me or I was going to kill him.

When he took a nap that evening, I slid the butcher knife from underneath his pillow. This was the perfect opportunity to chop his head off. I sat on the floor as hate for him began to build up within me. The desire to kill him was there, but something restrained me. *I'm the one that should die,* I thought. *I deserve all of this because I forsook God.* Instead, I turned the anger on myself and tried repetitiously to cut my wrist, but to my dismay, the blade wasn't sharp enough.

As if sensing danger, Drake eyes flew open. When he saw that I was trying to inflict harm on myself, he pried the knife from my grasp. It finally dawned on him how miserable he was making me. He rolled over out the bed and onto the floor next to me. He began crying as hard as I'd ever seen him do before. "I hurt you badly," he stammered. "You didn't deserve any of this, Crystal."

After letting him cry, I looked him straight in the face and whispered, "This might sound strange, but I forgive you." After speaking those heart-felt words, peace began to descend upon me. It felt like scales had just fallen from my eyes. Drake's mouth hung open in disbelief. He hadn't anticipated a response like that from me. This was the first time I had seen him completely speechless. I continued.

"Drake, I needed this to wake me up. God only used you to get my attention." I shuttered at the revelation. "Since I was a little girl, the hands of God were on me mightily. I felt like I was marked for a specific purpose. I allowed fear of totally surrendering to him hold me captive, thus causing me to run from him. It is because of my disobedience that God allowed you to do this to me," I said pointing at my face. "'The Lord chastens those he loves.'"

For a few minutes, Drake hung his head down in complete silence continuing to listen to all that I said. Afterwards, without a word, he got up and called his brother to take me to the emergency room.

Minutes later as we both sat in the living room with his mother, Drake announced, "I want to turn myself into the authorities. I was wrong for what I've done to Crystal, and I'm willing to suffer the consequences for my actions."

"I'm proud of you," his mother beamed. "That's the right thing to do." Shortly after, a horn honked outside.

"Come on," Drake said standing up. "That's my brother Robert." I followed his steps out the door and into the vehicle. I sat in complete silence as he and his brother talked and then drove off.

When walking into the doors of the hospital accompanied by Drake, doctors and nurses flocked around me. This buzz attracted nearby police officers to the scene. Everyone seemed to scrutinize my facial deformity. "What happened to you?" They all wanted to know. After seeing that Drake had changed his mind about turning himself in, I spoke up.

"A girl jumped me from behind," I lied. Drake looked at me in puzzlement as questions from the authorities continued to come. The police officers wanted to know all the details of what happened. They suggested I fill out a report, but I declined. I wanted so badly to tell them that it was Drake who had disfigured my face, but fear of him yet constrained me.

Once I made it into an examination room, X-rays of my face where taken. It was discovered that my orbital bone underneath my eye socket had been fractured. After accessing the wound, the physician told me it was too late to get stitches because I had waited too long to seek help. The new cells had already started to grow over the damaged ones.

"The only thing I can do now is write you out a referral to see a plastic surgeon," he said. The scent of his Old Spice Cologne filled my nostrils as he poked at the wound underneath my eye. "If you don't go, then there's a high possibility that the wounded area of your face would sink in."

I was stunned at the news. I didn't have any money to see a plastic surgeon nor did I want to walk around looking like the Loch Ness monster. Suddenly, it dawned on me. God was the best doctor I knew. He wasn't concerned if I had any money. He would heal me simply because I trusted that he would do it. He had spared my life, and even now, I knew he was capable of doing the impossible.

After leaving the hospital, Drake finally accepted the sad truth that it was actually over between the two of us and that he could no longer hold me against my will. When we returned back over to his mother's place, I silently packed my things and called my mother to come and pick me up. After hearing my voice, she exhaled a breath of relief.

When she and my brother Melvin arrived, I had on a pair of shades. My hair covered the side of my face that was disfigured, concealing any evidence of abuse. I acted as if everything was fine. It hurt to smile, but I managed one anyway. There was nothing different about me at least I thought. My mother's discernment saw straight through my masquerades: the makeup, the big earrings, and the smile. She saw straight to the pain that I was trying to cover.

Once inside the safety of our van, she questioned me about Drake's abusiveness. Due to embarrassment, I denied everything. I was ashamed. How could I let her know what I had just endured? How could I reveal to her that her daughter followed her same footsteps into an abusive relationship? Shame silenced me.

For the next few days, I tossed the recent incidents of terror in my head repetitively. I reminded myself of Jonah the biblical prophet (Please read entire book of Jonah). God had given Jonah specific instructions to carry out, but instead, he wanted to run as far away as possible from what God wanted him to do. God had a way of getting his attention. He had prepared a fish to swallow up Jonah, and for three days, he resided in its dark and pungent belly. During that time of reflection, Jonah contemplated on the plan and purpose that God had for his life. He realized that God was too big to escape.

While I ran from the call of God instead of a fish, God had prepared a man to hold me against my will for three days, so I could realize that I only had two options: life or death. And just like Jonah, in order for me to live, I had to accept his will for my life. We both had the Word of God in us. There wasn't any escape or consolation other than surrendering to God's plan.

There was no doubt in my mind that I was at the crossroads of my life. I had to dismiss the "Jonah mentality" and carry out the plan that God had purposed for me. I was going to have to forsake the path of destruction and walk the road less traveled.

The Transformation

One night, after having been in Wynne for a week, I was convicted to attend church, so I could thank God formally. Every time I thought about how he had spared me from death's grasp, I internally rejoiced. He deserved all the praise, and hopefully, mines would appease his anger towards me.

After putting on the proper attire, I caught a ride to the church with my mother for their weekly night service. Once there, I crept quietly into a back pew hoping to go unnoticed. The presence of the Lord greeted me, and within minutes, a flow of Hallelujahs flowed from my lips. I wanted to jump up and give a victory dance all across the front of the church, but my reluctance in surrendering my whole life to God yet restrained me. After all that I had just encountered, I still wasn't ready to give up the streets and everything that it had to offer. Internally, a war raged. I figured that praising God was enough to keep death from stalking me. It wasn't.

For about three weeks after being held against my will, I consistently tried to go to the small nightclub in my hometown. My life, I now realized would never be the same. Because of fear, I could no longer walk down the street at night by myself. I was paranoid and miserable. This left me imprisoned behind the walls of my home. Slowly, overtime, partying began to lose its appeal. Now that I was sick of myself or better yet, sick and tired of being sick and tired, I was ready for true transformation. Of course, as I began to get my life back on track, De Angelo re-emerged.

In March, I was hired as a Security Officer at the state penitentiary where I was paid extremely well. With my first check, I financed a Cadillac Deville. It was sky blue with a royal blue interior. I felt like I was on top of the world. Despite the fact that I wasn't truly happy, I marveled at how well De Angelo, and my relationship were starting to progress.

After almost four months of living in a void of unexplainable emptiness, it was time to choose who was going to be Lord of my life: De Angelo, or the True and Living God? Over the span of time, I would find out that the path of righteousness often required many hard decisions. Some would cause earthly possessions, family, friends, and/or relationships to be lost. "Those that follow me must deny themselves," Christ once said to his disciples (Matthew 16:24). Now, it appeared I had to follow the same steps.

My desire to serve God was fervent. I had gotten to a point where I was willing to do anything to be saved even if it meant walking away from everything that I had. I was tired of settling for less when I knew greatness was embedded within me. No matter how much I loved De Angelo, I had to give him up. *"Please Lord, Make a way of escape."* This became my daily prayer. I didn't see any way out. In the midst of my heartache, God continued stretching me. Where I would end up, I had no clue, but I did know that "[God] knew the plans that [He had] for me, to prosper me and to bring me to an expected end" (Jeremiah 29:11). Through the whole process of my metamorphosis, I continued to believe that my outcome would be far greater than my beginning.

June was almost over. I had just gotten paid. Once again, De Angelo and I got into a heated argument concerning my money. He wanted it, and I didn't want to give it up. I ended up giving him two hundred dollars to supposedly save for our anniversary that was coming up on July 4th. Of course I knew it would never make it to see that day. I dropped De Angelo off, not knowing that that was going to be the last day I would see him for a long time.

Before going to work that afternoon, I decided to stop by Tamar's house to see what she was doing. She was sitting on her porch. Without a word, she got up, opened the passenger door, and got in.

"Girl, I'm so tired of this," she burst into tears. "Derrick makes me sick. We got into it again." Derrick was her husband.

"Was it physical?" I asked already knowing the answer. She resorted to showing me bruises that had already become visible on her arms and neck. "I'm ready to leave him." Between breaths, she wiped at her tear-stained face. "I wish I could just leave everything and start over."

That was all I needed to hear. Her pain became my ammunition to leave everything behind and to start fresh with God in my life. I was going to be like Paul and count everything as dung.

"Are you serious?" I probed, looking for any signs of uncertainty.

"I'm very serious," she stammered. "Don't play with me, girl. I just got paid. We can leave right now." I said searching her face again.

"De Angelo and I just got into it too. I'm tired of being the one that has to make our relationship work. The only thing he seems to care about is partying." I griped. "I've been ready to leave a long time ago." I glanced over at Tamar. "Seriously, I want to be saved. I don't feel like I can do it here. My love for De Angelo has become too much of a stronghold for me. I don't care where we go; I'm just ready to leave."

"I know!" Tamar exclaimed suddenly remembering something. "Let's move to Atlanta. Janet Marshall has been trying to get me to move down there. I'll call her now and see if we can stay there until we can get on our feet." Janet was a girl that Tamar and I had grown up with. It seemed like a good idea to me.

After getting Janet's approval, Tamar and I both packed a

few belongings and stuffed them in the trunk of my Caddy. Next, we jumped in the car and drove to the gas station.

While pumping the gas, Tamar stuck her head in the window and said, "Get ready, hot 'lanta; here we come!"

"I can hardly believe it," I exchanged. Afterwards, we drove to Memphis, TN. where we spent the night over one of her brother's house.

The next morning before the sun had risen across the southern sky, we went to the store, bought a map, checked the oil in the car, and headed to Atlanta. We both took shifts driving. After about eight hours, we finally saw the sign that said Atlanta, Georgia. We had finally made it.

For almost two months, we resided at Janet's apartment. Her sister, cousin, two nieces, and her baby boy lived there as well. In my heart, I couldn't settle there. I wasn't ready to "pitch my tent in the wilderness." God was yet tugging me elsewhere. Despite all the partying that was going on, it wasn't until after trying to get various jobs with no acceptance. I accepted that Atlanta wasn't where God wanted me to be at least not for that season in my life.

After meeting a couple of people from upstate New York and being asked if Tamar and I would move there with them, I began pondering the question seriously. *Lord, is New York where you want me to go?* I prayed. I didn't have much to lose if I did move. My car had broken down a few days after moving there, so leaving it behind wasn't a big problem; and it wasn't like I had a job. *Lord, if this is your will, then let me find peace in it.* Peace was exactly what I got.

After promises of having a place to stay and our basic needs met, by faith, Tamar and I decided to go. Since neither of us had any money, we formed a scheme that would allow only one of us to purchase a ticket. I would accompany Tamar as her traveling nurse. Therefore, we would only need one ticket. I would be riding free. Our friends from New York sent the money for one ticket. When we went to purchase the ticket, I was amazed that they printed me out a free ticket as the accompanying nurse without asking for any identification or anything.

After packing our belongings and telling everyone goodbye, we started on our journey to the bus station. The sun was furious. The heat mingled with the air's humidity made me feel as if I were walking through a desert in slow motion. I carried two huge suitcases, plastic bags that contained food, one backpack that were filled with shoes, hair products, and books; my hands blistered. I tried not to think about how silly I must've looked. Since we didn't have enough money to catch a cab, walking to the transit station was our only option.

Along the way, I noticed Tamar having difficulty with her bags. I stopped to help her, so we wouldn't miss our bus. We were already behind our planned schedule. After minutes of struggling, we eventually caught the bus. Tamar and I, along with our luggage, took up the whole back seat. We were both excited about going to New York but were content with the fact that we were finally sitting in cool air. I wanted the bus ride to the greyhound station to last for a while, so I could rest while my body's temperature cooled.

We arrived at the overcrowded station a few minutes early. The bus hadn't arrived yet. Tamar and I took turns watching over one another's bags for a quick break. After staying overseas for a semester in college, I was very cautious of my surrounding. I knew how cunning people really were. I had watched many naive people get their pockets picked. I was one of the victims. .

The bus finally arrived. We grabbed our luggage and headed through the door that read *Departure: New York Gate* 6. Tamar and I stood in line with everyone else as we took out our tickets. My stomach tightened. One by one, each person that was ahead of us gave the attendant theirs. I held my breath as it came time for Tamar to give hers. He took it, and before I knew it, he had taken mines without saying anything.

Once outside, we handed our bags over to be placed underneath the bus's luggage compartment. We found two empty seats and took them. "So far so good," Tamar said gleefully. "Can you believe it? We're actually going to New York."

We carried on like a couple of schoolgirls until the bus departed. I was leaving behind the land of Egypt and was heading to my promised land. Egypt represented every obstacle that constrained me from reaching my full potential. Canaan represented New York—a land that flowed with milk and honey (countless of opportunities.)

Predestined to Reign

When we made it to New York, the long cold trip proved worthwhile. I stared in awe at the tall skyscrapers—the Twin Towers. It was still early, but I could yet make out the tall figures in the distance.

"Tamar," I breathed. "Look. I think those are the Twin Towers." After rubbing her eyes a few times, she squinted in the direction I pointed in. Someone sitting nearby said, "This must be your first time coming to the Big Apple."

"Yes, it is," I said yet talking quietly, so not to awaken sleeping passengers. A few sniggles erupted throughout the bus at our southern drawl.

"You girls must be from Texas," a chubby dark-skinned man across from us asked.

"No, we're originally from Arkansas," Tamar snapped. "Texas...Arkansas...what's the difference? They're both the same to me."

He continued to laugh causing others to join in with him. The remainder of the bus trip was hilarious. Tamar and I both joked with a few of the passengers about various slang Southerners use.

After finally arriving in Schenectady, New York, it didn't take long for us to get adjusted to our new surroundings. In the early hours of Sept. 11, 2001, I awakened to the feeling of uneasiness like something bad was about to happen. It was the morning that Tamar and I had decided to go look for jobs. While walking, Tamar stated, "I need some coffee. Let's go by the Salvation Army to get some." I agreed.

As we sat there amongst the homeless sipping on coffee, purpose stirred within me. "Look around," I whispered to Tamar. "We're supposed to be helping people like these. She shook her head, agreeing with my comment. "I know girl. I know."

While conversing with one another, an elderly man stepped up to us, I guess sensing our queasiness about being there. He walked like an old-school pimp. Before he opened his mouth, I knew he was about to throw some old, lame MacDaddy lines at us. I looked down at my attire. I stuck out like a sore thumb. I had on a leopard shirt, a black skirt with a slit up the side that stopped mid thigh, and a pair of black-sandaled heels.

Before he could open his mouth, I asked, "Do you know where we can get some clothes?" I soon realized I was drawing the wrong sort of attention to myself. I was seeking a job, not a man.

"The City Mission is around the corner. They have a women's shelter there. I'll walk you gals over there if you want," he stated obviously displeased I had hindered his pimping speech. Tamar and I accepted his offer.

When we stepped on the ground of the City Mission, I felt compelled to walk through its doors. As soon as I did, the announcement about the terrorist attacks on the Twin Towers was broadcasted on the television. Seconds later, the Lord spoke to my spirit audibly and said "I've called you for such a time as this." While he spoke, I knew destiny had pulled me to the very place I was standing.

After meeting the staff and finding out they had a Women's Discipleship Program, I knew this was where I belonged. I ended up joining the program and dedicating a whole year to God. During that year, like Esther, God prepared me for royalty.

By totally surrendering to the programs' standards, a portal was opened. I was able to regroup from the circumstances life had dealt me as I allowed God to revive my spirit. I was able to bring all my frustrations, my pain, and my misconceptions—all stemming from the same broken vessel—to be pampered and caressed through the Word of God, so I could be made whole. While there, I met women from all walks of life who had never been pampered and just like me were undergoing spiritual as well as physical restoration.

The Serenity House was where my life really began. It became the place where I stepped through the doors of destiny. During my year there, God equipped me with what I needed to break free from personal defeat. He taught me how to be real, he taught me how to deal with the root of issues, but most importantly, he taught me how to claim my spiritual inheritance and to walk in deliverance. Deliverance, after all, is a choice.

My life has been outlined with many hardships that God has enabled me to overcome. During those difficult times, I didn't expect to live to see the age of eighteen, but because of God's unfailing love, I made it! I'm now on my way to being thirty-one years old.

Although the devil had meant all of my heartaches and pains to be used against me, God showed me that they were all working towards my good. All of the debris of my past had left within me an astonishing faith in an awesome God. As I look back over my life, I can see how everything—the bad as well as the good—has strengthened my character and was essential for what God was getting ready to birth through me.

. Without a struggle, there's no refinement. Like a chemical reaction,. the only way a substance can change its chemical properties is by the process of heat. After the process, the new element gives off a different odor and takes on a new color. That is what God has done to me. He took that dirty, homeless, uneducated country girl and made a new creation. I am no longer arrayed with bitterness and animosity, but now clothed with the garments of praise. "If any man be in Christ, he is a new creature. Old things have passed away and all things have become new" (2 Corinthians 5:17). He has washed me, tried me, refined me, and glorified me for such a time as this, and might I add, this is just the beginning of my new life.

During my process of overcoming, God has blessed me. He has instilled various treasures in hidden places during those dark and lonely places in my life. Because I hungrily searched for those "jewels in the night," I gained wisdom during my process of becoming the person God declared over my prophetic destiny. When God spoke the words, "I've called you for such a time as this;" I now had a purpose to fulfill. Those words made me realize that I wasn't just on earth to live, get married, and then die. But it was much deeper than that.

God allowed me to break forth from my mother's womb in a specific time in history; because before the foundation of the world, he had already decreed my outcome. I was predestined to reign. Not so I could be in the spotlight but because I would be the vehicle to help disrobe the lies the enemy has spoken to those who "are the called according to his purpose" (Romans 8:28). I came to tell you that you are the head only and not the tail. You are a lender and not a borrower. You are above and not beneath. You are blessed going out and coming in. You are a royal priesthood, a chosen generation, and a peculiar people. You are the righteousness of God through Christ. You are all that God says you are!

I was spared so that I could pour into the lives of many. That's why abusive relationships didn't kill me. That's why I didn't die of leukemia as a child. That's why I didn't die from car accidents I was involved in. That's why cycles of addictions didn't leave me strung out in the streets, and that's why I couldn't commit suicide although I craved it many times. Destiny wouldn't allow me to. God had created me as a vessel of mercy in order to rescue the broken, the rejected, the abused, and the confused. Regardless of color, socioeconomic status, religion, age, or nationality, God sent me to break through your pain and pull you to your purpose—royalty.

In this book, it was necessary to expose the truths of my life, the whole truth, and nothing but the truth, so others would be healed. Now is the time to pull back the veil and expose real issues that so many of us face but are too afraid to admit. God seeks to rise up an army of people out of their brokenness. From your broken places shall raise power and royalty. Your pain will birth weapons to nullify the enemy, "for such a time as this." Daughter of Zion and Son of Thunder, although your road to royalty is painful, I pronounce your victory. You were predestined to reign! I decree that you shall live and not die. I decree that you shall not abort the destiny that God has spoken over your life. I decree that you shall be restored to your rightful place in the kingdom. I declare that you are free and delivered from all unhealthy relationships and addictive cycles in the name of Jesus Christ!

To Be Continued…

Dear Woman of God,

So many of us crave to feel loved, accepted, validated, and desired by a man. This yearning propels us to stretch ourselves above measure to get what we want, causing cycles of abuse to develop. We hook up with dysfunctional men; we try to change them; and after seeing that we can't, we start accepting their "flaws and quirks" and end up falling in love with their potential instead of their reality. Before we know it, we're addicted to the drama, and we're caught up in a cycle where we never truly get what we want. Why? Many of us don't know who we are and don't place value on the substance that God has placed within us. We readily cast our pearls amongst swine because we don't understand how valuable we are. Our neediness and insecurities cause us to lower our standards, and we find ourselves compromising with someone way beneath our morals in the hopes of not being alone. And because we lose the love that we have for ourselves, we neglect to establish healthy boundaries in our relationships. Failure to do so leave us opened and exposed to abuse and abandonment.

The majority of us women are bringing so much baggage into relationships that sometimes it's hard for men to deal with us. We bring suitcases full of bitterness and hurt from past relationships. We bring trunk loads of mistrust because every male figure in our life hurt us and let us down. We bring backpacks full of super hero magazines expecting our new mate to rescue us from debt, depression, and low self-esteem. We bring laundry bags full of old, molded attitudes because we think we're all that with our three different baby daddies and got-to-go-to-the-club-instead-of-watching-who's-fondling-the-kids selves. We dump all of our rage, bitterness, insecurities, and drama into the laps of our new man and have the audacity to think they have to make up for all the pain that everyone ever caused us.

We hold onto fear of being rejected, which causes us to appear clingy. We try to do all of the right things and dress the right way to ensnare a man, only to find that we can't keep him once we get him. We have been traumatized by pain, misused, and abused for so long that instead of trying to get healed from all of the pain, we try to medicate it. Relationships, sex alcohol, shopping, and/or drugs become our antidotes.

Women, God wants to heal us from the roots. The question he desires to know is, "Will thou be made whole?" We are his birthing instruments. He wants to teach us that it's only through him that our needs are fulfilled. He wants to take all of our emotional scars of being raped, molested, and disrespected by many rap lyrics and other instruments of abuse. He desires to delete our misconceptions of happiness: we have to have a man lying next to us even if he's broke and abusive as long as he can work it in the bedroom. The devil is a liar! God desires to delete our misconceptions of desirability: we must dress seductive, be thin as wasp wings, wear tons of make-up, wear fake eyelashes, fake nails, fake eyes, fake boobs, look like Barbie Dolls, and have fake hair. The devil is a liar! I am not against any of these things. It is the motives that I am against. We as women need to learn who we are and accept ourselves for who we are. A man can't define you. You define you! God wants to heal us where it hurts.

Discussion Questions:

Chapter One: From Bad to Worse

1. Have you ever felt like you were cursed? Why?
2. Describe your childhood. Was it pleasant or unpleasant? Why?
2. Have you ever had anything happen to you in your childhood out of your control that scarred you very badly?
3. How did you deal with it?
4. Have you or anyone you know ever been homeless? What was your/their experience.
5. Have you or anyone you loved ever battle with alcohol? How did it affect you?

Chapter Two: A New Start

1. Do you have any embarrassing school-years memories? What are they?
2. Have you ever met any celebrities? Who were they? Describe the experience?
3. Have you ever had dreams that came true? Discuss.
4. Have you ever had a near-death experience? Please Describe.

Chapter Three: The Trap

1. Was there ever a period in your life when it seemed God poured out his blessings upon you? Describe the experience?

2. Have you ever went in debt trying to keep up with the "Jones?"
3. Were you ever getting ready to do something but you could feel warnings go off? Did you take heed? What was the result?
4. Have you ever had a defining moment that changed your life for the worst?
5. How did you deal with the pain?
6. How was your first love? Describe the experience.

Chapter Four: It's a Setup!

1. Do you feel like your past is to bad for you to accept God's call.
2. Do you feel like God only loves you when you're doing "good works"
3. Can you identify any cycles in your life? Generational curses?

Chapter Five: The Cross Roads

1. What do you feel like is holding you back from walking in your purpose? Discuss.
2. Have you or is you running from the call of God?
3. What do you think it will take for you to totally submit to God's call on your life?

e|LIVE

listen|imagine|view|experience

AUDIO BOOK DOWNLOAD INCLUDED WITH THIS BOOK!

In your hands you hold a complete digital entertainment package. In addition to the paper version, you receive a free download of the audio version of this book. Simply use the code listed below when visiting our website. Once downloaded to your computer, you can listen to the book through your computer's speakers, burn it to an audio CD or save the file to your portable music device (such as Apple's popular iPod) and listen on the go!

How to get your free audio book digital download:

1. Visit www.tatepublishing.com and click on the e|LIVE logo on the home page.
2. Enter the following coupon code:
   29e2-9400-3981-def2-f963-b207-00c4-7725
3. Download the audio book from your e|LIVE digital locker and begin enjoying your new digital entertainment package today!